Additional praise fo
The Water Defender

"If you're in need of some inspiration . . . look no further than this crucial and absorbing account of the ordinary people in El Salvador who won big against a seemingly insurmountable international mining corporation."

—Karla Strand, *Ms.*

"The authors helped build the network of international allies that spearheaded the global fight against gold mining in El Salvador."

—Bill McKibben, *The New Yorker*

"It is rare, in the world of corporate power, to have a story where David beats Goliath. And rarer still to have one that reads like a fast-paced thriller. . . . In telling the story of how that happened, the authors have found a narrative gold of their own."

—Adam Hochschild, author of
King Leopold's Ghost and *Rebel Cinderella*

"An inspirational story that will echo around the world."

John Platt, Center for Biological Diversity

"This is a story about gold and water and activism. El Salvador is dangerously close to running out of clean water. Its rivers have been under threat from international mining companies for decades, companies that are after El Salvador's gold. But an unlikely alliance came together to stop them. . . . The inside story is the subject of [this] book."

—Marco Werman, *The World*

"Broad and Cavanagh . . . expose in granular detail and with great compassion the deadly, dangerous, and daunting legal and legislative juggernaut faced by those forced to defend and protect their most precious natural resource from the fallout of industrial greed and corruption."

—Carol Haggas, *Booklist*

"At a time when all caring people are seeking a new way forward out of a year of unimaginable death, destruction, and rampant inequality, along comes a book that gives us hope that a better world may be possible."

—Charlotte Dennett, *Toward Freedom*

"Demonstrates the potential of nonviolent campaigns to protect the interests of local communities against corporate powers."

—Kathleen Kollman Birch, *Maryknoll Magazine*

"The book is an environmentalist playbook, a how-to guide for activists seeking to defeat a power structure that is rigged in favor of their opponents."

—Sasha Chavkin, *The American Prospect*

"One of the most painstakingly—and lovingly—detailed case studies of people-based resistance to environmental depredation."

—Walden Bello, *Journal of Peasant Studies*

"Rife with valuable detail about the mobilizations, negotiations, alliance building, international campaigns, and legal maneuvers that stopped the Pacific Rim mining concession and led to the national ban."

—John Gibler, *Sierra Magazine*

"The authors' investigation took them to the hills of El Salvador, the halls of the World Bank and a community in the Philippines that faced a similar situation."

—Barbara Fraser, *National Catholic Reporter*

"Reads like a page-turning mystery novel . . . The best account I have read of the workings of an obscure global institution designed to undermine any obstacles to the mobility of global corporations."

—David Ranney, *Foreign Policy in Focus*

"This story of how everyday citizens, against implacable odds, managed to defeat a corporation that ravaged their community and polluted their water is one of the most inspiring I have read in many years. A blueprint for further global action . . . it is also exceptionally moving, full of unforgettable characters, intrigue, and surprising twists and turns."

—Ariel Dorfman, author of *Death and the Maiden*

"When the story of the courageous Salvadoran people came to my ears, I was full of pride and hope. Indigenous peoples everywhere are fighting for their water, and enlightened governments are valuing water over foreign corporate control. Our work . . . is a parallel struggle, and we are inspired by the people from the south. The Eagle and the Condor meet again."

—Winona LaDuke, author of *To Be a Water Protector*

"This captivating saga will help you envision who truly has power if we unleash our imaginations and act together."

—Ai-jen Poo, executive director of the National Domestic Workers Alliance

"In this gripping tale full of drama, plot twists, and, most importantly, the powerful and savvy dedication of ordinary people and their communities, Robin Broad and John Cavanagh have given us a terrific play-by-play handbook of how David can, in fact, beat Goliath."

—Dana Frank, author of *The Long Honduran Night*

the water defenders

HOW ORDINARY PEOPLE SAVED
A COUNTRY FROM CORPORATE GREED

ROBIN BROAD *and* **JOHN CAVANAGH**

BEACON PRESS
BOSTON

BEACON PRESS
Boston, Massachusetts
www.beacon.org

Beacon Press books
are published under the auspices of
the Unitarian Universalist Association of Congregations.

25 24 23 22   8 7 6 5 4 3 2 1

This book is printed on acid-free paper that meets the uncoated paper
ANSI/NISO specifications for permanence as revised in 1992.

Text design and composition by Kim Arney

Lyrics from "Water for Gold" reproduced with permission from composer
Joe Uehlein of the U-Liners, from the artists' album *Sweet Lorain*.

Library of Congress Cataloging-in-Publication Data

Names: Broad, Robin, author. | Cavanagh, John, author.
Title: The water defenders : how ordinary people saved a country from
    corporate greed / Robin Broad and John Cavanagh.
Description: Boston : Beacon Press, [2021] | Includes bibliographical
    references and index.
Identifiers: LCCN 2020030882 (print) | LCCN 2020030883 (ebook) |
    ISBN 9780807055403 (paperback) | ISBN 9780807029053 (ebook)
Subjects: LCSH: Pacific Rim Mining Corporation. | OceanaGold. |
    International Centre for Settlement of Investment Disputes. | Gold mines
    and mining—Political aspects—El Salvador. | Gold mines and mining—
    Environmental aspects—El Salvador. | Water—Pollution—Political aspects—
    El Salvador. | Environmentalism—El Salvador—History—21st century.
Classification: LCC HD9536.E47 B75 2021 (print) | LCC HD9536.E47 (ebook) |
    DDC 333.910097284—dc23
LC record available at https://lccn.loc.gov/2020030882
LC ebook record available at https://lccn.loc.gov/2020030883

*To water defenders everywhere,
especially to martyrs Marcelo Rivera,
Ramiro Rivera, Dora Sorto,
and Juan Francisco Duran*

Yo sabía que íbamos a triunfar, me lo dijo el río.
(I knew that we would triumph, the river told me so.)

—BERTA CÁCERES,

a leader in the indigenous Lenca people's campaign
to protect the Gualcarque River from a massive dam
project planned to provide energy for Honduras's
mining and logging industries,
assassinated in 2016

CONTENTS

INTRODUCTION

They came from the North with their money and their guns
for the gold in the hills where the Lempa River runs.
Marcelo Rivera, he'll never grow old.
Water for life, or is it water for gold?

—From song "Water for Gold,"
lyrics by Joe Uehlein

In late June 2009, the two of us received deeply disturbing news: Marcelo Rivera had been disappeared. We had never met Marcelo, but we had been looking forward to doing so. He and four other "water defenders," as they would become known to many, were scheduled to travel to our city, Washington, DC, to receive a human rights award.

At that point, we had never been to Marcelo's home country, much less to his hometown or the old house he was renovating. Nor did we have any plans of going there. To be honest, we did not know the difference between a tortilla and a *pupusa*.

For nearly two weeks, Marcelo Rivera's family could not find him. Then, on June 29, they received the phone call they had been dreading. The anonymous caller was brief. There was a body in an old, abandoned well just west of the Rivera hometown of San Isidro, Cabañas. The well was near the spot where Marcelo had last been seen some twelve days earlier, getting off the bus at a turnoff to the capital city.

During those twelve days, Marcelo's family and friends had been at wit's end, searching frantically, desperately, for him. They had spread news of his disappearance in all the barrios of San Isidro and nearby towns.

They had called the police for over a week, to no avail. The Rivera family had even filed a formal complaint with El Salvador's attorney general, pleading for him to conduct a search and an investigation into Marcelo's disappearance. But another poor person gone missing up in the rural north meant little to the authorities.

After the anonymous tip to Marcelo's family, the police finally acted. They pulled the remains of a body out of the dry, thirty-meter-deep well. So extensive was the torture that the body was unrecognizable. The face was grotesquely disfigured—no jaw, no lips, no nose. The fingernails had been ripped off. The testicles bound. The trachea had been broken with a nylon cord. In the assessment of the coroner, the death had been caused by asphyxiation. The public prosecutor disagreed, concluding that that death had come from blows to the head by a hammer. Whatever the cause of death, the torture bore eerie similarity to that inflicted by right-wing death squads during the twelve years of El Salvador's gruesome civil war in 1980–92.

Thus Marcelo Rivera became the first of several water defenders to be assassinated in the twenty-first-century fight over mining in northern El Salvador.

Though we never met Marcelo, we have been haunted by him and the circumstances of his death ever since. Who killed Marcelo? And why?

Perhaps you know the difference between a tortilla and a *pupusa*. Or perhaps, like we had done, you are entering this story without a clue. Perhaps El Salvador is not even on your radar screen. Or perhaps El Salvador is on your radar screen only because of gangs or immigrants who trek north. But, really, that does not matter. Certainly, on one level, this is a story about El Salvador. At the same time, it is not just about El Salvador. This is a David-versus-Goliath story about a battle between a country and a foreign mining company. But it is also about how global corporations—be they Big Gold or Big Pharma or Big Tobacco or Big Oil or Big Banks— move into poorer communities in countries all over the world.

Marcelo's story—before and after his murder—is about the struggle for clean and affordable water everywhere. It is also a story about workers and communities defending their air and land, their health and their climate, and their rights to defend themselves against corporate incursion. About how to prioritize those rights and the common good versus the usual prioritization of the profits of big corporations and their owners. It is certainly a story about gold—and when and why we should leave it in the ground. But it could be about coal or natural gas or other fossil fuels. About whether we measure progress in aggregate financial terms or through the well-being of people and the planet. About who gets to make the decisions that affect our lives.

To say that this story of the Water Defenders versus Big Gold holds keys to reversing the outsized power of global corporations today is not an exaggeration. You may find yourself surprised by the relevance of the strategies of the water defenders in El Salvador, whether your focus is on a Walmart in Washington, DC; a fracking company trying to expand in Texas or Pennsylvania; or petrochemical companies outside New Orleans. Along the way—however clichéd the quote attributed to Margaret Mead may have become—you may also find yourself inspired by a "small group of thoughtful, committed citizens" who stand up to corporate power.

We first heard of Marcelo in May 2009, just a month before his murder. He was a thirty-seven-year-old teacher who directed his hometown's cultural center, an avid reader, a person who loved theater and the arts and a good practical joke. We heard his name because he was a leader of the main coalition of Salvadoran groups opposed to mining—the National Roundtable on Mining in El Salvador, or La Mesa. The roundtable was not well known outside of El Salvador. But we learned of it because the group had been chosen to receive a prestigious human rights award from the Institute for Policy Studies where John works.[1] In 2009, the institute

---

1. Each year, a committee of human rights experts selects unsung heroes to receive this award in the names of Orlando Letelier and Ronni Karpen Moffitt, IPS colleagues who were assassinated in Washington, DC, in 1976 by agents of the Chilean dictator Augusto Pinochet.

selected the roundtable to honor its opposition to mining companies eager to exploit the gold deposits near El Salvador's major river.

On a misty night in October 2009, just months after Marcelo's body was pulled from that well, hundreds gathered at the National Press Club in downtown Washington, DC, to meet and applaud the Salvadoran water defenders. Among them was Marcelo's youngest brother and best friend, Miguel. Miguel had come in his brother's place, and his grief marked his face.

Accepting the award on behalf of Miguel and three other roundtable leaders was a farmer and community leader from the heart of gold country, Vidalina Morales. Vidalina looked small behind the podium. The US congressman who presented the Letelier-Moffitt Human Rights Award towered over her, making her look even smaller. Dressed unassumingly in an orange blouse and red skirt, her long dark hair pulled back in a simple ponytail, her face free of makeup, she at first appeared hesitant. Nervous before the large audience. Fragile even.

Then she began to speak. Her words filled the auditorium, almost as though she did not need the microphone. For nearly twenty minutes, Vidalina held the crowd spellbound as she relayed the saga of El Salvador's water defenders standing up to Big Gold. The Lempa River, she explained, winds through the country like a snake, providing water for over half the population. Water for drinking, for fishing, for farming. Water for the cities as well as the rural population. But the project of the Canadian-headquartered Pacific Rim Mining Corporation at its proposed El Dorado site in Miguel and Marcelo's hometown posed serious threats to the Lempa River. Key among the dangers was the toxic cyanide that Pac Rim would use to separate the gold from the rock.[2]

---

2. Throughout this book we typically use the name "Pac Rim" as shorthand for three related entities: "Pac Rim Cayman LLC," "Pacific Rim Mining Corporation," and "Pacific Rim El Salvador." The parent body is Pacific Rim Mining Corporation (headquartered in Vancouver). Exactly why there are these separate but connected entities with different legal names will become clear as our tale unfolds. On occasion, when we need to make a distinction among the legal entities, we will use the precise legal names. Overall, however, it is fine for the reader to think of Pac Rim as one entity operating in its Canadian headquarters, as a Cayman Island shell company, and on the ground in El Salvador.

Vidalina ended her acceptance speech with a seemingly audacious demand: that the government of El Salvador stand up to giant mining firms and choose water over gold by banning the mining of all metals. *All.*

Before this she had urged the audience to follow a related legal thriller unfolding four blocks to the west of where we sat, just past the White House, the site of a little-known tribunal in Washington. There, as Vidalina explained, Pac Rim had filed a lawsuit against the government of El Salvador right before Marcelo's murder. Pac Rim claimed that El Salvador had to either allow it to mine or pay it over $300 million in costs and foregone profits from future mining. Vidalina invoked the "upside-down" world summoned by Uruguayan writer Eduardo Galeano, in asking why it was not El Salvador suing Pac Rim, since the mining company threatened the water and well-being of her country.

But that upside-down world is the reality of global corporate power and economic rules that affect people around the globe. And, as we think back to that evening, we must admit that we each, separately and silently, found it just as far-fetched to imagine a national legislature passing a law to end mining as it was to conceive of this tribunal siding with Vidalina and the rest of the water defenders. Her demands just seemed implausible. So many had tried for so long to right that upside-down world, with relatively little success. But this reaction we kept to ourselves—we did not even tell one another.

Instead we shared what seemed like a more important and immediate reaction: being equal parts mesmerized by Vidalina and her words, and utterly outraged by Pac Rim and the prospect of the lawsuit.

At the reception following the awards ceremony, we huddled with Marcelo's brother, Miguel. Miguel was soft-spoken and gentle in his manner, understandably a bit shy as he asked for help. After all, we had just met. He seemed both incredibly focused on the details of what to do next and shell-shocked by the chain of events—by his brother's murder and the lawsuit. But his appeal was urgent, direct, and heartfelt: "We don't know this tribunal or how it works. We don't know what to expect. Can you help us find out about this lawsuit?"

The suit had been filed by Pac Rim at the luxurious and sprawling headquarters of the World Bank, one of the global institutions set up after

World War II by the United States, the United Kingdom, and other leading powers. We had done decades of research on the Bank. Robin had
written a book and many articles on the World Bank in the Philippines
and other countries, and John had pulled together researchers to examine
impacts of its policies on poor people around the world. We knew the
Bank well, yet so hidden was this tribunal that we did not realize it was
officially part of the World Bank Group. At that point, we did not know
that its cases could drag on for seven years. We did not know that most of
what transpired was done in secret.

But we did know that Pac Rim's claim—that a government could not
adopt environmental rules that deprived a corporation of future profits—
could well stand up in that court. We knew that such lawsuits could be
initiated against El Salvador or Canada or even the United States. We
also knew that global corporations typically prevailed in their lawsuits
against governments like El Salvador. And, given this reality, that governments often caved in under the financial costs of such suits, settling outside
of court either by paying the corporation or removing the problematic
regulation.

More to the point, we knew that we could not say no to Miguel.

On that foggy evening in October 2009, who could have guessed that
Miguel's questions and Vidalina's call to action would pull us two—and
thousands of others around the world—into the vortex of three intertwined unknowns for nearly a decade to come?

First, there was the on-the-ground mystery: Who killed Marcelo
and why? Not just who carried out the brutal killing. Who was the
mastermind?

Second, there was the mystery at the national level: Could El Salvador
possibly become the first nation on earth to ban mining—or at least move
closer to that goal? Or did all this hoopla about stopping mining simply
mean, as many assumed in 2009, that Pac Rim had not paid a high enough
bribe to top officials in the national government?

And, finally, the global legal thriller: Could little El Salvador possibly
prevail against the gold mining industry in Washington, DC? Would El
Salvador, a poor country, even have enough money to pay for its legal and

related costs? To hire a lawyer savvy enough to take on what would un-doubtedly be a top corporate law team hired by Pac Rim?

We had no idea then how these mysteries would play out. But, as we joined the hundreds of people who streamed out of the National Press Club after the award ceremony, we knew we were hooked. We knew we needed to find out more about this tribunal—at least a day or two of re-search to answer Miguel's questions. And we were intrigued by the pros-pect, however unlikely, that a poor country might actually choose to halt mining to save its water. Perhaps the one thing we felt fairly certain about was that the question of who had killed Marcelo would be unraveled by others in El Salvador within months or, at most, a few years.

We also had no idea just how involved we would actually become. In the years that followed, we would travel to El Salvador eight times. We would become uncomfortably familiar with the road on which Marcelo made his last journey. On each trip from San Salvador, our eyes would look to the right when we passed the turnoff that led to the well where Marcelo's body was found. To the left when we passed the Pac Rim mine site.

Over those years, we spent many days in the communities that were standing up against mining, as well as those whose mayors were actively supporting it. Given the lack of hotels, we slept many a night in the small town just north of the mine site at the dormitory of the social research and action center where Miguel and Vidalina worked. We talked late into the night with whichever one of them or their colleagues stayed with us. Only belatedly did we realize that they were staying there not necessarily because they liked talking to us but because it was not safe for them to travel home after dark. We walked up and down the streets of Marcelo's and Miguel's hometown of San Isidro, where youth painted their oppo-sition to Pac Rim on murals on the exterior walls of homes, just minutes from the El Dorado mining headquarters.

Over these years, we ate countless *pupusas*—the typically cheese-filled fried tortillas ubiquitous in El Salvador—with farmers and townspeople as they told us their stories. We munched local cashews with them as we walked through their fields to see for ourselves the problems created by Pac Rim's test wells. Sweating in the tropical heat and trying to keep up with Miguel and others, we hiked down steep volcanic embankments to the streams below to see the water defenders' projects to bring piped water to communities high above. Women and children passed us politely as they scampered down the hillsides each morning, trekking back up somewhat more slowly—but still far faster than our pace—with heavy, water-filled urns on their heads.

We traveled to the far northeast of the country, to a mine that was shuttered years ago. There we learned about the sulfides in certain mines that turn into deadly sulfuric acid every time it rains. As a result, minerals leach into the land and water, and on some days the spring water below this closed mine emerges rusty orange. Other times the water appears cranberry red. An environmental nightmare of toxic water, land, and air—and the one place in El Salvador that makes us shudder.

We also spent much time in air-conditioned offices in San Salvador, often waiting for hours to meet with busy national legislators and government officials who explained their views on the pluses and minuses of mining. We talked mining with ministers as well as the vice president and president. And we sat in churches and parish houses with priests as they explained how they and their parishioners came to oppose mining. We learned how this opposition was in keeping with the history of support for social justice from El Salvador's church community, continuing the legacy of the martyred Archbishop Oscar Romero, whose photo is omnipresent in this country.

Vidalina's speech and our initial research efforts to answer Miguel's questions also led us to understand that this was a global fight as well as El Salvador's. We were hardly alone in this understanding. In 2011, we joined with others to set up a network of groups from around the world, the International Allies Against Mining in El Salvador. The International Allies coordinated research, letters, petitions, and actions with Americans, Canadians, Australians, Germans, and others. It brought pressure to corporate and World Bank suites and to the streets. It protested outside Pac Rim's headquarters in Vancouver, outside shareholder meetings in

Toronto and Melbourne, and outside the World Bank. And we helped with several educational tours for Vidalina, Miguel (until his multi-entry visa to the United States was inexplicably canceled by the US embassy in El Salvador), and others.

The two of us also returned to the other side of the planet twice (in 2013 and 2017), to the Philippines, a country we knew well from the years we worked there during and after another dictatorship backed by the United States. In 2009, we did not expect that our experience and contacts in the Philippines would connect to this Salvadoran drama. But a sister mine of El Dorado stood hidden in the mountains of the northern Philippines, a project the mining company in El Salvador touted as an example of its "green" and "responsible" mining that the poor people of El Salvador were sadly missing out on. We traveled twelve hours from the capital city of Manila along steep, winding, and dusty roads to find out if the mining company was telling the truth. In 2017, one of us would return to El Salvador with a Philippine governor, himself a farmer, for a week-long tour that included his testifying to the Salvadoran legislature on the deadly impacts of mining in his province.

All this activity culminated seven years later as the World Bank's tribunal ruled on the corporate lawsuit, and six months after that as a bill to ban mining finally reached the floor of El Salvador's legislature for a vote. But that is getting ahead of our story.

The more we spent time with Miguel, Vidalina, and ordinary people in northern El Salvador, and the more we learned about the dangers of mining and the rules rigged in favor of the mining firms, the more we found ourselves confronting daunting questions whose answers appeared as elusive as they were compelling. These questions also brought home to us the relevance of this story to communities in the United States, Canada, Australia, and elsewhere.

The popular wisdom on the environment is that it is wealthier people in richer countries who care the most. The poor, it is often argued, cannot afford to worry about the environment. What then led Marcelo, Vidalina, and other ordinary, poorer farmers to become water defenders, to lead the charge to protect watersheds in El Salvador?[3]

This question led us into deeper discussions with mining proponents and mining opponents about a set of related queries: What is "progress"? What is "development"? To phrase that differently: What constitutes a better life for oneself, for one's community, and for one's country? We found strongly felt and divergent answers to this essential question. These conversations often reminded us of discussions that are consuming—and often dividing—communities across North America, debates about whether "progress" or "development" can be catalyzed through fracking or tar-sands pipelines or big-box stores or public subsidies to supposedly job-creating entities such as Amazon.

Central to this book are questions about that most basic of resources—water—at a time when ordinary people from Michigan to the Sahara struggle for access to clean and affordable water. In 1995, Egyptian environmentalist Ismail Serageldin warned, "The wars of the next century will be fought over water—unless we change our approach to managing this precious and vital resource." Since then, around the world, water defenders have stood up in numerous epic struggles. The Standing Rock Sioux of North Dakota and South Dakota. The people of Flint, Michigan. Others, starting in North Carolina, who have put the right to clean water center stage as they build a twenty-first-century version of Martin Luther King Jr.'s Poor People's Campaign in the United States. Farmers in India fighting Coca-Cola's attempts to take their water. Inhabitants of hundreds of cities and towns in the United States, Bolivia, France, and Canada fighting big corporations that seek to privatize public municipal

---

3. Across the Western Hemisphere, organizations and individuals struggling to save their waterways from mining, from fossil fuels extraction and pipelines, from new dams, and from other harms have often been called—and have often called themselves—either water protectors or water defenders. When we asked Vidalina and her colleagues what term they and their allies across El Salvador used, they responded: "Defensoras y defensores del agua"—water defenders. In the chapters that follow, you will get to know water defenders in organizations such as La Mesa and International Allies. You will also meet like-minded people and groups who are not officially part of these organizations but who also fall under the collective umbrella term "water defenders."

water systems. Towns from New York State to New Mexico that are protecting their land and water from fracking for natural gas. And, from El Salvador to Indonesia, from Argentina to the Philippines, communities valuing water over mining—even rallying under the same cry: "Water is life!" "Agua es vida," as we are told time and time again in El Salvador.

Our questions about water led us to questions about whether corporations in El Salvador, the United States, or anywhere could ever safely mine gold and other metals. As we learned more about what lies beneath the earth and the dangers of extracting it, we found ourselves pondering the metals that seem central to our modern lifestyles. Imagine trying to get through the day without the steel in our buildings, bridges, and railways, the aluminum in our cars, computers, and cans, the rare earths in our cell phones. Gold, the most precious of minerals, is central to jewelry and most electronic devices—even cell phones—and other industrial uses. Gold has also been highly attractive as a financial investment for centuries, and its value rises in uncertain and turbulent times. Walmart and Amazon have become among the largest firms in the world because of our seemingly insatiable demand for stuff. Much of that stuff is put together from minerals that are scattered randomly around the world, most in remote mountains such as those in Nevada and Maine, or those that cross northern El Salvador into Guatemala on one side and Honduras and Nicaragua on the other. Some—"conflict minerals"—are extracted from, and finance conflicts in, lands like those of the Democratic Republic of Congo and the Central African Republic.

Yet millions of people in mining communities face the dangers of mining accidents, the contamination of their water, and the conflict—the violence—that mining invariably brings. Millions of people do not want their water or land contaminated by toxic substances such as the cyanide used by the mining companies or the other poisons that are released from the rocks along with the gold. Might we do better to keep some minerals in the ground? Are there areas where mining should be banned? And can we mine the rest in less harmful ways?

Growing corporate control of water and minerals led us to questions about rules, regulations, and laws, and about who establishes them and on whose behalf. From the first research about the World Bank tribunal we undertook at Miguel Rivera's request, much of what we contributed had to do with what we knew—and learned—about the rules and institutions of the global economy. For close to four decades, since the elections of Ronald Reagan and Margaret Thatcher, thousands of rules have been written into trade and investment agreements—agreements signed by governments—that favor globe-girdling corporations over communities, indigenous peoples, human rights, and the environment. Notable among these is the so-called "investor-state" clause that allowed corporate "investor" Pac Rim to sue the "state," the government of El Salvador. That very same rule written into a trade agreement allowed fossil fuel giant Canadian TransCanada to launch a jaw-dropping $15 billion "investor state" lawsuit against the US government when President Obama stopped its pipeline due to the pipeline's predicted impact on climate change.[4]

Can we, like Vidalina, imagine transforming such pro-corporate rules as these, without sounding like we live in la-la land?

We became intrigued with questions about the often unusual tactics and the alliances of our new Salvadoran friends as they took on giant corporations far more powerful than they. Some of these alliances reminded us of a distinguished senior colleague of John's at the Institute for Policy Studies (IPS) in the 1980s. Jorge Sol was a man born into one of the fourteen wealthy families that dominated El Salvador for decades. He went to Harvard, was appointed minister of finance of his country, and was chosen to be an executive director at the International Monetary Fund, the sister institute of the World Bank in Washington. At a certain point, he chose to leave that world behind and came to work at the IPS. There he joined groups working to end the Salvadoran civil war and working for social justice for the country's poor majority. Would anyone follow in his footsteps and cross class lines to join the water defenders today? Some would, and you will meet such people in this book.

We also found ourselves wondering whether there are ways to predict who would look beyond short-term interests of the few to the good of the majority. As Pac Rim and other mining companies entered El Salvador,

---

4. The TransCanada lawsuit was halted only because the next US president, Donald Trump, allowed the pipeline to proceed.

the people of El Salvador would elect a conservative president in 2004 and then progressive ones in 2009 and 2014. At first we jumped to the assumption that the "good guys" would appear only with the progressive administrations. But we—and the water defenders—discovered a more interesting truth. There would be people on both sides of this fight in all three administrations. What motivated some government officials to take risks and to stand with the water defenders, while others sided with the mining companies? And what lessons do such unlikely allies hold for campaigns in other countries, including our own?

Finally, there were profound questions about a country like El Salvador and whether it could overcome its history. As in many poorer countries around the world, from Guatemala to Zaire to Chile, El Salvador's history is one drenched in the blood of US-backed coups and interventions and corporate incursions. The Washington, DC, award ceremony in 2009 and our trips to El Salvador brought us back a quarter century. Like many of our generation, we knew El Salvador through its brutal civil war of the 1980s during which the US government of Ronald Reagan sustained a dictatorship there. In that final decade of the Cold War, the Reagan administration poured money into ruthless regimes and right-wing armed groups across Central America and elsewhere in the name of fighting communism. Thanks to journalists such as Ray Bonner of the *New York Times*, we knew of the US government's complicity in massacres in El Salvador. And we were continually reminded. Indeed, a number of our meetings in San Salvador took place at the Jesuit university where six priests and two workers had been executed in 1989, most in the gardens outside where red roses now replace their blood.

El Salvador is still known to many for this civil war, during which over seventy-five thousand on both sides were killed. As a percentage of the population, this would be comparable to killing five million people in the United States. Joan Didion in her searing 1983 book *Salvador* wrote: "Terror is the given of the place." And today El Salvador is one of those countries known as a place of gangs, drug trafficking, and violence, legacies of this history of US intervention. Marcelo and others were assassinated in a province where justice was scarce, and where the murky world of global corporations would merge with the interests of local elite politicians and with the reality of jobless gang members. In this climate, would the water defenders be scared into silence? With this history and present reality of conflict, could the people of El Salvador possibly choose water and the common good over potentially large financial rewards of mining for the few? If you were a water defender and you received a text message that said "You are dead . . . you goddamn dog," what would you do?

In the years after 2009, the assassination of a thirty-seven-year-old teacher who directed a cultural center and a corporate lawsuit catalyzed actions in Washington, DC; Manila; Toronto; Melbourne; and elsewhere. Actions by labor unions, environmentalists, faith leaders, artists, and others coordinating with farmers across northern El Salvador, far off the beaten path.

This work has changed our lives as well as our sense of the possible. And it has changed our views of what is required to win when the odds seem stacked so heavily, as they often do, on the side of the wealthy and powerful. It has also motivated us to dig back in time to the beginning of this story, before we appeared on the scene, when Marcelo, Miguel, and Vidalina first met the miners from Big Gold in the early 2000s.

Along the journey of this book, you will also meet people you might not have expected to choose water over gold, people who became central players in this drama. Luis Parada, El Salvador's lead lawyer in the lawsuit, went from the Salvadoran military to West Point, to become a skilled lawyer, a champion of the environment, and an archrival to Pac Rim's smug corporate lawyers. We play law students of a sort with Luis—discussing and debating various possibilities of what might happen in the lawsuit. He teaches us that one can often get confidential updates on machinations around the government's positions and the lawsuit by hanging out in the extravagant lobby of San Salvador's five-star Sheraton Hotel, a world away from our dorm room in mining country.

You will meet archbishops, right-wing government officials, legislators, and farmers who decide to act in ways that may surprise you.

Of course, you will also hear from those who chose gold over water. While officials of the mining firm Pac Rim refused to meet with us, a principal figure in this story will come to life through his testimonies to the tribunal and through emails made public through the long court battle. He is Thomas Shrake, the Nevada-based Pac Rim executive who attempts to woo Salvadoran mayors and government officials and even farmers. Shrake's email traffic reveals Pac Rim's almost comical self-importance when he suggests enlisting support from the pope and US president George W. Bush.

In addition to our interactions with these and other main characters in this drama, we spent a great deal of time with dozens of other key individuals in El Salvador. We spoke to most of these people through an interpreter, and their quoted words that appear throughout this book are our interpreter's English translations of the original Spanish.[5]

Looking back, it feels as if the two of us were somehow fated to wander into the drama surrounding Marcelo's disappearance in 2009, to become a part of it, and then to share it with you.

We two had long been drawn to David-versus-Goliath fights. In most cases, though, Goliath had won.

When we first met, in graduate school, Robin was just back from a fellowship year in the southern Philippines. There she lived and worked with an indigenous community trying to protect its ancestral land from an expanding Del Monte pineapple plantation. Del Monte eventually won. The land is now submerged under water from a series of foreign-funded hydroelectric dams that provide energy to the plantations.

John was just back from his first year working at the United Nations in Geneva. There he joined a small research team digging into the unchecked power of global corporations. Once again, the corporate Goliaths prevailed. As John's team raised the idea of cracking down on misleading marketing practices by tobacco and alcohol corporations in poorer

---

5. We conducted these interviews over eight trips to El Salvador from 2011 to 2019. When the precise time of our interviews is not important to the story, we do not mention the exact date. We also shared Spanish and English versions of the relevant chapters with key individuals in El Salvador to make sure we were not misconstruing or misquoting anyone. See the acknowledgments section at the end of the book for the names of the people we interviewed in El Salvador and elsewhere.

countries, the Reagan administration pulled the plug on the funding for that work.

In graduate school, we bonded over our quest to learn more about working with communities to counter the power of global corporations. Some couples gel over drinks or dances. We gelled over self-initiated study sessions during which we learned everything we could about topics like the abysmal wages and working conditions of the Asian women who stitch together our sneakers and shirts, be they in Indonesia or in New York's garment district. We clicked as we linked with others in attempting to convince the president and board of Princeton to divest the university's financial holdings from the racist, apartheid government in South Africa. We connected over social justice in a moment in history when dictators ruled from Zaire to Chile but also when popular movements against such dictators were on the rise from El Salvador to the Philippines to South Africa.

Since Robin fell in love with the Philippines before she fell in love with John, our marriage was a package deal. With Robin came off-hours work against Philippine then-dictator Ferdinand Marcos, whose wife had a legendary weakness for shoes. We became experts on the private corporations that dominate the global economy as well as on the public institutions that set the rules in favor of those corporations.

In 1983, with a graduate degree in hand, John landed his dream job at the DC-based Institute for Policy Studies, where he has worked ever since. Robin's perches varied—from the US Congress to the US Treasury Department to, in 1990, teaching at American University in Washington, DC, where she finally (as a parent might say) settled down. Some summers and vacations we spent working to document abuses of nannies, caregivers, and restaurant workers, many of them immigrants, in this country. Others we spent returning to the Philippines and elsewhere where people, many of whom would become close friends, were fighting against overwhelming odds to make their world a better place. We coauthored books, articles, a comic book, op-eds, blogs. Somewhere along the way, we had a son who, at a young age, jokingly complained that we talked shop a bit too much over family meals.

This work prepared us—at least somewhat—for the struggle we would join after Marcelo Rivera's murder. Beyond our knowledge of the World

Bank, we knew how to dig up information on secretive institutions and how to research corporations, and we had contacts inside the Bank. Years of working with farmer groups in other countries and participating in broader coalitions had also taught us how crucial it was to build relationships of trust for this kind of cross-cultural and cross-border work. Yet we could not have imagined in 2009 all that we and our allies would still need to learn.

Then the story's plot twisted and turned, with us in it.

This story began several years before Marcelo's disappearance and murder, in a small town in the northern mountains of El Salvador when "white men in suits" arrived. The unknown men said they had come to talk about mines. As a local farmer who became a town official recounted, when the men in suits started trying to talk about mines, it created some confusion for him and his fellow townspeople: "We told these white men in suits that the United Nations had already come through and taken out all the mines—that is, the land mines from the civil war. There were no more land mines. But the men in suits said: 'Oh, no, we're looking for another kind of mines, ones with gold, silver, and iron.' That is when our struggle against mining began. That is when the companies' lies began."

CHAPTER 1

White Men in Suits
(2002–2004)

Thomas Shrake picked the right moment to search for gold in El Salvador. In 2002, the country dangled a new mining law jam-packed with enticements for foreign firms. And the price of gold was surging, thanks to a boom in global sales of mineral-laden electronics and a roaring Chinese economy. It would climb from $270 an ounce in 2001 to $1,400 in 2010, the year after water defender Marcelo Rivera's ghastly murder.

A new gold rush had begun. Confident "white men in suits" from Canada, Australia, the United States, and elsewhere jumped on airplanes to El Salvador. Many set up shop at the luxurious InterContinental Hotel in San Salvador, the capital. It was the hotel of choice for the economic and political elite during the years when the right-wing ARENA party held power—the place to catch up on the latest insider news and gossip. The men in suits would start the day at the hotel's lavish buffet breakfast. And then they would travel a few hours north in shiny, private vehicles to the mountains of gold country, at which point their vehicles were no longer shiny.

We could not help but wonder: Did Shrake and the rest of them, as did we, breathe a sigh of relief as they escaped the traffic and heat of the congested San Salvador streets and entered the fresh mountain air of the north? Once in Marcelo's province of Cabañas, were they reading dry mining prospectuses? Or did they stare out of the car windows at the cornfields, the over-logged hills, and the modest but well-kept cement and adobe houses, painted with pretty earthen and pastel colors and surrounded by carefully maintained flower gardens? As they drove on, did they stop to gaze at the streams and rivers that flow north and east into the mighty Lempa River—Central America's third longest—the lifeblood and lifeline of this country? Or did they focus only on the rock formations they passed, mentally calculating the mineral wealth that lay beneath?

Tom Shrake would drive past these streams into Miguel and Marcelo Rivera's hometown of San Isidro many times. Silver-haired, broad-shouldered, and standing erect, Shrake looked like a man whose photo would grace the pages of an outdoor retailer's catalog. Indeed, he called himself "an avid environmentalist and outdoorsman." He also exuded the confident air of a top corporate executive accustomed to getting his way. A US exploration geologist and CEO of Vancouver-based Pacific Rim Mining Corporation, he worked out of the Pac Rim office in Reno, Nevada, the state that dominates gold mining in the United States.

Decades of successfully sniffing out gold deposits in the United States, Costa Rica, Mexico, and Chile prepared Shrake for his Salvadoran gambit. Gold buried beneath the soil does not advertise itself from the roads or from planes flying overhead. Shrake was trained in economic geology, which he described as "the science of mineral deposits." His early research and work in Nevada focused on the characteristics of rocks near gold and copper deposits, which, he bragged, "enable[d]" him "to recognize and assess potentially mineable orebodies."

After twenty years in the field working for companies focused on minerals exploration, Shrake had been tapped by a third-generation Canadian gold mining executive in 1997 to become head of Pac Rim, then a small company with a silver mine in Argentina. Shrake immediately went on the road in a quest for new, profitable, Pac Rim mine sites. He hired two senior geologists, and together they explored sites in Argentina, Mexico, and Peru but failed to hit pay dirt.

Although he was a man with a good eye for gold, Shrake's big find for Pac Rim did not happen out in the field but instead in an air-conditioned

convention hall. Modern-day mine owners woo others to invest in their
projects at conventions held in cities like Toronto, Vancouver, and Melbourne, home to many mining company headquarters. Shrake learned
about a promising mine site in northern El Salvador, enticingly named
El Dorado, from a US miner named Robert Johansing at a Prospectors &
Developers Association of Canada meeting in Toronto in 2001. Johansing
had been manager of the El Dorado project since 1993, and he would go
on to find gold in a nearby province in the years to come. That El Dorado
was then owned by a company sharing a board member with Pac Rim
undoubtedly helped pique Shrake's interest in pursuing this lead.

After the convention, Shrake hopped on a plane en route to San Isidro,
where the El Dorado mine had been opened over a half century earlier
but had lain dormant for several years. A hilly town, San Isidro has a
population of about ten thousand. The town's densely populated center
is only five blocks by four blocks, and over half the population is spread
out in surrounding farms. The old adobe houses, with their thick walls,
are slowly being replaced by cement and brick houses, and a few small
stores line the paved roads. San Isidro's streets often bustle with schoolkids,
women carrying baskets on their heads or umbrellas to shade them from
the sun, and farmers walking to and from their corn and bean fields and
their small cattle farms. Long gone is indigo, planted centuries earlier for
its midnight blue dye.

While in El Salvador, Shrake carefully studied El Salvador's new investment and mining laws. He was favorably impressed by the welcoming
attitude toward foreign mining companies. He visited the El Dorado site
a second time, and he left convinced that the land held more gold than
its then-owners estimated. Shrake met with the director of El Salvador's
Bureau of Mines—a key contact for any prospective mine owner—and
he recalled in a witness statement years later that she "expressed great enthusiasm for the El Dorado project and the possibility of the Pacific Rim
Companies' investment in the country."

Over the many years that we traveled back and forth to El Salvador,
we reached out to Shrake and other Pac Rim executives several times
for interviews. We were turned down or ignored every time. But we
feel we know Tom Shrake rather intimately from the extensive cache of

documents—written testimonies, transcripts of oral testimony, emails, memos, and other communications concerning Pac Rim—that became part of the public record.

As we read Shrake's testimonies and communications, we were reminded of the risk-taking and gold-sniffing "man in a suit" from the United States who first brought large-scale industrial mining to El Salvador over a century earlier, Charles Butters. Born in Massachusetts in 1854, Butters studied metallurgy at the University of California and became an expert on what were then the state-of-the-art techniques. In 1885, he moved to the tiny town of San Sebastian in the northeast of El Salvador, and there he built a sophisticated plant that used chlorine as part of a process to separate gold from surrounding rock. Butters and his operation helped kick off the early Salvadoran gold rush.

In the late nineteenth century, modern gold mining was in its infancy, but a network of gold engineers was spreading around the world. Butters interacted extensively with metallurgists and miners from the United States, England, South Africa, and elsewhere. These men competed with each other one day and collaborated on new profit-making ventures the next. Butters got pulled from El Salvador to South Africa just as Scottish chemist John Steward MacArthur figured out that if you mix the toxic chemical cyanide with water, it dissolves gold out of the surrounding rock much more efficiently than does chlorine. MacArthur was issued a British patent for the technique in 1887.

It was Butters who further improved the cyanide process during his years in South Africa. He quickly proceeded to build cyanide-based gold-processing plants near mines in the United States, Mexico, and Nicaragua, eventually perfecting the process and thus creating a flourishing gold mining industry. Butters's process remains the primary technology of gold mining today, but the process carries substantial side effects—as water defenders would learn.

Butters could not forget his early experience at the San Sebastian mine in northeast El Salvador. He pronounced this mine a "great property" that had been "grossly mismanaged." He returned to El Salvador and paid $100,000 for the mine. Within a year, he had mined $1 million in gold.

He went on to construct several cyanide-based gold mines in El Salvador and Nicaragua, opening both countries to Big Gold—and making a lot of money in the process.

Then came 1927, during the two-decade US military occupation of Nicaragua and the resulting popular uprising led by revolutionary leader Augusto Sandino. After Sandino brought a band of armed men to Butters's Nicaragua mine and gave Butters the choice of a bullet to his head or banishment from the country, Butters wisely chose exile. After all, he had found an extremely compliant government in El Salvador and had made a fortune there.

The path between Charles Butters opening up El Salvador to Big Gold in the early 1900s and Tom Shrake setting up shop there in 2002 is rocky, reflecting the ups and downs of capitalism. The Great Depression of the 1930s shuttered Butters's mines as well as others the world over. After World War II, many mines picked up. Indeed, it was just after the war, in 1947, that a US mining firm found gold in San Isidro and opened the El Dorado mine. This company, New York & Honduras Rosario Mining, had already mined over $100 million in gold and silver—a handsome sum—in neighboring Honduras and was in expansion mode. The company operated the El Dorado mine profitably before shutting down in 1952 after only five years, as gold prices fell.

As with Big Gold in major mining countries such as China, Australia, Russia, the United States, Canada, and Indonesia, the profitability and fate of El Salvador's gold mines after World War II waxed and waned depending on the vagaries of global gold prices and local political conditions. Gold prices remained low from the mid-1950s till the mid-1970s. When gold prices jumped, drilling at El Dorado resumed in 1974, only to be interrupted again, this time by political events. From 1980 to 1992, the brutal Salvadoran civil war brought "security concerns" to foreign mining companies and halted mining everywhere in the country. After the civil war, the conservative ARENA party won the first of three consecutive presidential races, and these right-wing governments actively courted foreign investors. As a result, mining exploration at El Dorado picked up again briefly in 1996. But world gold prices plunged again between 1997 and 2001, and mining exploration in El Salvador again halted.

The gold price cycle kept repeating itself, and mining firms came and went. But prices seemed to spend more time down than up and global gold mining companies more absent from El Salvador than in the country actively mining.

Tom Shrake arrived in El Salvador just as the latest wave of low prices was ending. China had developed a voracious hunger for minerals as its economy expanded, driving gold prices skyward. But it was not just China: across the globe, our cellphones, computers, and other electronic devices required gold, the most efficient conductor of electrical charges. The world's romance with gold was entering a new era, and Big Gold was beginning its most lucrative period. Global mining firms, most headquartered in Canada, Australia, and South Africa, began reexamining mines closed over the preceding century. Mines in Nevada, Alaska, Colorado, and South Carolina, as well as in El Salvador, Russia, Indonesia, and elsewhere.

Something else changed by the end of the 1990s, and not just in El Salvador. In the mid-1990s, poorer countries around the world—from El Salvador to the Philippines—were pressured by the richer countries' governments and the global institutions they dominated, such as the Washington-based World Bank, to change national mining laws to be more welcoming to foreign investors than they already were.

Big Gold had grown in sophistication since Butters's time in South Africa. At the top stood ten giant firms, with annual sales in the billions of dollars, employing tens of thousands of workers around the world. Closer to the bottom were explorers like Shrake and Johansing, each working with a small ("junior") startup company—each trying to strike it rich by finding gold veins. Typically, such junior mining firms make a nice profit finding gold and then selling out to so-called senior companies that have the capital and expertise to do the actual mining.

Seldom strangers to one another, junior and senior firms' executives often overlap on boards, and the firms frequently share investors. The executives meet at lavish gatherings of miners, prospectors, and representatives of corporate networking bodies like the World Gold Council, where they

share tales of rich strikes and compare notes on political allies in governments around the world. The World Gold Council consists of twenty-five
of the world's largest mining firms, from Canada's Barrick Gold Corporation to Colorado-based Newmont and Australia-headquartered multina-
tional OceanaGold. Like Big Pharma, Big Tobacco, Big Banks, Big Oil,
and now Big Internet, these mining giants have translated economic riches
into political influence in Washington, Ottawa, Canberra, and other capital cities around the world.

Big Gold executives also weave a narrative—for themselves and the
public—in which mines not only enrich themselves and their shareholders
but also bring great benefit to the communities and countries where they
mine. In the words of the World Gold Council: "Gold mining often takes
place in remote areas where there is little existing infrastructure, so companies invest heavily in building power supplies, piped water and roads,
which can create important benefits for local communities. Infrastructure,
from roads to power stations, is part of the legacy that responsible miners
leave beyond the life of their mines, and is a major component of their
beneficial impact on developing and middle income economies."

Thus, in 2010, Shrake recalled of the El Dorado site: "The deposit was
located in one of the poorest regions of El Salvador, which desperately
needed foreign investment and which, because of its poor soil and remote
location, held little promise for agricultural development or other projects
of economic worth." One of the most striking things about Shrake's argument is its confidence in the rightness of his mission, not only for the
stockholders of Pac Rim but also for the people of El Salvador. To Shrake
and to the many executives and consultants of Pac Rim, the merits of
large-scale mining were obvious. Mining would bring jobs and revenues,
which would bring prosperity to all. With this worldview, Shrake thought
it would be easy to generate enthusiasm from local people near the mine
site. Who would possibly stand in the way of an industry that brought such
progress to poorer communities and countries?

In 2002, after Shrake convinced himself and then his board that more
gold lay beneath San Isidro's cornfields and cattle-grazing lands than anyone suspected, Pac Rim merged with the firm that owned El Dorado. In
so doing, Pac Rim also acquired the exploration licenses for the El Dorado

site. It then began to scout on the outskirts of the Rivera brothers' home-town with apparently little local attention—at least initially.

The exploration stage of mining involves more than just surveying the rocks and the landscape. The exploration licenses gave Pac Rim the right to sink wells to obtain core samples to determine how lucrative a site under consideration might be. As Shrake explained: "The core is a cylinder of material retrieved by drilling below the surface of the ground. Geologists study the core for mineral percentages and the location of the minerals within the rock formations, which give them the information necessary to begin or abandon mining operations in a particular area." Pac Rim started drilling those holes in El Salvador in May 2002. According to one report, Pac Rim drilled "more than 670 holes—up to 2,300 feet in length, across a 34-square-mile exploration zone."

These drillings produced long cylinders of gray and brown rock, which Pac Rim packaged in wooden boxes and sent to Reno, Nevada, for testing. The result would be the moment of truth for Shrake and his gold-sniffing abilities. And presumably for the future of Pac Rim in El Salvador.

What did the Rivera brothers, Marcelo and Miguel, think when the men in suits appeared in their home province of Cabañas? We gingerly asked Miguel this one day toward the end of one of our first stays in Cabañas. We were sitting on wooden benches in the shade of a majestic tree, a ca-cophony of birds and insects exploding around us. Miguel looks a lot like the photos we have seen of Marcelo, but with more hair. With his broad shoulders and muscular arms, he gives the impression from afar of being taller than he is. So too, from afar, do the T-shirts and baseball caps that he typically wears give him an air of youthfulness—belied, on closer view, by his large, deep-set eyes. Much as he might look like Marcelo, Miguel is not a center-stage type of guy. He wears a gentleness about him and, at times, a fragileness that made us even more leery about entering the pain-ful parts of his personal terrain.

When we asked Miguel about the men in suits, he sighed, fidgeted with his cap, and looked down at his sneakers. Then he surprised us by recounting a different story of white men arriving in Cabañas. "A story my mother told Marcelo and me long ago, when we were kids," he said. His story took us back to the 1950s when there had briefly been mining at the site that Pac Rim wanted to reopen in the twenty-first century. "Our mom rented a room in her old adobe house to a miner who was nicknamed Pig. Pig told my mother that, at the end of every month, when the miners got paid, the devil would come to the mine. The devil was a white man with red eyes on a black horse. And fire would shoot out of the horse's mouth wherever the horse stepped.

"And every time the white man with red eyes on the black horse arrived, three people would get stuck in the mine and die." Miguel's voice dropped to a whisper. "That was the deal the miners made with the devil in order to be able to mine there. It was a pact with the devil." Miguel paused, his moment of being center stage in the conversation coming to a close. The bench creaked as he leaned back. Then he looked directly at us and said: "That's the very first time Marcelo and I heard about mining."

There was more to the pact with the devil. Their mother also told Marcelo and Miguel stories about how the river in town near the mine used to be full of shrimp and fish, but, after Pig came and the mine was operating, they had died.

We thanked Miguel for sharing the story but wondered why he had done so, and at such length, rather than more directly answer our question. He smiled briefly, as if reading our minds. "It's a Salvadoran tradition," he offered. "There are stories to explain how things happen."

As we heard more stories that mentioned fish dying, we realized that we, probably like Shrake, had entered El Salvador without much knowledge about its rivers and the many threats to its clean water. Fourteen million people in the United States do not have access to clean, affordable water. That number rises to billions at the global level. The situation in each country is, of course, different. As we learned, El Salvador's water crisis is severe in terms of both quantity and quality—and rooted in decades of corporations excessively logging its watersheds and polluting its rivers. At the time of our first trip, as Miguel told us, the country held the dubious distinction of being second in the hemisphere behind Haiti in deforestation and first among countries worldwide in terms of overall environmental vulnerability, with 95 percent of its population living in areas at high risk. Most Salvadorans worry every single day about securing and affording enough clean water for drinking and cooking and washing and farming. Hence, water looms large in most families' concerns. Protecting that water is vital.

When Shrake and Pac Rim's men in suits first came to Cabañas, Marcelo, Miguel, Vidalina, and other water defenders were already paying attention to water but not yet to mining. They were busy trying to ensure that other so-called modernization and development projects did more good than harm. Their initial alarm regarding water was a proposed landfill for trash. In El Salvador, most trash ends up in landfills rather than being incinerated or going to recycling centers. Since many batteries and other toxic materials get dumped in the trash, the toxins invariably seep into the surrounding soil. And the proposed landfill was not to be small: the plan envisioned tons of trash trucked daily from more than twenty municipalities into San Isidro.

While one might not immediately think of a landfill in terms of water contamination, Marcelo and other community leaders had learned that the landfill was to be located close to the river that went through San Isidro. And that river was not just the primary source of water for the townspeople, their cattle, and their farms but also a key site for family gatherings and fishing. Moreover, it eventually flowed into El Salvador's main river, the Lempa, which then wove its way toward heavily populated southern El Salvador.

As Marcelo came to understand the threat of the landfill to water and thus to the community, he began to meet with farmers and others from organizations in nearby towns. In campaigning against the landfill, the water defenders took on a powerful opponent: the mayor of San Isidro, José Bautista. The landfill was his project, his baby, and, as mayor, he may well have thought he would be viewed as a hero when he told the community that he was going to bring thousands of dollars a day and jobs to the town by building it. Like most mayors in Cabañas, Bautista belonged to ARENA, and a photo of Roberto D'Aubuisson hung on his office wall. D'Aubuisson was the party's cofounder and leader of El Salvador's infamous death squads during the civil war. The water defenders' opposition to the landfill pushed them into the middle of the political fray.

Marcelo and the mayor had had "business dealings" for years before the landfill proposal. Indeed, Marcelo's first entry into community work had involved getting the mayor's permission for a project he and his kid brother Miguel cooked up. As Miguel explained after he recounted Pig's story of the pact with the devil:

> I was the last of nine siblings. I remember when I was eleven and Marcelo, the brother immediately above me, was eighteen. There was nowhere in San Isidro to get books. You had to take a bus to another city to get books. So we talked to others and we founded what we called the San Isidro Foundation for Culture and Arts. Marcelo and I went house to house to ask for donations of books. We got lots of books, maybe more than thirty. But where to put them? My mom agreed that we could put them in the living room of our very small house. We cut wood to make shelves for the books.

Miguel grinned. "I remember the day Marcelo and I opened our cultural center in our living room. But, the library kept growing, and our house wasn't big enough. That's when we went to the mayor's office." A municipal official who happened to be there reminded the brothers of an uninhabited public building in town. The long, single-story structure facing San Isidro's central square had been vacant since the civil war ended in 1992. There was just one problem that explained its vacancy. "During the war, bodies from a nearby place were brought to that building, so nobody wanted to use it," Miguel told us. "When we asked if we could use it, this municipal officer said, 'Well, there are ghosts there, and we are not taking responsibility if something happens to you there. But if you want to clean up the space, you can use it.'"

The brothers quickly went to work with their friends. As Miguel recollected, the biggest stumbling block was who would be brave enough to first risk an encounter with the building's ghosts. "I remember opening the door. Nobody wanted to be the first person to enter. But I ran through to the other side and back. And I remember crying."

Now they had a place to house the books, haunted or not. But who would staff the cultural center, and how could they continue on a volunteer basis as they had for their living room library? To their delight, a solution proved fairly easy. A government official happened to be in town, Miguel told us. "He surprised us by saying that the government would pay the salary of one person. That's how Marcelo became the director of the cultural center, a position he held until he was disappeared."

By 2004, Marcelo's influence extended beyond the cultural center. He was also directing a local nonprofit in San Isidro. The very existence of this nonprofit reveals the love and fierce loyalty that many born there have for their hometown. People from San Isidro who migrated north to California sent donations back home, which allowed the group to pay salaries to a small staff—beginning with Marcelo—and support community projects. As the landfill debate heated up, Miguel, who had been working in San Salvador as an accountant, quit his job to volunteer at the nonprofit.

Soon thereafter, Mayor Bautista waved another so-called development project in front of his constituents: a giant hog farm that also promised jobs and money to locals. And lots of hogs: as many as seventy thousand. But the prospect of countless tons of hog waste dumped into the river horrified Marcelo and the other water defenders. So, as Pac Rim vigorously drilled its holes, the hog farm and the landfill diverted the water defenders' attention.

Through community gatherings large and small, and in conversations with neighbors, the water defenders created enough community pressure to defeat the landfill. They were not successful in the fight against the hog farm, which gave them the taste of defeat. Both conflicts put them on the mayor's not-my-friends list. But the win against the landfill infused Marcelo and the others with collective self-confidence, and the San Isidro group made connections with like-minded groups in several other towns that would help in the struggle still to come.

"At the time of the landfill fight, we didn't know anything about mining," one of the water defenders revealed to us. "I talked to a friend in the Ministry of the Environment. He said: 'Worry more about mining than the landfill.'" That grabbed the water defenders' attention.

———

From their initial base in San Isidro, the water defenders expanded to other towns in the province through the Association for Economic and Social Development, ADES. Ever since the end of the civil war, ADES has been the central organization in the province of Cabañas to educate farmers about organic agriculture and convene forums on reducing violence in the area. It also started the community radio station run by youth. ADES became the water defenders' new home base in Cabañas.

The ADES central office is nestled in the hills of a small town just north of San Isidro, not far from the El Dorado mining site. The almost impossibly steep incline of the office's driveway stymies all but the most expert drivers. Once inside the big metal gates, one finds a compound of a few buildings—an office, an eating area, modest guest rooms above a large meeting room—and an oasis. Tropical flowers and trees, some with fruit, spill over neat walkways. The constant chatter of birds and insects fills the air. Just below the open-air eating space, staff have planted a small field of amaranth, a protein-rich grain that flourished in Mesoamerica before the Spanish conquistadors. In the post-Columbus world, Spanish colonists banned amaranth, claiming its association with "pagan" religious ceremonies. The Spaniards' real concern, some say, centered on the physical strength that amaranth gave the indigenous people. But groups like ADES have been helping farmers reintroduce the crop.

Both Miguel and Vidalina would end up working at ADES. But it was Marcelo who first brought mining to ADES's attention. Antonio Pacheco, the long-time executive director of ADES, explained to us that he started hearing about mining exploration in Cabañas as early as 1997 but did not then see a role that his group could play: "I thought [a mine] would solve employment problems and help the community overcome poverty." Antonio, a slight, bearded man, looked and sounded like an all-knowing academic as he waved his eyeglasses and hands to punctuate his points. In this case, he readily admitted that he had been behind the curve on mining, at least until Marcelo had approached him. Marcelo was not a stranger: "[He] had supported ADES by giving workshops on culture and theater." And, Antonio continued, Marcelo "was like the lead bloodhound, far ahead of the rest of us on the trail of the harmful impacts of future 'development' projects. He was the one who convinced us to take up mining. We made that decision at the end of 2004."

ADES's decision "to take up mining" pulled Vidalina into the work. The daughter of a Salvadoran father and a Honduran mother, Vidalina and her husband ended up living far north in Cabañas near the banks of the Lempa after the civil war. Her face, accentuated by high cheekbones, can shift in a split second from dead serious to a captivating smile. Vidalina wakes early each morning to make sixty-odd tortillas in an open-air kitchen for her husband and five sons. Then her commute of an hour or more begins. She walks from their small hamlet to the town center and then catches a bus to the ADES headquarters.

We were eager to hear more from Vidalina about the early years of the water defenders. We did so at what then served as the closest restaurant to ADES: a residence just down the hill where we feasted on a five-star breakfast of homemade tortillas, homemade cheese, and fresh eggs in the living room. We knew from past experience that Vidalina would eat little and have most of her food packaged to bring home for the rest of her family. She sat down, dressed as usual in a simple but colorful outfit, her blouse lit up with embroidery, her hair pulled back neatly as usual. No makeup. No high heels. Unpretentious and immaculate, without a hint of long dirt roads and hot buses. She has an ageless look that hides the wear and tear of her youth and her hard work in northern El Salvador.

In our conversation that day over breakfast, Vidalina reinforced that when Marcelo and others started to raise concerns about the mining companies in 2004, the local people were not against mining. Vidalina readily recollected how she first reacted to the news that Pac Rim was interested in opening the old El Dorado mine. It was as Shrake had predicted. "Initially, I—and really the rest of us—thought mining was good and . . . was going to help us out of poverty . . . through jobs and 'development.' . . . We were celebrating that mining was going to come. We were really totally unaware of mining's environmental, social, and economic downsides at that early stage."

Vidalina's honest recollection surprised us, but it should not have. El Salvador is one of the poorest countries in Latin America, and the northern provinces whose mountains contain the gold are the poorest of the provinces. Outside of government jobs and growing corn and beans, there are few formal, regular jobs. In most of those jobs, wages are low. So, many from Cabañas end up taking the two-to-three-hour bus ride back and forth to San Salvador, often for temporary and low-paying jobs. Or they join those heading north to the United States.

Pac Rim geared its initial sales pitch in Cabañas to this reality. As one water defender explained to us: "The mining company said: 'If you have natural resources, why don't you want to use them?' Pac Rim said: 'Mining equals jobs equals development equals happiness.' They said mining is development."

But then some odd things happened. Pac Rim offered money—a blank check—to ADES. Antonio remembers the Pac Rim official stating, "[It's] from a fund we have so that you can continue working on projects for the people." Later, Pac Rim tried another approach, sending three attractive "ladies of the night" to ADES—more than once. The ADES director said no to all such offers. Then Pac Rim offered thousands of dollars per month to the youth-run community radio station affiliated with ADES. The youth there also said no. Then, we were told, Pac Rim tried to hire a former mining company worker who had become critical of mining to spy on the other water defenders—offering a generous thirty dollars a day. He too turned down the money.

Certainly by then, Marcelo, Miguel, and Vidalina knew they had to learn more.

Cabañas was not the only province to be suddenly swarming in men in suits, and its citizens were not the only ones to realize that they needed to learn more about mining. At about the same time that Pac Rim began trying to sell the merits of mining to Marcelo, Miguel, and Vidalina, men in suits descended on the next province to the northwest, the equally mineral-rich province of Chalatenango.

The drive into Chalatenango from Cabañas is breathtaking: one descends from the mountains toward a panoramic view of the Lempa River at some of its widest expanses. But crossing the bridge over the river is crossing a vast political divide. Chalatenango was long a stronghold of the progressive FMLN party, named after Farabundo Martí, who led an unsuccessful mass uprising against the giant coffee plantation owners in the 1930s. In the late twentieth century, the province was a center of resistance to the US-backed military regime and right-wing ARENA in the twelve-year civil war. Whereas Marcelo's province of Cabañas was dominated by mayors like José Bautista of ARENA, Chalatenango was largely run by FMLN mayors whose constituents were wary of foreign investors.

One of the foreign miners in suits who descended on Chalatenango was Robert Johansing, the man who told Shrake about El Dorado at the Prospectors & Developers Association of Canada convention. Johansing is a self-described mineral exploration geologist with a degree from Colorado State University. Picture a salt-and-pepper handlebar mustache and the thick neck of a football linebacker—someone who looked like he knew how to get what he wanted. Johansing had been project manager of the El Dorado project in Cabañas from 1993 (after the civil war ended) until 2002, when Shrake and Pac Rim bought the company he worked for. Johansing left soon after Pac Rim management took over—"fired," in his rendition of events.

As gold prices rose from $343 an ounce in 2002 to $513 an ounce in 2005, Johansing sought his next gold adventure and venture but not via a Prospectors & Developers convention. Rather, like explorers of the past, he traversed northern El Salvador looking for a lucrative site—low-cost and high-profit. He found one in San José Las Flores in Chalatenango, not far from the border with Cabañas.

As we followed Johansing's trail, we tried to imagine what thoughts passed through his mind as he first entered San José Las Flores to meet with the local officials. Did San José Las Flores charm him as it did us—with its narrow streets, its central plaza, its ubiquitous flowers (as the name suggests) and its one main restaurant where everyone seems to know each other?

Johansing must have been struck by the difference in ambiance between Cabañas and Chalatenango that accompanied their political differences. As he approached the center of town, how could he help but notice that, unlike Cabañas, Chalatenango wears its FMLN political identity proudly and loudly? The central square greets visitors with abundant red and white paint, the colors of the party—and with a centrally placed mortar launcher from the FMLN side of the civil war. Across the street, painted FMLN logos cover the municipal building—should you forget who runs this town. Looking back at the plaza from the front door of that building, one sees that the plaza includes a playground populated by cement animals. Did Johansing notice the large lion and tiger baring their fangs?

Just as did Johansing, we entered the municipal building. Inside, a handful of officials greeted us, and soon they were recounting their memories of when the men in suits came a-wooing. One town official regaled us with the story about his initial bewilderment, a story that he clearly loves to tell and retell: he thought the men in suits were talking about land mines rather than gold mines. The same man then described meeting with Johansing and two others from that mining firm. Proudly wearing a polo shirt proclaiming him an official of the town, he took us back in time to that encounter: "I remember the meeting in this very same room. The mining company created a picture of the beautiful world they would create for us with development from mining. But we told them that we had our own plans for our own development." These were plans very different from Johansing's.

Unlike their compatriots in Cabañas, people in Chalatenango were leery of the gringos from the very start. The water defenders of Chalatenango immediately began organizing, something they knew well how to do from their war experience. "From that day on, we started working full-time, nonstop, to stop mining. We got a computer, a projector . . . we went to the communities, we did our homework at night to prepare for the next day. We got calls to get to meetings that the men with suits were holding before they ended, and we drove so fast that sometimes the screws would be flying off our cars."

When the people of Chalatenango and Cabañas decided they needed to learn more about mining, they knew whom they could trust. And they realized that they did not have to travel far. Thousands of people from both provinces had spent years during the civil war in refugee camps across the Lempa River in Honduras. Successive conservative governments in Honduras had embraced foreign mining companies, and so there were a number of possible nearby sites in Honduras where Marcelo, Miguel, Vidalina, and the other Salvadoran water defenders could learn about the impacts of industrial mining.

The waters of the Lempa divide Cabañas from Honduras for a stretch, long after those waters emerge in Guatemala, curl into Honduras, and traverse Chalatenango. Most of the people we met in northern El Salvador who live near the river and hence near Honduras do not think much about being from a different country than Hondurans. Vidalina explained to us: "My mother was Honduran and my father Salvadoran. I live in El Salvador. But, Honduran or Salvadoran, we all come from same origins. Many of us are descendants of the [indigenous] Lenca people of this region."

Vidalina brought us to her town in the far north of Cabañas, where the entire population of thousands was forced to evacuate in the second year of the civil war, 1981. Various-sized modest houses lined the one main dusty street. Posters of Archbishop Romero appeared everywhere on the outsides and insides of buildings. It was Easter Sunday, and we were leery of disturbing the town on this holiday. But we were immediately ushered in to meet a town elder, Don Carlos, a handsome and distinguished-looking man with a flock of white hair and a big tan hat. From how Vidalina and others treated him, it was clear he was revered.

We had come to talk about the townspeople's 2004–5 mining-research expeditions to Honduras. But Don Carlos would not let us start in 2004. "Our history is very long," he warned us. We sat back. Neighbors joined us, some who clearly knew the story firsthand and others who must have heard the story dozens of times.

"We lived in a state of poverty—you could say slavery in the 1970s," Don Carlos began, describing years before the war. "We farmed the land of large landowners who told us where to live and where to plant. We began to investigate and study to understand our persecution."

He paused. "Then the military operations against us began in the late 1970s. . . . This got worse when the war started. By 1981, the government was pursuing a 'scorched earth policy' against us. The military came in with seven thousand troops. So we didn't have a choice but to flee."

"My wife had given birth to twin daughters just days before," Don Carlos continued, his eyes flickering. "One died. We were fleeing with our [surviving] infant daughter and another young child. It was mostly elderly people, women, and children fleeing. Gathering only a few belongings, 7,500 of us fled north as the US-funded Salvadoran military burned our houses and fields. But we reached the Lempa . . . and it took us two days to cross the river."

"Two days," he repeated. He paused again, to make sure we understood, and then continued: "As we crossed the river, Salvadoran soldiers fired on us and dozens were killed. . . . Unfortunately, the Honduran army received us in the same way. For two weeks, we were surrounded by the Honduran military. We finally reached a place in Honduras where we could build a refugee camp. The Honduran people there received us with open arms." The people did, even if the government did not.

We knew the broad outlines of this war—and of the US government involvement and complicity in such atrocities. But we did not know the excruciating, on-the-ground details. We looked at Vidalina watching us, as we realized that she had brought us to Don Carlos in part to make sure we knew the history—the past horror—of the Cabañas communities that were now standing up to save their land from mining.

A 1981 *New York Times* article succinctly described what happened as the Salvadoran refugees crossed the Lempa River: "It was a massacre." Thus began six years of exile for this community and others from northern El Salvador in the refugee camps of Honduras. Many who live in northern El Salvador today were born in these camps. So too did many from Chalatenango live through similar atrocities and then in exile in Honduras, including some of the officials with whom we—and Johansing—met in San José Las Flores.

As Don Carlos said to us, there were a number of bad things but some good things about the six years in those camps: "On one side, no freedom. . . . On the other, if we hadn't been in those camps, we wouldn't have the organizing skills needed when we crossed the Lempa back to El Salvador . . . skills also necessary for the water wars to come." Don Carlos and Vidalina both chuckled as they saw us digesting his optimistic musings: "You could say that we made the most of the situation."

Twenty-three years after this first exodus across the Lempa into Honduras, Marcelo, Miguel, Vidalina, and others crossed the river again to learn everything they could about the gold mines in Honduras. Among the mines they visited was a giant open-pit mine owned by a Canadian heavyweight member of the World Gold Council. That mine began operations in 2001. And it used the highly toxic chemical cyanide—in the technique perfected by Charles Butters nearly a century before—to separate gold from the surrounding crushed rock. Pac Rim planned to use the same chemical in El Dorado, so the Honduran mine offered a close-up view of what might come.

The close-up shocked the travelers. The water defenders returned from Honduras with horror stories: of rivers poisoned by cyanide, of dying fish and skin diseases, of displaced communities, denuded forests, and corruption and conflict catalyzed by mining company payoffs. But it was the mining companies' use of water—the central environmental concern around which Marcelo and his fellow water defenders had already been organizing in their anti-landfill and anti–hog farm campaigns—that seized their attention. As Miguel told us, they learned about the effects of mining on water quality and quantity: "We learned how much water the mining companies would use to mine, and that became a big issue. Mining uses a lot of water, and we had little."

There were a number of such trips. The town official from San José Las Flores shared a bit of what they learned: "We saw with our own eyes those huge craters where they had cut off mountains. The mountains looked like a snail with trucks at the bottom, trucks looking so small. We saw the green leeching pond with the wastewater. And we also went down and looked at the river, and there was not one single thing living in the river."

In our conversations years later, we were struck by how often water defenders mentioned the impact of what they had seen in Honduras. It became the example that took what they were already beginning to sense and crystallized their thinking. Many in richer countries tend to think of poorer farmers like those in Chalatenango and Cabañas as not caring about the environment. And many tend to think of them as needing our help to put these pieces together. The story of the water defenders of El

Salvador shows how capable Marcelo and his friends were to start the inquiry on their own. And to persist.

The water defenders were vigilant researchers, thirsty to know more. So they did not stop after Honduras. Rather, they headed east across three provinces in El Salvador to continue their quest. Little did they know that they were walking into a nightmare created by Charles Butters just over a century before.

CHAPTER 2

A New Pact with the Devil (2005)

What gold-sniffing Charles Butters did not know and probably would not have cared about a century ago—but what Marcelo, Miguel, and Vidalina would learn—is that these ancient mountains contain not only gold. They also contain a toxic combination of materials that should never be exposed to air or water—a combination that can haunt for thousands of years once they are.

After returning from Honduras, Marcelo, Miguel, and Vidalina decided to expand their research with a visit to the site of Butters's old mine at San Sebastian, where underground mining had been practiced for over a century. The Cabañas water defenders had a much better understanding of the reality of open-pit mines thanks to their travels to Honduras. But Pac Rim now claimed that, while it might build an open-pit mine in Cabañas, it would largely extract gold through underground mines like Butters's—which the company insisted would be less destructive of the environment. So Marcelo, Miguel, and Vidalina knew they needed to learn more about mines built by tunneling underground.

San Sebastian was the place for that.

What Marcelo, Miguel, Vidalina and others saw when they traveled to San Sebastian in the middle of the first decade of the twenty-first century—and what we witnessed ourselves when we retraced their steps years later—would not have been out of place in an apocalyptic disaster film. Even though mining had been halted years before, the spring water below the San Sebastian mine emerged rusty orange, laden with iron and other minerals. Other times, the water appeared cranberry red. It flows into what is now a lifeless stream that empties into a river that then flows southeast into a larger river. Many communities use that contaminated water before it empties into the Pacific Ocean far to the south. Experts from the Salvadoran government's Ministry of Environment and Natural Resources would visit the mine site more than once and find shockingly high levels of cyanide and iron in nearby waterways. In 2006, they would order the mine closed—but the damage had already been done.

The science behind the rusty orange and cranberry red water is as simple as it is horrifying. It turned out that there are sulfides in the mountain on which the town was built. Once mining excavation exposes the embedded sulfides to the air and rain, they convert to sulfuric acid. With each new rain, the sulfuric acid eats away at the rock, releasing previously embedded toxic substances that then flow down the mountain into streams. This is a trick played by the gods of gold—or a pact with the devil, if you prefer—in an estimated half of the gold mines in the world. Scientists call it acid mine drainage. And one cannot know for sure in advance if and when acid mine drainage will occur. If you want to extract the gold, you have to accept the strong possibility that arsenic, iron, and other poisons will leech into your waters and land every time it rains. That is the pact.

The acid mine drainage that results when sulfides are exposed through mining is not just a short-term problem that can be fixed later with mining profits. Acid mine drainage has plagued mine sites from Pennsylvania to the Philippines for a long time.

Indeed, some communities near ancient Roman mines in England and Spain continue to suffer the effects of acid mine drainage over two thousand years after those mines were closed. To repeat: the poisoning of the water has continued for over two thousand years.

And remediation—or cleanup—is technically and financially challenging. Similarly red-orange streams have dotted the landscape around abandoned mines across the United States for a long time, prompting community activists to pressure the US government to pass the Surface Mining Control and Reclamation Act of 1977. Through this act and similar actions by state governments, hundreds of millions of dollars have been spent attempting to rehabilitate land, streams, and rivers in Pennsylvania, Kentucky, and elsewhere across the United States where sites have been poisoned by acid mine drainage. One university study estimated that coal mines in Pennsylvania contaminated over three thousand miles of streams in that state—and would cost millions of dollars to remediate. If the challenge of cleanup is difficult in the United States, imagine the challenge in a poorer country like El Salvador.

So, the water defenders of Cabañas added one more item to their growing list of concerns.

Years after their initial research trips, we were also able to visit the old San Sebastian mine, thanks to a priest from a nearby parish who had become an authority on acid mine drainage. We asked him how he and the community first came to understand that the mine had polluted the local water supply. He began his answer by explaining that he was not always against mining. Indeed, his father was a miner in a nearby area. But then, eleven years prior to our visit, he was assigned to this parish. He and others noted San Sebastian's high incidence of kidney failure, cancer, skin problems, and nervous system disorders. "My first clue," he reported, "was that I would visit farms in this community, and I would wash my hands and notice that there were no suds from the soap. The water was too acidic to make suds. This is how we made the link between the mining and the water." And then they made the link to people's health.

The priest drove us toward the mine. Along the way, we picked up a man who, it turned out, had worked at the mine. The old miner noted various landmarks as we wound our way up the mountain: "After Butters, a Spaniard came who took over the mine. He lived in that house," the man said, pointing, "and is buried here." He pointed again.

The old miner paused and stared at us intently, as if wondering if we would understand what he wanted to say.

"The Spaniard had a pact with the devil . . . so that this mine could be productive, profitable. He got 24-carat gold out of the deal. But lots of people died in the mine. Workers came from all over, from Nicaragua, from Honduras, from Guatemala, but many of them never came out of the mine. That is because the Spanish man wrote down their names on a piece of paper. He had a pact with the devil."

The old miner glanced at the priest as if fearing disapproval, but the priest's face was not registering any disagreement. And so the old miner repeated: "Mining is a pact with the devil."

The priest drove up to the mine's main entrance, past a locked metal trailer he and others informed us contained cyanide, to the mining site that Charles Butters discovered over a century earlier. Near the summit, we reached one of the mine's entrances: a large jagged hole carved into the mountainside, with piles of rock below. Here and there a glint suggested the ore that lay within.

As we reflected on the miner's story and descended into this century-old mine, we were reminded of what we knew from our own research: because of accidents, disease, and exposure to toxic chemicals, mining is one of the deadliest occupations on earth. But reading such statistics is one thing. Seeing the reality for one's self is another.

Nobody we met who visited San Sebastian returned unchanged. You need only see a child wading in the stream or a woman washing clothes to start to shudder. For Marcelo, Miguel, and Vidalina, the visit removed any doubts about their growing opposition. So too for the others from Cabañas whom the water defenders brought to see San Sebastian for themselves. The old Butters mine made one think hard about progress based on the idea that a country should focus on economic growth first and worry later about cleaning up environmental damage. And we found ourselves pondering the much larger question about the need to stop industrial mining in many parts of the world. Having seen the after-effects of mining on this local level, we wondered: what would that mean for the public's addiction to gold and other minerals that are integral to so many products deemed essential to modern living?

Buoyed by what they had learned in Honduras, from their neighbors in Chalatenango, and from the bright-colored deadly streams of San Sebastian, the water defenders now knew they had science on their side. But they still strove to learn more. Vidalina traveled to San Salvador every Saturday for four months for a course on mining. Others soaked up information on hydrology and related subjects. Just as the Rivera brothers had been thirsty for books years before, the water defenders read everything they could get their hands on related to mining.

With their expanding knowledge, Marcelo and others began to spread the word. They rode motorcycles to far-flung communities, intending to knock on every door. They also knew that they needed to popularize their findings, to make them accessible to a wider group of people in Cabañas. One of the leaders of the Cabañas community radio station, Radio Victoria, described how they did this: "For the people to make a decision, they need access to quality information. We needed to bring scientific information to a level that people could understand. Make it accessible. We had to frame the mining issue culturally. Through radio, art, song, we made it accessible to youth. Speeches aren't enough. So we cooked up a radio soap opera on water scarcity. We did a show with 'Mrs. Jug and Mr. Faucet' on the problems of water."

As head of the local cultural center, Marcelo took the lead in organizing theater and artistic festivals. Explained a young man, a former theater student of Marcelo's who then got a job at Antonio, Vidalina, and Miguel's organization: "We used theater, songs, murals, and other cultural forms to show resistance. We used laughter."

Laughter, we learned, defined Marcelo's personality and outreach. He especially relished performing in the guise of the Salvadoran folk hero Cipitio. Cipitio is the Peter Pan of Salvadoran folklore, the child who will never grow up. He is small and big-bellied, costumed always in a giant sombrero, depicted often with feet pointed backwards. Cipitio loves to laugh and play practical jokes that do no harm. But also, as Miguel told us, "Cipitio reminded children of things that they needed to do in a positive way." And Marcelo's Cipitio did this without lecturing them. It is no surprise, then, that Marcelo stood out in the public eye, though not everyone who knew San Isidro's Cipitio knew his real name. Indeed, years later, during the twelve days of Marcelo's disappearance, a little girl would come forward to say that she had seen Cipitio being hurt by some men. Yet another would call him Cipitio at his funeral.

Through such cultural activities and their door-to-door canvassing, Marcelo, Miguel, and their friends spread the word about what they had learned in Honduras and San Sebastian. And in Cabañas, the water defenders' renown grew.

The assassins robbed us of the opportunity to meet Marcelo. Initially, we were hesitant to ask Marcelo's closest friends and family questions about him, fearful of the pain we would evoke. But we eventually found ourselves able to raise the topic with Miguel and then with his wife and daughter. We learned little things first: when not dressed in his white Cipitio attire, he favored black and gray T-shirts. He loved chicken soup, especially his mother's. He was a connoisseur of fried chicken—both KFC and the local Pollo Campero. And he was an active participant in the FMLN.

One day, when we knew Miguel better, we walked through San Isidro with him expressly to ask people about Marcelo. We wanted a fuller sense of who he was and what the people of San Isidro felt about the work of the water defenders. An older woman was sitting on a chair in the shade outside the front door of her house. Years earlier, in the wake of Marcelo's murder, her family allowed the water defenders to paint a mural across an exterior wall of the house. The painting's right side depicts the water defenders' early history: the pollution from the landfill and hog farm flowing into a river. But the left side features the hoped-for future: clear blue water flowing from the beak of a white dove.

At the mention of Marcelo's name, the woman offered a flood of passionate memories of him, relating incidents as if they had happened the day before. Marcelo had convinced her to join the theatrical work that was central to the fight against mining. She burst out in song—a rhyming ditty—from a play Marcelo had directed. As she explained, it was not only Marcelo's work that made him special. "He was like a father to my son. . . . I would say everyone in town loved him. It didn't matter who you were. If you needed something, Marcelo was there. He would take you to the doctor, buy you medicine if you didn't have the money, check in on you." "And, remember," she added quickly, "it was not as if Marcelo had much money. If he bought you medicine, he would be foregoing something for himself."

We moved on, two houses down this narrow central San Isidro street. Here we heard a neighbor refer to Marcelo as a "natural leader." We learned of Marcelo's love for planning birthday parties and celebrations for elder members of the community. "He was humble, honest, a visionary, and fearless." And he loved a good laugh. He even made what could have been grim and determined "anti-mining" work fun—such as when he termed a march a "caravan of laughter" and helped participants don red clown noses.

At the next house, three men called out to us before we even saw them. They seemed to know us even though we did not recall meeting them before—a sign of how few gringos come to San Isidro. "He was a good guy, a fighter." A fighter not in the literal sense but in his doggedness in taking on the landfill, the hog farm, and Pac Rim. And "he told a lot of jokes." They started laughing as they shared their memories. Once, they told us, Pac Rim sponsored a soccer tournament as part of its community "outreach" work. Marcelo not only recruited a skilled and determined team of locals but also cooked up one of his schemes. The water defenders raised contributions for team uniforms: black jerseys with the words "OUT WITH PAC RIM" on the front and the team name "NO TO MINING" in gold letters on the back.

Pac Rim had made sure the local media was covering the match. Undoubtedly to Pac Rim's consternation but, Miguel claims, not to the water defenders' surprise, the NO TO MINING team won the tournament. Part of the winning team's prize was fancy uniforms promoting Pac Rim. And the water defenders' team lost little time figuring out how to make use of this prize, adding "OUT" to "Pac Rim" on the shirts. Marcelo's former teammates chuckled as they re-created the scene for us. But then they grew serious: "It was a game, but we didn't see it as a game. To put that differently, we saw it as a chance to beat Pac Rim at their own game."

The tales and adoration, almost a decade after Marcelo's brutal murder, made it clear why he had become a target of the pro-mining forces.

Tom Shrake and other top Pac Rim officials and owners had expected neither the creative determination of the likes of Marcelo nor the water defenders' protests. After all, the US Geological Survey told readers: "El Salvador [is] regarded as one of the lowest risk profiles in all of Latin America for investment in all parts of the economy, including the mining sector because of the stable political-economic climate." What could possibly go wrong?

Pac Rim thought it could nip the growing community concerns in the bud by adapting its message and tactics. Shrake shifted his pitch from focusing mainly on jobs to asserting how "deeply committed" he was to "the environment and to sustainable development." Pac Rim's on-the-ground efforts in Cabañas shifted accordingly. Suddenly, the job-creating company became a trailblazer of socially and environmentally "good" mining. In 2010, Shrake looked back to this period and bragged that "we held numerous community meetings . . . so that we could describe our plans for the mine as well as listen to the community's concerns. One of the cardinal rules of Corporate Social Responsibility . . . is to maintain an open dialogue with the local communities where the corporation intends to work."

At the top of the checklist of community environmental concerns about water contamination in 2004 and 2005 was the chemical that Pac Rim would be employing to separate the gold from the surrounding rock—cyanide, just as Butters had used and that the original El Dorado miners had used after World War II. Many community members had seen for themselves the impacts of cyanide from the mines in Honduras and at San Sebastian.

Pac Rim officials tried to pacify them. At one of their community meetings, a Pac Rim official boasted that cyanide was so safe that he was more than happy to drink a glass of a favorite local drink, *horchata*, laced with a white powder he claimed was cyanide. The official, we are told by Miguel, backed down when community water defenders insisted on authenticating the cyanide sample before the liquid was drunk. "The company thought we're just ignorant farmers with big hats who don't know what we're doing," Miguel explained. "But they're the ones who are lying."

Mining CEO Robert Johansing launched a similar public relations offensive focused on "green mining" in Chalatenango, with even less success. "I saw that same [man in a suit], and he told me about 'green mining,'" a

Chalatenango water defender recounted. "I replied: 'Your mining can be green, blue, red, or black. . . . We don't want it. Your interest is economic and ours is social.' I told him: 'We aren't going to let you in.'"

According to several people who experienced the Pac Rim public relations blitz, the words rang hollow, not only on environmental issues but even on the basic economic issue of jobs and financial benefits. The water defenders may not have held PhDs in economics, but they certainly had done their research. Antonio Pacheco, the ADES director, explained: "As we investigated deeper, we found that after the two years of mine construction were over, there would only be 148 jobs for the six years of the mine's operation, the majority of them foreign. Then, in the final two years of closing the mine, only 60 jobs."

What jumped out at us as we read Shrake's words, and as we heard these stories and spent time with the water defenders, is two totally different visions of progress. For Shrake and his mining allies and competitors, every piece of mining equipment, every water pump, every drill they brought into the mountains was modernization, progress. And the gold at the end of the rainbow would bring revenues, a small share of which would go to the local government and a small share of which would go to the national government. Who could turn this down?

We have heard similar corporate reasoning for decades in our travels and research in the United States. From coal mining executives in Kentucky. Oil company CEOs in Oklahoma. Copper mining officials in Apache lands in Arizona. Amazon corporate lobbyists in New York, Maryland, and Virginia lobbying for tax breaks and other financial incentives. Walmart public relations teams in inner-city neighborhoods in Chicago and Washington, DC.

For the farmers and townspeople in northern El Salvador, protecting their scarce water is a unifying priority, just as it has been in Kentucky, Oklahoma, and Arizona.

For these people, "water is life" is not just a slogan. It is everything.

Water and land mean food and livelihood and culture—a good part of which centers around the ancient grain corn in El Salvador. One evening after we had known Miguel for some years, he informed us he was bringing us "crazy corn"—*elote loco*—to the dining area at ADES. We were not sure what to expect. After a tropical evening rain, he, his wife, and their teenage daughter appeared carrying big pots and pans filled with corn. And we proceeded to eat corn in many different forms. Corn on the cob that we were instructed to dip into a variety of "crazy" sauces colored red and green and white. Homemade corn tortillas. Homemade corn tamales. Endless presentations of corn. Our stomachs were bursting, but we did not want to stop—in part because Miguel was laughing more than we had ever seen before. And, in part because Miguel was sharing his joy and his culture; he was showing us that corn is integral to life here. If the rivers are poisoned by cyanide and arsenic and acid mine drainage, the corn and other crops cannot be grown. And life stops.

On another afternoon, Vidalina brought us back to her community. This time, we had not come to hear the community's history or about their trips to Honduras. We came to see how neighborhood groups here were spreading sustainable farming techniques as an alternative to mining becoming the community's economic foundation. "We reject the image of us just as anti-mining. We are for water and a positive future," explained Vidalina. "We want alternatives to feed us, to clothe us." One of Vidalina's local coworkers led us to the riverbank and pointed to communal land where organic farms were being built. Three large greenhouses already contained plump hydroponic tomatoes, green peppers, and other vegetables. Such initiatives could make their town self-sufficient in vegetables.

Like parents everywhere, Miguel and Vidalina want their children to have a better life. They want good schools and health care and an end to violence in their communities. But they are at least one step closer to their land and water than most of us, and they understand that the preservation of the land and those rivers is paramount to their own and their descendants' well-being.

Shrake and his men in suits appeared destined never to understand this as they focused on the roads, the jobs, and the profits from the gold. Might these conflicting visions ever be reconciled? Or was a collision inevitable?

Remember the 670 holes that Pac Rim had dug and the rock cylinders extracted from the holes that were on their way to Nevada for testing? The wait for the results must have been excruciating for Tom Shrake. But, to his great relief, the El Dorado tests came back overwhelmingly positive for both gold and silver. Shrake's predictions were right. Pac Rim had found its low-cost and high-quality gold in El Dorado. As a result, Shrake and his colleagues were champing at the bit to get government permission to start mining.

But so too were the holes becoming a major topic of concern to those living near El Dorado. As Pac Rim's exploration wells spread, people started noticing strange things about their water supply. When we let it be known that we wanted to hear stories, far more people than we expected came to share their experiences with us. One day alone, eighteen farmers appeared on the back patio of the small home-turned-office housing the Environmental Committee of Cabañas, a water defender organization. Some had walked for hours over unpaved rural roads to get there. One after another, each stood up to tell his or her story, some clearly fearful of going public. Their stories focused on several small rivers that ran through or near the El Dorado site as part of the Lempa River watershed. One man talked about how one of these rivers flooded one of his three hectares—fully a third of his arable land—as a result of a small dam that Pac Rim built during exploration. Another recounted watching the river near his farm dry up in the wake of Pac Rim's drilling: "This was very strange as it had never done this before. So we walked up the river to see why." The culprit was a Pac Rim pump that was drawing water for exploratory wells.

Miguel and Vidalina decided that we needed to meet another farmer, a fellow water defender named Lidia Urias. This time we were the ones to make the journey down a long, potholed road far off the main road to Lidia's isolated farm. Brown and wilted flowers lined the dirt driveway. Lidia greeted us on the covered patio in front of her house and, in the gracious local traditions of hospitality, served us a homemade sweet snack along with a cup of coffee.

She then began to tell us of two visitors who had preceded us. The second was a gringo like us, a white man who visited Lidia's father at this farm around 2005 during Pac Rim's exploration period, and his visit was the story she started with. He was not just any man in a suit, but the president of Pac Rim El Salvador, a man who reported to Shrake. The president of Pac Rim El Salvador came all the way here to meet the owner of this small, dirt-floored house. He "walked up to the house," Lidia told us, "and, when he arrived, the first thing he said to my father was: 'I had to go through a whole desert to get here to paradise.'"

The family farm was indeed a paradise then. The house was the same: simple, without electricity. But it was surrounded by vegetables, flowers, and beautiful trees, a thriving fruit grove. "My father had 500 fruit trees down there," she said, pointing north. The paradise received some renown: "He won first prize for El Salvador from an American environmental group for his soil conservation and restoration work here, after he built stone barriers to prevent erosion. He was supposed to go to the United States to receive the award, but he didn't want to leave his thirteen kids behind."

"We continued my father's work and dreams for this farm." Lidia's voice quivered. "It was truly a paradise."

The first visitor who had come to paradise hoping to seal a pact, she told us, some years prior to the visit of the president of Pac Rim El Salvador, was the local mayor. He had approached her father to buy the land where a spring bubbled up from the earth to provide water for their farm. The mayor offered what he thought was a great deal: to bring electricity to their home in exchange. Her father told the mayor: "This spring has given me life. To sell it would be to take away the lives of my children and grandchildren."

Lidia shifted back to the day that the man from Pac Rim arrived during the company's exploration years. She repeated: "He walked up and he said: 'I had to go through a whole desert to get here to paradise.' You see, he saw that it was paradise. My father fed him our fruit. He ate our fruit." And then he told them that he wanted to explore for gold on our farm. He explained "how we would all get richer, and our lives would be better, filled with beautiful things." But they responded just as with that mayor and his promise of electricity. "We told the man from Pac Rim that he could not dig wells on our farm. Why would anyone want to do anything to disturb paradise? What he did not say was that the mining exploration would bring the desert with it."

Indeed, the desert came, even though Lidia's father said no. "Pac Rim came and dug an exploration well just down the hill." The well was just beyond her property line. "And, within a year, the spring began to dry up. Now there was no water coming from the spring." Miguel, who was one of the water defenders to study hydrology, surmised that one of several things could have happened. Most likely, Miguel explained, there was a subterranean aquifer where internal pressure had been pushing the water out as a spring. The drilling likely created holes that changed the pressure and dried up the spring.

Telling her saga and hearing Miguel's explanation drained Lidia. She took Robin's hand and walked her to a wooden bench surrounded by withered vegetation. "This was my favorite spot to sit and look out at our farm . . . at paradise. But now look at it." Lidia concluded, her voice weary: "Now because of water scarcity, if we water our plants, we can't take a bath. We used to have pigs but now just one goat. Before we could plant in dry season, and now we can't. If we don't get water, we'll have to leave."

As we drove back to ADES, Vidalina told us that other local farmers and communities—beyond the eighteen and Lidia—had experienced similar things. Some had complained to local officials and even to Pac Rim about the impacts of the wells on their groundwater. Shrake, when asked about this, acknowledged one such case—that of a local businessman. Pac Rim sent him bottled water—a gesture that the man found to be preposterous: "Are they going to send me water for the rest of my life?"

In Lidia's desperation, she also complained to the company. But in her case, it was to no avail. The man who ate her father's fruit was no longer interested in visiting or following up. Or even sending her water. Rather, she found herself not only without sufficient water but also concerned about her security. Looking around nervously during our visit, she whispered her fears beyond the future of her farm to her and her children's and grandchildren's safety.

Pac Rim's map of its hoped-for El Dorado concession, which we discovered in its 2007 annual report, revealed the company's plans. The map showed a wide area north and south of the main road that ran smack through San Isidro, with wormlike streaks running north to south in many places. The streaks represented the mining company's best guesses at and silver veins lay, deep beneath the surface. Presumably the map had been pieced together from the information gathered from the 670 exploration holes Pac Rim had drilled.

But it was hard for us to connect Pac Rim's wormlike streaks—the squiggles of the likely minerals below the surface—to the aboveground reality of San Isidro. So, during one of our later trips, when it felt safe to walk around San Isidro, we showed the map to Miguel, who seemed immediately to make the connection. As we started querying him about what was where, he decided that the best solution was to take us on another tour of San Isidro and its surroundings.

Thus, on a hot July afternoon, we found ourselves walking around the outskirts of San Isidro with Miguel. We began at the expansive soccer fields just south of town. Determined boys and girls of various ages peppered goalies with hard-kicked shots. We wove our way through the players—kicking the soccer ball back to them as they paused to interact with the gringos. Miguel stopped at our destination: a curious, small, square, redbrick and gray concrete structure just a couple of feet in length, width, and height. Like a chimney-top sticking up from the ground. Fairly innocuous until one thought about what heavy equipment it took to drill down through solid rock at this spot. As Miguel explained: Pac Rim "brought in machines to dig. . . . Every place they dug, they placed small brick-and-concrete structures."

Miguel pointed out another small brick structure about fifty yards away housing some pipes buried in cement. Here Pac Rim was attempting to win people over by drilling a well that would be used to pipe water up the small hill to the houses above. But, Miguel continued, "the company found naturally occurring arsenic in the rock, so it scrapped the idea of the water well."

We walked back to the first brick structure and asked Miguel to confirm exactly where the suspected gold vein under the bricks continued. "Straight through town. They were following the ore vein direction, and that was going through town," Miguel answered, pointing in the direction of the church and its surrounding residential areas that mark the town center. "The miners would have dug up the town had Pac Rim been allowed to proceed."

We grabbed Pac Rim's map of the hoped-for concession from our backpack where we had put it for safekeeping, to take another, more careful look. How did we miss this when we first looked at the map? We found out how, reexamining the map. The town and surrounding neighborhoods of San Isidro—the people and their houses—are invisible: they do not appear on the map. In the plans of Tom Shrake and his colleagues at Pac Rim, they simply did not exist. What mattered was where the gold lay and in what direction the vein headed. As we watched a determined duo weave toward the goal passing the soccer ball back and forth, we tried to imagine the field disappear into endless piles of toxic pulverized waste rock from a mine.

While Lidia and other people in Cabañas were beginning to feel the effects of exploratory drilling, their counterparts just to the northwest in the FMLN-controlled province of Chalatenango stepped up the pressure to stop Robert Johansing. According to a resident of San José Las Flores, Johansing's company was "doing their exploration right in the middle of towns," right where people lived. "They were all over, breaking fences and disturbing property. We told them they couldn't break our fences."

We learned more in our conversations in the San José Las Flores town hall: "It was a struggle," one man told us. "We told the workers who were cutting brush to stop. Another day, at seven in the morning, we stood in the road and closed the road. It was an intense debate. We told them, 'Either you leave, or you will suffer the consequences.' We had everyone from the community out that day, even the ex-combatants who had only one leg."

"I would prefer to live through twelve years of civil war again than have mining," added another man. "The rivers we have here are some of the only clean rivers in El Salvador, and so we've got some tourism here." "This is sacred land to us," stressed another.

Bolstered by the fact that their local elected officials were behind them, the farmers and other townspeople took increasingly bold actions against the company. As one woman recounted: "We have the advantage that our mayors' offices have been in resistance with the communities . . . versus the situation in Cabañas. But still it was a huge task for us to educate the population on the effects of mining." Their efforts came to a head in October 2005. Community members surrounded miners from Johansing's company and escorted them out of the province. By the end of that year, the communities of Chalatenango had thwarted mining exploration in the province.

Meanwhile, back in Cabañas, with the results of the test wells revealing abundant gold and silver, Pac Rim took the next step on the path to getting its permit to set up a large-scale mining operation by applying for an "exploitation license"—or the actual mining concession—for El Dorado. In most countries, mining companies must submit an environmental impact assessment report to the relevant government agency. Mining companies hire experts—geologists, hydrologists, chemists, and engineers—to do the technical side of the assessment. Some also hire other experts, managers, and so-called compilers, who decide what to leave out of the assessments before they are sent to the government regulatory agencies.

Pac Rim contracted with a Colorado-based firm to conduct the environmental impact assessment of the proposed mine. Pac Rim submitted what it considered the final version of that assessment to the Salvadoran Ministry of the Environment in September 2005. El Salvador's law required that the public be allowed to review the assessment and submit written comments. And so, in keeping with the apparent letter of the law, the Ministry of Environment announced that it would make available to the public one copy of the fourteen-hundred-page document at its San Salvador offices for ten working days in October 2005. Fourteen hundred pages. Only one copy. Only in San Salvador. And for only ten working days. No photocopies allowed.

Marcelo, Miguel, Vidalina, and their colleagues at ADES knew that they had amassed a great deal of information from their research trips to Honduras and San Sebastian and from their studies. But, with San Isidro's Mayor Bautista and other local ARENA officials aligned with Pac Rim, the water defenders realized that they needed help to take on a fourteen-hundred-page technical document in ten days. They needed a "heavyweight," as Antonio expressed it, ideally a water scientist, to read the Pac Rim assessment and help the community understand what it said.

That job fell to Robert Moran, a Colorado-based hydrologist and geochemist. Earlier in his career, Moran had done such work for (by his own calculation) more than two dozen "mining companies or their attorneys" around the world, including major mining corporations like Newmont, Unocal, and Union Carbide.

"How did you come to know of Moran?" we asked Antonio years later. Once again, the answer—which Antonio told us in his usual professorial manner, waving his arms around for emphasis—seemed more like fate than serendipity: "By May [2005], we knew that Pac Rim's environmental impact report would be coming soon, and we knew we needed a heavyweight to respond. So I asked a young Canadian who was volunteering at ADES on organic farming to do some research. Some days later, she came back and said: 'You know, there is a mining project in Argentina, and there's a man named Robert Moran who did a study, and he basically brought down the project.'"

Antonio and the volunteer figured out that—amazingly—Moran would be essentially next door looking at a project in Guatemala in June. So, using ADES's Guatemala contacts, they arranged to go meet him. Prior to the meeting, Antonio had no idea how much a "heavyweight" like Moran would cost, and ADES had not raised a cent. Moran explained that he typically charged $30,000 plus expenses. Antonio could not recall if he flinched, but he did recall that the two men hit it off. Moran seemed intrigued with what Antonio was telling him about Pac Rim's El Dorado and about the water defenders' work. Moran proceeded to grill Antonio. "If I do a study for you, what will you do with it? What is the action plan?" Moran, it turns out, was weary of doing studies that simply ended up gathering dust. He was not for or against mining. But he was for the decision being based on honest environmental impact assessments. Realizing that his work truly might make a difference, Moran told Antonio (in Antonio's words), "Well, I'm liking the idea [and] you're kind of swaying me your way," and he dropped his price to $10,000 plus expenses, including three professional technical translators. Antonio readily agreed, without blinking an eye. As he explained to us, he knew such a study could be critical. And he set about raising the funds—successfully, to his great relief. He was not sure about the three translators but, in Antonio style, figured that would resolve itself.

Bob Moran—whom we would meet some years later—came to El Salvador in early October 2005, and read Pac Rim's fourteen hundred pages. He did so with the help of one professional translator and two volunteers. All of them, to ADES's great relief, proved capable of translating the technical details that Moran knew would be in the submission. They quickly produced a twenty-two-page *Technical Review of the El Dorado Mine Project Environmental Impact Assessment*. Moran's report more than validated the water defenders' concerns. In the report, Moran summed up Pac Rim's assessment this way: "Many of the environmental impacts routinely encountered at similar gold mining sites are being neglected. . . . [This assessment] would not be acceptable to regulatory agencies in most developed countries."

Moran also expanded the water defenders' list of concerns. One of these was "tailing ponds." Extracting minerals from rocks leaves "tailings" in the form of crushed rocks covered with toxic chemicals. A challenge at mines the world over is how to dispose of these tailings. In most instances, the tailings are placed in rubber- or clay-lined pits and covered with water, to create "tailings ponds." Pac Rim promised lined tailings ponds, with assurances that nothing could go wrong.

Moran's report raised questions about that conclusion. Could floods push water over the edge? What about earthquakes in this seismically active area? As Moran knew and as the water defenders would learn further, these were not hypothetical concerns. A case in point was a disaster at the Philippine mine site of the Marcopper Mining Corporation, a Canadian company. In the early 1990s, Marcopper opened—to much fanfare—the largest open-pit mine in the Philippines on an island in the center of the country.

However, in 1996, a breach in a drainage tunnel under a giant tailings pond at the mine sent two to three million gallons of contaminated water and tailings into a nearby river. The tidal wave of contaminated sludge buried a third of the sixty towns downstream—displacing some twenty thousand people, and killing countless fish and cattle. A United Nations team declared the river biologically dead. Beyond losing homes and live-lihoods, those living along the path of the toxic water would subsequently suffer from shockingly high levels of zinc and copper in their bloodstreams.

Be it Marcopper in the Philippines or Pac Rim in El Salvador, Min-ingWatch Canada's Jamie Kneen reminded us: "The only question about tailing ponds is not if they will leak, but when."

Moran's succinct technical report quickly became hot reading in Cabañas in October 2005. That same month a top Pac Rim official, Fred-erick Earnest, agreed to share the stage with Moran at a public forum billed as "Mining: Opportunity or Threat?" Earnest, one of two top Pac Rim officials in El Salvador, reported directly to Tom Shrake. The debate took place in the Cabañas capital city of Sensuntepeque—a city of four hundred hills, if the indigenous meaning of its name is to be believed—just northeast of the El Dorado mine.

Picture this: Over five hundred farmers and others from all around Cabañas gathered in a covered basketball court with a concrete floor, three sides open to the elements. On one side, a larger-than-life painted mural of Archbishop Romero stared down at the court. Picture sombreros, lots of sombreros and other hats. An estimated fifty people in the audience had been bussed in by Pac Rim to applaud Earnest. Over five hundred pairs of eyes locked on the stage. Over five hundred pairs of ears were about to listen to two gringos—a hydrologist and a Pac Rim executive—debate one another, along with Antonio and the former head of a Honduran uni-versity who had witnessed the impacts of mining firsthand.

Moran, almost a decade later, described the substance of the de-bate: "As part of Mr. Earnest's presentation, he stated that no significant water-related impacts were anticipated." Taking issue with that, Moran recalled that he had "stated that projects similar to this one often gener-ated water-related impacts such as: lowering of water tables; drying up of springs; increased competition for water; [and] possible contamination of local water resources; and that such operations normally used cyanide to extract the gold (and silver)."

Moran further recalled: "Following these presentations, the audience began to ask questions. It was clear . . . that the citizens in the audience had not previously been informed [adequately] about the possibility for such impacts. A significant portion of this audience voiced concerns about possible impacts to the water resources if the project became operational."

Rather than trying to refute the substance of Moran's response, a Pac Rim consultant would later try to brush him aside as "a known anti-mining advocate." To which Moran responded with clear professional disdain: "False. Apparently . . . [Pac Rim] believes it is only acceptable for a scientist to write positive statements about projects and to work only for industry clients. My criticism of this technically-inadequate EIA does not mean I am anti-mining."

Who won the debate that day? The answer depends on whom you talk to, but let us call it unclear, perhaps even a draw. According to observers, Moran left feeling good, as did Antonio. If Pac Rim had agreed to the debate thinking that Earnest would pummel Moran, the company's officials had miscalculated. But Earnest also received some applause—and it was hard to decipher if those applauding included people who were not part of Pac Rim's entourage. Earnest spoke in Spanish. Moran did not. Some of the water defenders and allies left worried, fearing that the economic power, the muscle and sway, of the global company came through all too clearly. Even Antonio admitted that he was worried, at least in terms of beginning to understand the enormity of the task at hand to stop Pac Rim. But so too did Earnest seem to grasp that he had not quelled the opposition. According to Antonio, Earnest left saying "From what I can tell, the water's already divided here."

The more important question would turn out to be not who won the debate that day but the impact of the Moran Report, as it came to be known, in the longer term.

What was at stake was becoming clearer in northern El Salvador. Opposition in mining country had mushroomed. In less than two years of self-education, the Cabañas water defenders had learned a prodigious amount about mining and its impacts. By the end of 2005, they knew the details of the new pact that the devil was offering.

Little did they realize how far they still had to go or what they were truly up against having taken on Big Gold. As the water defenders' ranks swelled in the north, Marcelo, Vidalina, Miguel, and their allies began to recognize that they faced two big problems.

First, the water defenders in Cabañas and Chalatenango remained largely invisible to the rest of the country. Few in the big cities of El Salvador had any idea they existed. There was no reason to think that the elite of San Salvador—the fourteen or so families who had historically controlled the country economically and politically—would share their concerns. The water defenders sensed that the time had come to move beyond door-knocking in Cabañas.

Second, the water defenders had kicked a hornets' nest among those who stood to gain from mining, starting with the mayors of the mining towns. José Bautista, for one, the ARENA mayor of San Isidro, he of the ill-fated landfill and the thriving hog farm. As one water defender described the scene after October 2005, in the aftermath of Moran's study and Chalatenango's kicking out of the men in suits: "When we fought back and came out against mining, the threats started. The mayor was mad. The community became divided into those for and [those] against." Suddenly things had changed. "In our communities, you did not know whom to trust, even neighbors and long-time friends."

People began to lock their doors at night—something they had not done since the end of the civil war. But Marcelo was still alive, ever more well-known as he performed street theater in his Cipitío costume. And, while the desert had come to his friend Lidia's once verdant farm, the water defenders had largely kept intact the oases of paradise that made up Cabañas.

On the other side, Pac Rim had financial resources, power, and the connections in town halls, in San Salvador and beyond. Even with news of the negative aspects of mining spreading through such events as the Moran-Earnest debate, Pac Rim was feeling confident, even cocky.

Little did any of them know that a "state of siege"—as mining CEO Robert Johansing would later term it—was about to begin.

CHAPTER 3

State of Siege
(2006–2008)

Pac Rim CEO Tom Shrake was not naïve. He knew well that mining companies seldom open up mines in poorer countries without some sort of a fight. Indeed, as he explained later, in his 2010 testimony to the Canadian Parliament, he had expected as much when he moved to El Salvador almost a decade earlier. "I've done systematic exploration programs in Argentina, Chile, Peru, Costa Rica, El Salvador, and Mexico over the last twenty-five years," he said in 2010, and he acknowledged that community opposition to mines was "not a very unusual event. Armed mobs have taken over exploration camps in three countries that I know of."

However, Shrake continued, in those early years he absolutely did not foresee what he termed the ensuing "nightmare." Or, the "state of siege," as his fellow mining CEO Robert Johansing put it. Nor did the water defenders foresee what a nightmare those same years would prove for them.

Shrake entered 2006 confident that the odds were in Pac Rim's favor.

When the dust settled from the Moran debate on the packed basketball court in late 2005, both Tom Shrake and ADES director Antonio Pacheco knew that their respective sides had been able to present their cases. The water defenders were pleased but unsettled. Five hundred people had just been exposed to presentations on the stark realities of mining. At least some doubt had to have been seeded in those peoples' minds about the safety of their precious rivers and streams.

Yet the daunting obstacles stacked against the water defenders were coming into focus. Restrictions on mining by the national government, some combination of the executive branch and the legislature, both far away in San Salvador, would be necessary.

When Antonio surveyed the national political landscape, he found no clear allies. The right-wing ARENA party, with its support of all kinds of foreign investment, controlled the presidency. Worse in some ways than ARENA control of government, many of the leaders of the FMLN—the party that most water defenders supported—did not oppose mining. Rather, some in the FMLN believed the revenues and jobs Pac Rim promised the mines would bring outweighed any environmental costs. So ARENA seemed aligned against the water defenders while debates raged in the FMLN as to whether mining could be a key to a brighter economic future.

As to the broader public outside of Cabañas and Chalatenango, most Salvadorans knew little if anything about metals mining. An arch-conservative archbishop ruled over the Catholic Church, a key bully pulpit for reaching the public in this heavily Catholic country. If the mining companies were throwing money into the towns near the gold veins like San Isidro, exciting mayors with the prospect of ending up with that 1 percent of the mining profits in their pockets, how much more were the companies spreading at a national level?

Tom Shrake and Pac Rim had another advantage. In their line of work, finding the gold was the hard part, and they now knew the true bounty that lay beneath El Dorado. The next stage, the charm offensive—backed with generous handouts—usually smoothed over any rough spots in obtaining the actual mining concession. Shrake knew that key government officials nationally, including the vice president, welcomed their presence. As for the environment minister, Shrake knew that he was a businessman and a founder of the ARENA party. So Pac Rim executives felt no worry about the eventual acceptance of the environmental impact assessment needed to obtain the mining concession.

Plus, the price of gold, and hence the potential rewards to both the mining company and El Salvador, continued to climb. How could a na-

tional government in a poor country like El Salvador possibly turn its
back on the projected revenues? And, should it be absolutely necessary, a
mining company could always sweeten the deal by agreeing to increase
the percentage paid as a mining tax to the Salvadoran government—as
companies in some other countries were doing.

Internal mining company documents revealed that a top Pac Rim concern at this moment was what appeared to be an insignificant mining law
requirement. By Salvadoran law, in order to mine on a specific parcel of
land, a company needed to either own that land or have the permission
of the landowners. But Pac Rim recognized several mitigating circumstances. The executive branch had not really enforced this part of the law
in the past, certainly not rigorously. Moreover, should Shrake and his
team run into resistance due to that legal requirement, they were confident that they could use their top-level government contacts to convince
the national legislature to amend the law. Pac Rim could probably even
draft the amendment themselves. Finally, if that somehow failed, they
knew that the Salvadoran constitution granted subsoil rights to the government. So, they figured, they could simply tunnel underneath people's
lands, backed by a sympathetic national government. Patience might be
required by Tom Shrake and his Pac Rim team, but they had all these
fallbacks in place.

Corporate lobbyists open similar grab bags of incentives, from larger
shares of profits to partial government ownership to outright bribes, to sway
elected officials around the world—albeit with different permutations in
each country. Indeed, as we listened to Antonio list the odds against them,
our minds returned to communities around the world fighting Walmart,
fracking companies, oil pipelines, and factory shutdowns. Was the water
defenders' chance of succeeding better than theirs—or worse?

With the deck stacked against them at a national level, the water defenders
of Cabañas divided their forces into two flanks. Marcelo, who was already
well-known locally, would remain focused on popular outreach and education in their home province. But others—especially Antonio and Vidalina—would reach out to likely allies in San Salvador.

Much of the national work required outreach to groups that knew little or nothing about mining. The Moran Report helped greatly. By late 2005, word about mining's deleterious impacts was spreading. "We sent the Moran Report to everyone we knew," Antonio told us. The fact that the Lempa River supplied water to over half the country's people, combined with the fact that gold country was upriver of the rest of the country, helped animate the slogans: "Agua es vida" and "Sí a la agua; no a la minería." ("Water is life." "Yes to water; no to mining.")

When Antonio said that they sent the Moran Report to "everyone" as part of the outreach work, he really meant everyone. The water defenders reached out not just to likely allies such as environmental and human rights groups but also to businesspeople whose economic interests might well be adversely affected by mining. Among those was the conservative environment minister, Hugo Barrera. Beyond sending the report to Barrera, they asked the minister to meet with them. To Antonio, Marcelo, Vidalina, and Miguel, this was clearly necessary. They had no chance to stop mining if they did not win over some from the Right.

Yet for many water defenders, as Antonio reminded us—as he wielded his neon green, battery-powered, plastic mosquito zapper, reaching out to "the enemy" was tantamount to treason. The Salvadoran civil war—which pitted the left FMLN against the right-wing government forces that would subsequently form ARENA—remained fresh in people's minds. Of the seventy-five thousand people killed in that conflict, many died in brutal massacres committed by government troops or right-wing death squads, some of whom were trained by US military advisors. Barrera had not only cofounded ARENA, he had run for vice president with infamous death squad leader Roberto D'Aubuisson, another ARENA cofounder. While Barrera sometimes played the sage older businessman and government official dressed in an expensive tailored suit, he could also be seen sporting a red, white, and blue ARENA jacket and hat—the word ARENA embroidered in black on a white cross. The very attire was an affront to water defenders. If your sibling or parent or child had been tortured or murdered by government soldiers, would you feel like approaching the likes of Barrera, whatever the cause?

Thus opened a decade-long debate among those opposed to mining. Was it worthwhile to reach out to influential people from ARENA or other conservative pockets of the country, people who could be useful if they could be convinced?

Regardless of the water defenders' dispute about Barrera, to nearly everyone's surprise he almost immediately agreed to a meeting. On October 19, 2005, just two weeks after the Moran debate, Antonio and other community leaders journeyed to the Environment Ministry in San Salvador. To their amazement, Barrera had prepped for the meeting by reading Moran's report. As Antonio recalled the meeting to us years later: "Barrera gave us a big thank-you. He said: 'Your report lifted a big weight off of us. We didn't know how to respond to Pac Rim's environmental impact statement. Now we do.'" And, true enough, the Environment Ministry sent a series of new questions and concerns to Pac Rim that were based on Moran's report.

Reaching out to a former enemy seemed, at least initially, to be paying off.

Useful as a tactical alliance with the likes of Barrera might be, the Cabañas water defenders knew that they needed a national-level network of trusted allies—just as they had built one locally in Cabañas. Even this posed challenges. Earlier in 2005, they had knocked on the doors of the two largest national environmental groups, whose directors were pillars of the country's environmental movement. Antonio was taken aback by their reaction or lack thereof. "Both said: 'Why mining?' Mining simply was not on their radar screen." Actually, this should not have been surprising. Had not Antonio reacted the same way to Marcelo's first warnings?

Those initial overtures to likely allies did not augur well for scaling their campaign up to a national level. Yet the local and provincial water defenders were undaunted. They found an early ally with mining expertise in Oxfam America, which had placed the coordinator for its Central America extractive industries work in San Salvador. And they reached out to others. After the Moran forum, they launched a monthly gathering of would-be collaborators in San Salvador. Around the table sat leaders from local, provincial, and national groups, from lawyers and researchers to farmers and organizers. Environmental groups, including the Salvadoran Ecological Unit, were there, as were human rights advocates, representatives of Catholic organizations, and Oxfam. They were a diverse bunch in many ways, but, as Vidalina pointed out, almost all were men.

The sectoral diversity of the group and the lack of expertise in mining among the majority made for complicated and lengthy discussions, with speech-making by some and listening and learning by others. They met through the early months of 2006. One of the key early discussions entailed not only whether there should be some kind of national coalition but also the very scope of their joint work. They settled on gold and other metals mining, deciding to leave out the mining of rocks for cement-making and road-building.

Meandering into discussion topics beyond that central focus got them mired in sticky debates. Some around the table argued that a goal of actually kicking out mining firms was unrealistic. Instead, these folks argued, the groups ought to focus on the goal of gaining tight government regulation of mining firms and then seeing this implemented and enforced. Among those arguing against this limited goal were representatives from Chalatenango and Cabañas who were in the process of trying to kick out the likes of Tom Shrake and Robert Johansing, with notable success in Chalatenango in 2005. They argued that a focus on regulations was a move backwards. There were long hours of what often felt like repetitious debate.

Eventually someone suggested that everyone around the table step back and, with no more pontificating, see what they could agree on. "In the end," Antonio told us, "all groups agreed they did not want metals mining in the country, and we agreed on the name." They would be the National Roundtable on Metallic Mining—La Mesa Nacional Frente a la Minería Metálica. La Mesa, for short.

Two of the goals they agreed on were unsurprising: help community-level water defenders build resistance at local levels, and link with similar struggles in Honduras and Guatemala, since the Lempa River starts in one and winds through the other. But a third seemed like a pipe dream in 2005: get the Salvadoran Congress to pass a new national law banning metals mining. It was exactly the kind of policy proposal that many would likely toss aside as not being pragmatic.

Depending on one's definition of "gringo," one gringo joined the early meetings: Andrés McKinley, the person in charge of Central America mining work at the Oxfam office in El Salvador—a direct, opinionated, and knowledgeable man. Andrés hailed from the Irish-American neighborhoods of Boston, where he spent his childhood as "Andrew." In his early twenties, his commitment to the struggle for social justice led him to become a teacher in northern Liberia. Andrés had come to El Salvador in 1982 to work with a development organization and had quickly become enmeshed with progressive political forces during the country's civil war. By 2005, he had been in El Salvador for so long that, while his lighter complexion still marked him as a gringo, he largely thought of himself as Salvadoran—and eventually became a Salvadoran citizen.

Andrés's directness irritated some in La Mesa. But anyone who has worked in coalition circles knows that tension among members is unavoidable. Andrés's work at Oxfam allowed him to witness the destructive impacts of mining across Central America and in other countries. And he creatively deployed some of Oxfam's resources to create learning spaces for La Mesa members to meet counterparts from other countries, especially in Central America.

In Andrés, Antonio found an ally for pushing the boundaries on tactics. The two delighted in scheming how to reach out to and sway powerful forces to their side. Even so, they would often disagree. The usually serious Antonio chuckled as he recounted years later his hours-long attempt in 2005 to convince Andrés to have Oxfam chip in on funding for Moran's visit. "Why are you hiring this man? It's not urgent," Antonio recalls Andrés arguing. "A couple of hours later, Andrés said, 'I see you won't budge.'" So Andrés agreed to help fund Moran, but, as Antonio says, "gave . . . only $2,000 toward the cost." A full four years later, Andrés would realize the importance of the Moran trip and report and would tell Antonio: "You were right."

As ADES revved up its anti-mining work nationally in 2006, it brought on Vidalina full-time. Vidalina had moved to northern Cabañas with her husband and sons years earlier. At that point, she looked up Antonio, whom she and her husband knew from the time in exile in Honduras during the civil war. "Listen," she told Antonio, "what's going on? I can't just sit still. I need to be participating in something. I need to do something useful." She began doing work in conjunction with ADES in her northern Cabañas town and later joined the ADES board. Upon joining the staff in 2006, she became a regular at La Mesa meetings. Vidalina admitted to us that she had not enjoyed all La Mesa meetings and disliked the macho attitudes of some of the men. However, she quickly emerged as a national leader—with a range of skills from public speaking to figuring out the logistics of how to bus farmers from northern El Salvador to events in San Salvador.

With the goal and name settled, La Mesa founders needed a game plan. They needed to make a splash, to catch attention. Again, lengthy discussions and debate ensued. But, by late spring in 2006 they had reached agreement to burst into the nation's consciousness through a weeklong series of high-profile events. It was an ambitious plan for a new organization.

The National Action Week on Mining, as it was called, was publicized well enough that one Big Gold company trying to mine in El Salvador wrote up an internal five-page summary of events. The week opened on a Monday in mid-June 2006 with a La Mesa press conference, as would become a La Mesa tradition. That same day, a popular television show featured a two-hour interview with Andrés of Oxfam and a La Mesa researcher who also knew a great deal about gold mining. The host was Mauricio Funes, who was considered center-left although he was not an FMLN member. He had built a large following and was making a name for himself as a broadcast journalist who hosted a show that took on serious and sometimes controversial issues. The water defenders viewed it as quite a coup to convince Funes to devote an entire show to mining.

Here is how that internal mining company memo assessed the impact: "The June 12 interviews gave a very negative impression on the TV audience and even on [the] host of the program." The anonymous writer of the memo continued, "During a [subsequent] visit to the office, our landlady commented upon the program and the tremendous environmental damage produced by mining." Imagine: a landlady recounting this to her corporate tenants. The mining company memo does note one "positive" result from the two-hour show: Pac Rim's Frederick Earnest, the man who had debated Moran in October 2005 in Cabañas, called in and succeeded in getting Funes to agree to host him as a guest on the show three days later.

On day two of the National Week of Action, the water defenders moved their venue to the prestigious Catholic University of Central America (UCA). UCA holds a sacred spot in Salvadoran history. It was here, during the civil war, that a death squad murdered six Jesuits and two women who were denigrated at that time as communist FMLN supporters and later mourned by many as martyrs.

The forum that day was billed as an informational event, with speakers from government and civil society. Oxfam played a key role, while the Jesuit rector of UCA, as host, did the inviting, offering an aura of neutrality. The event featured Oxfam's Andrés (who years later would become a researcher at UCA), a La Mesa representative from San Salvador, and a water defender from Chalatenango. Representatives from the government included lawyer Yanira Cortez, the deputy attorney for the environment for El Salvador's Human Rights Ombudsman's office. The Jesuit rector also invited both the minister of economy and Barrera, the minister of environment. To the surprise of hardly anyone, the minister of economy did not show. To the surprise of most, including the organizers, Barrera did.

Roughly five hundred people packed the auditorium. Among them, thanks to the careful planning of the organizers, were several hundred who had come in crowded buses from gold country in the north. Many of these had traveled from San Isidro, the site of Pac Rim's coveted El Dorado mine, in a Vidalina-organized bus. According to the internal gold company memo summarizing the week, a mining company informant, who "attended the forum as a student and recorded most of it," was also in the audience.

Barrera, looking out from the front of the room, was truly impressed by the size of the audience and its strong unity in opposition to mining. When he took the podium, as he told American University researcher Rachel Nadelman years later, "I asked them who among them owned the land, and many people [indicated that they] owned the land. [I explained] therefore that the law also establishes that for a mining project to operate, the company—in this case Pacific Rim—[needed to] check who is the owner of the territory and then procure the authorization of these land-owners to be able to go ahead with their projects. Right now, they do not have [this authorization,] and, if the communities are not willing to give permission, the problem is solved." "Solved" meaning no mining allowed, no further debate necessary.

If Barrera's view of the Cabañas water defenders and of El Salvador's mining law came into clearer focus during the forum, so too did Barrera transform the water defenders' understanding of the power that local people held to keep mining out of Cabañas. Vidalina and Yanira Cortez both recall being stunned by what Barrera said publicly. They had expected Barrera to sound pro-mining or at least middle-of-the-road and uncommitted. After all, Barrera was once considered, in the words of a *New York Times* reporter, as "the No. 2 man" in ARENA, the party of the death squads. But here he was, Vidalina recounted, "providing us with incredible, useful information." As she added: "Even we at the center of the work learned that we had a very powerful [legal] tool at our fingertips." Barrera, whom most had not expected to attend, never mind be sympathetic, ended up making it a momentous event.

What was going on in the head of this pro-investment, anti-FMLN, right-wing minister in 2006? Did something change after he became minister of environment? A former colleague at the ministry told us: "Barrera was a simple solutions man. He had common sense." Oxfam's Andrés, who got to know Barrera fairly well, emphasized Barrera's respect for the law: "In the forum, Barrera said: 'My job is to apply the mining law.' And, the more he listened to the opponents, the more he became skeptical." Skeptical of Pac Rim's legal right to mine, that is. Before Barrera filled the post, it may not have been the intention of the Environment Ministry to apply the letter of the law. However, that appeared to be Barrera's intention now that he was minister.

But did Barrera really care about water? Or did he care about making the ministry, and thereby himself, more powerful? In terms of power, Environment had been a relatively minor ministry after its founding in 1998, compared to powerhouses such as the Ministry of the Economy. Antonio remained more dubious than Andrés about what led Barrera to offer his July 2006 advice. "Barrera was the general manager of Diana, the big drinks and snacks company owned by his family," Antonio said. "The company's profits depended upon water." In this regard too, the water defenders of Cabañas gained an important insight from the UCA Forum regarding how to approach possible allies, and it harkened back to where Marcelo began: water. Rich or poor, progressive or conservative, water was valued by all.

Whatever the reasons behind Barrera's surprise pronouncements, the National Week of Action generated huge press coverage on mining, bringing the issue to living rooms, kitchens, porches, and community gatherings around the country. La Mesa had made itself and concerns about mining known nationally beyond its wildest dreams.

Barrera's public pronouncement at UCA shocked Shrake, Johansing, and other Big Gold executives. They knew that decisions on mining exploration permits and actual mining licenses were made both by Barrera in the environment ministry and the minister of the economy. Was Barrera speaking also for the minister of economy and President Tony Saca? That was the million-dollar question as far as Big Gold was concerned. Another internal mining company memo offered some reassurance for the mining companies. According to the memo, someone who spoke with President Saca's secretary of communications reported that the president "was furious" over Barrera's "abrupt" announcement. Barrera's statement, the memo relayed, "does not represent the President [or] the Government position" as a whole. And, "his removal as Minister could take place by the end of the year."

Pac Rim wanted to hear this in person from the minister of the economy and President Saca. The economy minister at the time was Yolanda
Mayora de Gavidia, a woman who had met with mining executives in the
past. In their view, she was positively predisposed toward mining. But,
unlike Barrera, during this time Gavidia had remained silent in public on
her views on mining. Recall that, unlike Barrera, she had declined the
invitation to speak at the June forum.

Internal mining company memos reveal that Shrake and Johansing actively courted her. One of the results was her early July 2006 meeting with
Pacific Rim El Salvador president Fred Earnest. Earnest wanted Gavidia to
get him an audience with President Saca to clarify the exact government
position on mining. But Gavidia informed Earnest (according to one of
the memos) that the president was not available to meet with him. The
response left Earnest fuming, and he made his anger apparent to Gavidia.
As the memo continues: "[The] Pacific Rim CEO has already warned
that if the exploitation concession is denied, they will make lobbying to
discredit the country."

By now, Tom Shrake was paying close attention to the moves of the government as well as to the water defenders. Shrake's team, like Johansing's,
moved into a higher gear in the weeks and months after the National
Week of Action, setting up more meetings with both Barrera and Gavidia.
And they stepped up their efforts both in the north and in the rest of the
country to make their case for mining. Internal memos also reveal that the
mining companies had numerous "informants" in anti-mining marches,
in mining country, and in the government.

Big Gold was particularly interested in a late July 2006 march, when
over one thousand water defenders traveled from Chalatenango in the
north to the front door of Gavidia's Ministry of the Economy. To the
amazement of the marchers and of Big Gold, Gavidia opened the doors
of the ministry and allowed at least some of the activists to come inside.
Those who entered reported with surprise that Gavidia listened attentively
to their demands, responding in ways that echoed Barrera.

Just days after Gavidia met with those marchers, mining executives from a handful of different firms—among them Pac Rim—gathered in her office. Gavidia assured the group that "the Minister of Environment['s] opinions against mining were personal and had been taken out of context." She went on to tell the group (in the words of a memo by a mining executive present) that the government "has heard the NGOs, religious and community leaders who oppose mining."

In another surprise for the convened mining executives, Gavidia informed those assembled that the government was seeking outside advice and had hired an environmental consultant who was a legal expert on mining. According to the memo, she assured those gathered not to worry, saying, "Since most companies act with much social and environmental responsibility . . . we are certain that no one will oppose this law review." Moreover, in response to a Johansing question, she adamantly stated (again, in the words of the memo's author) that the move was not political: "I do not want to mix politics with legal-institutional issues."

The consultant whom the government hired was Peruvian lawyer and environmental expert Manuel Pulgar-Vidal, a man who would later become environment minister of Peru. Merely two months after the June 2006 National Action Week on Mining, Pulgar-Vidal recommended that the Salvadoran government stop permitting any new mines and rather conduct a rigorous "strategic review" of the environmental and economic impacts of mining. While a typical government study might analyze the economics of a proposed project or development path, Pulgar-Vidal was suggesting something far broader. Yet Barrera and Gavidia agreed with him, saying that they would issue no further mining permits, either for exploration or actual mining, until such a detailed study could be carried out. Later, Pac Rim would claim it did not know of this until a couple of years later—but these documents clearly reveal that they knew in 2006.

While Shrake and Johansing were actively engaging with national government officials in San Salvador, Pac Rim continued in its attempts to win over water defenders in the north, in mining country. Shrake, like Johansing, had great faith in his powers of persuasion. After the Moran debate, Pac Rim had realized that ADES was a key organization to win over. Antonio received quite a few visits from top company executives in 2006 at the ADES office. "There may be some differences between us," Antonio remembered an executive saying, "But we want to support you." None of this surprised Antonio or us. Distributing cash around community projects and organizations is a key tactic of corporations of all stripes, from Walmart to tobacco firms to mining firms as they woo community support. The intent was "winning hearts and minds," as US president Lyndon Johnson repeated many times during the Vietnam War.

How did Pac Rim think it could win over the hearts and minds of the Cabañas water defenders in 2006? Years later, in 2018, we asked Antonio exactly what and how much the company had offered. "A blank check." We thought we must have misunderstood, but we had not. Antonio elaborated: "They said: 'So how much money do you want? Tell us.'" He turned them down, and "then they arrived with three young women. Some 'fancy' women. They kept coming back, with different women. I kept sending the women away and saying: 'Let this be the last time you come.'"

Antonio and the core water defenders had stood firm. But he frowned as he remembered one friend's amazement that ADES had turned down Pac Rim's offers. Antonio recalled, "There was no way for us to win, [the friend had concluded]." And the friend had asked: "When are you giving in? Are you not interested in getting something out of the company?" "I got really upset," Antonio said. "I told him: 'No matter what they offer, we aren't going to change. We're not going to betray the people.'"

Not only were the water defenders not caving in; they had bigger battles in sight. From their early success with Barrera, they started researching another possible ally, one even more unlikely than Barrera.

To say that the Catholic religion and the pronouncements of the Catholic hierarchy are influential in El Salvador is an understatement. No religion in the United States has such influence. On the rare occasions when the Salvadoran church hierarchy speaks out on an issue, it carries weight akin to that of the pope globally. A significant portion of the population listen to weekly radio homilies of the top Catholic officials, and they also pay attention to pastoral letters and church pronouncements.

The most widely revered figure in El Salvador over the past forty years has been Archbishop Oscar Romero, who was assassinated by a member of a right-wing death squad in 1980 while performing Mass. Romero's status was—and remains—somewhat akin to that of Martin Luther King in the United States, and Romero was canonized in 2018. Posters and photos of Romero are omnipresent in homes across the country. Many of the people with whom we met still talked about how they had looked forward to Romero's weekly radio homilies in the late 1970s.

The contest between the water defenders and Big Gold for the support of the Catholic Church began in Chalatenango. Mining CEO Robert Johansing, a Catholic himself, understood the church's importance. Both he and the water defenders courted the church's top official there, the bishop. But the water defenders had deep roots in the communities. In early 2006, the bishop of Chalatenango became the first Salvadoran bishop to go public in opposition to mining.

Emboldened by their successes, Antonio, Andrés, and others in La Mesa decided they needed an ally high up in the Catholic hierarchy. They selected the most unlikely target: the archbishop of the country. Archbishop Fernando Sáenz Lacalle was a conservative, pro-business priest from Spain who had come to El Salvador in 1962, become a citizen in 1966, and been named archbishop in 1995. Sáenz Lacalle belonged to the far-right Opus Dei order. Indeed, he had come to El Salvador to be at San Salvador's Opus Dei center. Founded in Spain in 1928, the order was widely known for its support of and participation in Franco's fascist government in Spain. Criticism of that history had been only enhanced by Opus Dei's continued secrecy and political conservatism. In popular culture, Opus Dei was demonized in the book and movie *The Da Vinci Code*. By the mid-2000s, Sáenz Lacalle had made himself known as a conservative and pro-business man-of-the-cloth—a stark departure from Romero.

Shrake had realized the importance of the archbishop and begun meeting with him. One might have thought that the Opus Dei connection would have been enough to cement Sáenz Lacalle as an ally of Big Gold.

As they had with Barrera, most in La Mesa scoffed at the notion of wooing the Opus Dei–connected archbishop. After all, when he had been named archbishop in 1995, he had announced, "[A] bishop does not speak of politics; he speaks of religion. I am not thinking about talking about politics." Still, a few water defenders started reaching out to the archbishop. They were not surprised when they heard nothing back. But Andrés and Antonio—who do not easily take no for an answer—kept trying, until finally the archbishop agreed to meet with them.

To nobody's surprise, the conversation did not start well. In words and body language, the archbishop made it clear that he was not interested in hearing about mining or taking up the Romero mantle. As Andrés recalled, it looked like it was going to be a very brief meeting, not much more than hello and good-bye. Then someone mentioned that industrial mining uses cyanide to separate gold from the surrounding rock, and "cyanide" proved to be the password. According to Andrés, the archbishop's "ears perked up and his entire countenance changed."

Unbeknown to the water defenders, there was more to Sáenz Lacalle than Opus Dei. The archbishop held a degree in chemistry. He knew well the toxic impact of cyanide. And with that knowledge, he did a 180-degree flip on mining. While Sáenz Lacalle would never allow his church to be one with the water defenders, he would lead his church on a parallel track. He would even invite Andrés to give talks on mining and water to his priests and nuns.

In the summer of 2006, just as Environment Minister Barrera was handing the water defenders a key tactic at that UCA forum and Economy Minister Gavidia was welcoming anti-mining marchers into her ministry, the archbishop spoke out publicly for the first time on mining, stating his unequivocal opposition. Rather than frame his opposition in theological terms, Sáenz Lacalle focused on the science and especially on the threat of cyanide-based mining to the country's precious water. And he continued to do so: "It is unjust to risk people's health and damage the environment so that a few people who don't live here can walk off with 97 percent of the profits and leave us with 100 percent of the cyanide." So much for Sáenz Lacalle's vow to not "speak of politics."

Pac Rim was livid and quick to counterattack. Pac Rim supporters protested at the Office of the Human Rights Ombudsman, the Ministry of Economy, and even at Oxfam. Protestors with signs proclaiming themselves to be the Pro-Mining La Mesa of San Isidro started appearing outside the national cathedral on Sundays while the archbishop was saying Mass. This caused a media stir. The protestors told media that they came from gold country, specifically from Miguel and Marcelo's hometown of San Isidro, Cabañas.

When La Mesa learned about these weekly protests against the archbishop, they thought something smelled fishy. One Sunday Miguel and others traveled to San Salvador to investigate, to figure out who these "protestors from San Isidro" could possibly be. San Isidro is a close-knit town, with a population of only some ten thousand people. But when Miguel approached the protestors, he recognized no one. Miguel showed his own ID to a reporter, saying "I'm from San Isidro." And he suggested that the reporter ask a protestor for an ID. As Miguel remembered, the protestor "didn't even know where San Isidro was; I could only smile." When Miguel and his fellow water defenders returned the next Sunday, the pro-mining protestors looked at them and their banners and started packing up. "We went for four more Sundays," Miguel told us, "and they never came back." Shrake admitted in an April 2008 email to his board that Pac Rim had organized the weekly protests. As Robert Johansing, whom Shrake had fired back in 2002, told researcher Rachel Nadelman: "You can buy protestors [in El Salvador]. Pac Rim did it. I did it. They charge you $5–10 per person, plus transport."

We cannot think of another country where a year began so favorably for the gold industry and within eight months had become such a nightmare. A bad week in June was one thing. But being at odds with two ministers and an archbishop and unable to get a meeting with President Saca comprised another. Pac Rim had entered 2006 knowing that there was substantial gold under San Isidro, Cabañas, and in other parts of the north. With a seemingly compliant government, they believed they were poised to lead and benefit from a great new gold rush in El Salvador. But the announcement by the ministers of environment and economy that there would be a pause in mining concessions as the country carried out a "strategic environmental review" meant, at a minimum, costly delays for the mining firms.

It was now anyone's guess which side would ultimately prevail. If one were placing bets, Big Gold would always be the favorite. Big Gold still had money on its side, money that could buy consultants, PR firms, local elites, and friends in government, never mind pro-mining protestors. By the fall of 2006, Big Gold realized that it might take all of these tactics to win in El Salvador.

Pac Rim needed a new battle plan, a multifront counterattack. The company dropped attempts to woo the likes of ADES's Antonio Pacheco with ladies of the night, stopped inviting such organizations as ADES to meetings, and started playing tough. Ad hominem attacks began: water defenders were said to be pawns of foreigners with dubious motives. Oxfam, ADES, and other members of La Mesa were called "rogue" organizations and "anti-development."

On another front, Pac Rim laid out a plan to strengthen its ties with key government and business figures. El Salvador's vice president, Ana Vilma de Escobar, in charge of attracting foreign investment, was Pac Rim's key top-level contact. She and Pac Rim were especially focused on getting El Salvador's legislature to amend the mining law to remove the land titling problem. Were that stipulation to be removed, Pac Rim and the vice president thought that the company would be able to move forward quickly at El Dorado.

As for the Salvadoran national business community, Big Gold belatedly recognized a key flaw in its entry into El Salvador years before. Global mining firms had not nurtured local elite support. In many countries with minerals, the foreign mining executives form close ties with local business leaders, sometimes setting up joint ventures with them. By giving local elites a piece of the mining pie, Big Gold wins domestic political support in difficult interactions with government. But Shrake, Johansing, and other top executives of the Big Gold corporations intent on mining in El Salvador had done precious little outreach to Salvadoran business leaders. Who needed them in such a small poor country that would certainly be desperate for mining revenues?

This mistake had to be rectified, and Pac Rim did not mess around. The company hired Manuel Enrique Hinds, a former finance minister and a man well connected in both government and business. Hinds was also connected globally, having worked at the World Bank for a decade and served as a fellow at the Council on Foreign Relations, a prestigious gathering place for the US foreign policy elite.

Pac Rim released Hinds's consultancy report—*Gold Mining in El Salvador: Costs and Benefits*—in May 2007. With no equivocation, the report laid out the case that the financial rewards of mining were higher than understood, that the environmental costs were lower, and that the risks of mining were far fewer than risks to be expected with many other ventures. "There are very few projects [for El Salvador] that could generate a wealth as immense as gold," the report asserted. "Given the enormous potential benefits of mining and the modern technologies that reduce environmental risks, renouncing gold mining would be unjustifiable and globally unprecedented."

Economists like Hinds pretend that economics is an exact science, and they often hide their unrealistic assumptions while broadcasting supposedly indisputable economic benefits of projects. In this case, the Hinds report determined that a whopping 36,000 jobs would be created by Pac Rim. But how did Hinds come up with this number? He began with the 450 jobs that Pac Rim argued it would initially create during construction, the most labor-intensive stage of mining. Hinds then assumed, without justification, that three other mines would also open and that the job-creation benefits from all these mines would multiply into other sectors of the Salvadoran economy. Voilà! The already optimistic 450 jobs ballooned eighty times into 36,000 jobs. Hinds's 36,000 became the number waved around by Pac Rim and its supporters as the number of jobs the Pac Rim project would create in El Salvador.

Even if one accepted the highly inflated figures that Hinds presented as guaranteed and certain, his report assumed away differences in definitions of progress and development at the core of the debate. So too was Hinds silent on questions about who would benefit. These were the very questions that had led the water defenders to oppose mining in the first place.

Hinds also lobbied for Pac Rim—meeting with Archbishop Sáenz Lacalle, among others. In addition to deploying Hinds, Pac Rim also found an ally in El Salvador's richest man, oligarch Ricardo Poma. Poma advocated for Pac Rim and the mining industry in the corridors of power. A top lawyer of the Poma Group, Fidel Chávez Mena, and his son Rodrigo, joined Pac Rim's lobbying efforts in El Salvador's legislature—pressing for pro-mining changes to the national mining law. For good measure, Pac Rim hired a very close relative of the vice president. Perhaps not surprisingly, years later, Pac Rim would refuse to supply a list of those the company had paid over the years.

Pac Rim also sought to mobilize allies outside the country. Documents reveal that the company was trying to get the George W. Bush administration to "intervene" (Shrake's word) to pressure El Salvador to let the company mine. Pac Rim was also attempting to pull Pope Benedict XVI to their side—or at least have him silence that pesky archbishop. In 2008, Shrake emailed his board of directors: "While in Washington I met with the former US Ambassador to the Vatican. We discussed the possibility of getting to the Pope with our issue. The Pope is anti-liberation theology and the statements by the ES [El Salvador] archbishop contradict the statements of the Pope made in January. We are identifying the right person in the Vatican for help."

Pac Rim complemented all these activities with several major public relations campaigns in newspapers and on the air. In this PR work, the company at times demonstrated political sophistication, aiming separate messages at the right ARENA party and the left FMLN party. Pac Rim executives knew that many in the FMLN followed other progressive leaders in Latin America, several of whom were funding their social agendas with mineral and fossil fuel revenues. One observer summed up the company's advertising pitch to FMLN supporters this way: "Castro [in Cuba], Putin [in Russia], Chavez [in Venezuela], Ortega [in Nicaragua], they all want mining. Why don't you?"

In 2007, Johansing suggested in a three-page internal memo that the campaign was having an effect: "Aided by Pacific Rim's aggressive radio campaign bringing to El Salvador's attention that mining is viewed differently in other Latin [American] countries, we have seen a subtle change in the FMLN's attitude about mining. . . . [T]here appears to be a subdued recognition that our industry would play a role in their government if they are elected [in the presidential election] in 2009."

Indeed, water defenders noticed that when politicians came back from travel abroad, they were more likely to be pro-mining. For ARENA government officials, this followed trips to the United States especially but also to Canada. For FMLN politicians, the change of heart—or at least misgivings about saying no to mining—followed trips to meet with socialist allies.

Pac Rim also launched a major advertising campaign on the benefits of "green mining," which was how the company had begun to brand itself in El Salvador. Since the water defenders were leading with the environment, Pac Rim officials realized that they needed to make the case that theirs was a "responsible" and "green" mining company. It placed ads on radio and on the sides of buses touting the economic, social, and environmental benefits of mining.

Pac Rim executives made one crucial miscalculation in this campaign: their ads did not mention the company by name as sponsor. Several people with whom we spoke in San Salvador mentioned that almost everyone knew that Pac Rim was the "backer." The fact that Pac Rim did not publicly own up to the ads made some who were sitting on the fence about mining suspicious of the company's motives. If mining was truly a good thing, why would Pac Rim not stand proudly behind its media campaign? Why the anonymous ads? Johansing later told Rachel Nadelman that he had found the campaign to be "patronizing" and "overdone."

The massive Pac Rim PR efforts won some converts from across the political spectrum. But, overall, the campaigns were too little and too late to stop what Gavidia had told those with whom she had met in late July 2006: the government was halting new mining licenses while it studied the issue.

In late 2007, the University of Central America decided to launch a public opinion poll on mining. The poll asked residents of eight gold-rich provinces their views on mining. Before the results were in, some water defenders were very nervous. Just a few years earlier, many of the respondents likely had no idea what mining was, never mind an opinion on whether or

not it belonged in El Salvador. Or, like the man we interviewed in Chalatenango, they might have confused the term "mining" with land mines.
What would happen, some water defenders quietly asked one another, if
the polls showed overwhelming support for Big Gold rather than for La
Mesa's position against mining? Yes, Marcelo and other water defenders
had led countless educational sessions on the environmental, social, and
economic dangers of mining, but how many people had been convinced?
The worry was dispelled when a stunning 62.5 percent expressed opposition to mining in El Salvador.

With the public and the church opposed and with 2009 elections starting to loom, reigning President Saca of ARENA stated publicly in March
2008 that there would be no mining permits issued in his final months in
office. This simply reinforced the mid-2006 government policy—which
had been shared with mining CEOs at the time—of no mining permits
until the strategic environmental review proposed by the Peruvian consultant was done. But Pac Rim found Saca's public statement disconcerting.

The next month, in April 2008, Shrake wrote Saca a three-page letter, laying out the impasse: "Pacific Rim in El Salvador finds itself in a
very critical and precarious situation." The company still had "no answer
acceptable to [its] rights as an investor" regarding approval of its mining
concession (and environmental impact assessment). Thus Pac Rim has no
choice but to contemplate legal action on a global level. In case Saca did not
grasp the significance of this threat, Shrake added: "The afore-mentioned
situation would be very negative for the image of El Salvador in international capital markets and in the eyes of other foreign investors."

Shrake and Johansing and many of the rest of the mining executives were
trained geologists and engineers. And, as geologists and engineers, they
had indeed succeeded at what was expected to be their hardest job: finding
the gold. But over the period from 2006 to 2008, it was becoming clearer
and clearer that they often blundered in their public relations efforts and
did not seem to have much insight into the future.

The one exception we came across was an internal October 2007
memo titled "The Potonico Brief" by would-be Chalatenango miner

Robert Johansing. In the memo, Johansing presented what seemed like the most informed analysis of that time regarding how things would play out in the short term versus post-election for Big Gold in El Salvador. At that time, with elections coming up in early 2009, Johansing acknowledged that Big Gold was under a "State of Siege" in El Salvador. "We are currently under assault from both sides," he wrote—"both sides" meaning both left and right parties.

But Johansing boldly predicted that global mining companies seeking to mine in El Salvador would be fine after the election. Big Gold just had to wait out that "State of Siege." Post-election, global mining companies would simply need to play the game of whichever party won the election. If ARENA won, he predicted, it would demand "greater control of the exploration licenses . . . a greater stake in the 'game'"—that is, more of the revenues. And should the FMLN somehow prevail, unprecedented but possible, that party would also support mining but with "changes to the rules and an 'acceptable' socialization of the industry."

In other words, wrote Johansing, whichever party won, that party would revert to its true nature and focus on the economics of how to get a bigger slice of the profits from Big Gold, be it via higher mining taxes or some kind of joint ownership or both. This seemed especially likely given the record-high prices that gold was then fetching. As for the concerns of the water defenders for the environment and the communities, concerns both parties were also raising: these would disappear after the election. In Johansing's words, either the FMLN "Red Miners" or the ARENA "Red, White and Blue [M]iners" would silence the calls for environmentally responsible "Green Miners." Thus, Johansing confidently concluded, "Of course we, as a sector, will be invited to play regardless of who writes the new rules."

Big Gold just had to play the game well, mostly behind the scenes, until the election. Whatever the "nightmare" of 2006–2008 for Big Gold, after the election it would be "game over" for the water defenders, Johansing foresaw confidently.

CHAPTER 4

Local Terror, Global Extortion (2009)

Since you never abandoned us, we will not abandon you. . . . Your [river], with your hills free of mines, will stay behind. Here we follow your path and we will defend our inheritance with pride, so that tomorrow, when we come across a child reading calmly below the shade of a tree, [we] will tell everyone that he has your face. Your face is still alive.

—From "Eulogy for Marcelo Rivera," by a close friend

Thanks in part to the water defenders' unlikely allies, they had gained valuable ground against Big Gold, but 2009 would change that.

The year began with a jolting and ominous reminder to Marcelo Rivera and the water defenders of the high-stakes game they were playing. On one of the narrow streets in his hometown of San Isidro, a car appeared out of nowhere and sped up, veering straight toward Marcelo, his brother Miguel at his side. Miguel reacted in a split second. He grabbed Marcelo and pulled him out of the car's path.

Neither brother could believe what had happened. To add to their shock, they recognized the driver. They knew he worked as an employee of long-time San Isidro mayor José Bautista, the mayor with the photo of ARENA death squad leader Roberto D'Aubuisson hanging in his office. Under the photo were the words: "Leader of yesterday, today, and forever. There for the fatherland." Like most ARENA mayors in El Salvador who ruled with an iron fist, Bautista enjoyed virtual impunity. Bautista was the water defenders' first major political opponent, and they had clashed with him for years as they had tried to halt his environmentally destructive pet projects, first the landfill and pig farm and then Pac Rim's mining venture.

As 2009 rolled in, gold prices continued their unprecedented rise. For Bautista, this made the El Dorado mining project even more enticing. The mayor fully expected that Pac Rim would eventually be granted the right to mine, and he knew he would be a primary financial beneficiary since the local government would get 1 percent of Pac Rim's revenues. Plus, he was already benefiting significantly from Pac Rim via company-sponsored English and sewing classes and other community projects. "It's resource management," he explained to a visiting human rights delegation. "We send notes to companies asking them to sponsor activities, and there are many activities in the cantons. I don't call that corruption."

But Marcelo and the other water defenders had been making Bautista's life complicated.

Just two days prior to the car incident, San Isidro had held its elections for mayor. Bautista had expected to emerge victorious in his reelection bid, while Marcelo and other local activists had been warning people for weeks of possible fraud in the local elections. They reminded the public that in the 2006 local elections, some in the ARENA camp had transported Hondurans over the Lempa River to San Isidro to cast illegal votes for Bautista. Marcelo and his allies had expected similar shenanigans in the January 2009 elections, and they had brought a number of observers to the polling place on election day. As these observers, along with official poll monitors, witnessed numerous fraudulent voters from nearby Honduras and elsewhere showing up at the polls, they blew the whistle. The police responded by closing the polls that day. Bautista stood alone among the candidates for mayor in arguing to keep the polls open. The electoral tribunal disagreed and postponed the election one week.

In the week between the postponed local election and the rescheduled one, according to a respected Salvadoran human rights group, Bautista and another local official hired over one hundred gang members from San Salvador and elsewhere to intimidate the local population. The intimidation worked. Bautista won reelection in San Isidro with 52 percent of the vote.

Bautista's friend Tom Shrake wrote a statement on a prominent human rights website, in August 2009, professing Pac Rim's noninvolvement in these elections: "Democracy was convincingly demonstrated in these elections in Cabañas. Mining was a major issue in the Cabañas elections and the people overwhelmingly voted for candidates that favored the proposed project." Lest anyone think it odd that Shrake had anything to say about local elections in Cabañas, he added: "Pacific Rim has never contributed to any campaign of any electoral candidate from any party anywhere in El Salvador or anywhere else."

So why, just two days after the postponed local elections, had that car veered straight toward Marcelo Rivera, the most prominent opponent of Pac Rim in Cabañas?

The drama of the mayoral elections went largely unnoticed outside San Isidro and Pac Rim. But even those not really following events in El Salvador might well have heard news of the national elections two months later. That was the case for us.

Remember the television personality Mauricio Funes, who hosted Andrés McKinley and another water defender on his show back in 2006? Well, in 2009, Funes had to retire from his show. In March of that year he was elected president of El Salvador, running for the FMLN as a "moderate leftist" candidate. El Salvador received global attention for electing its second-ever progressive president, just a couple of months after Barack Obama became the first Black president of the United States.

In 1931, El Salvador's first progressive president—Arturo Araujo—was overthrown by the Salvadoran military, less than a year after his term began, and the first of many military dictators seized power. In 1932, that first dictator, Maximiliano Hernández Martínez, oversaw an infamous massacre. Tens of thousands of coffee workers and small farmers, many of them indigenous, had decided that they could take no more. They had risen up to demand better conditions and democracy. The landed elite, led by fourteen families, and the military government responded quickly and decisively and brutally. Accounts vary, but roughly thirty thousand people were killed. The massacres targeted people based on their indigenous

heritage and appearance, effectively criminalizing the surviving indigenous peoples of the country.

For many Salvadorans, the 2009 election of Funes seemed as unlikely
a victory as Obama's did for many in the United States. Until that year,
ARENA had handily won all three presidential elections held since the
bloody civil war ended in 1992. From global news reports in 2009, we
knew that Funes was a popular TV host and "left-wing but moderate."
He referred to himself as a "center-leftist." Reports stressed that although
Funes's FMLN-member brother had fought and been killed in the civil
war, Funes himself had not been an FMLN party member until deciding
to run for president. He had needed a political party at the same time that
the FMLN was looking for a candidate with a broader, less ideological
appeal. The word on the street, as well as in a confidential briefing from a
former ARENA minister to a US embassy staffer, was that such a politically independent president might be one to broker compromise policies.
But nothing we read mentioned that Funes had hosted members of La
Mesa on his show as they launched their national campaign in 2006. Or
that, for an incoming president, he was exceptionally well versed on Pac
Rim and the mining debate.

The presidential election campaign had been ugly. In the run-up to
the election, ARENA focused less on Funes and more on the specter of
Latin America's "pink tide" inundating El Salvador, the purported next
Latin American domino to fall to a leftist government. ARENA, as the
New York Times reported just days before the March election, "linked the
F.M.L.N., the party of El Salvador's former guerrillas, to Latin America's
far-left leaders. Images of [Venezuelan president Hugo] Chávez appear
during almost every ARENA commercial break in montages of grainy
clips that also feature scenes of street chaos and camouflaged soldiers. The
message is less than subtle: Elect Mr. Funes as president and the F.M.L.N.
will 'surrender' the country to the socialist camp."

After Funes won in a tight count, the *New York Times* reminded its
readers, Funes's "immediate concern will be strengthening El Salvador's
tiny economy to withstand the buffeting of the global economic recession." The *Times* did not suggest that, with the high price of gold continuing its ascent, mining would be one obvious way to increase revenues. But

the *Wall Street Journal* had linked the two in its election coverage starting a few months earlier. Pro-ARENA, pro–foreign investment *Journal* columnist Mary Anastasia O'Grady had dined with Tom Shrake, a Pac Rim lobbyist, and Salvadoran government officials in El Salvador in 2008. A Funes win, asserted O'Grady in the *Journal*, "would be tragic for the tiny, market-oriented Central American nation." And she added: "Take the case of Pacific Rim Mining Company," writing that the delay in allowing mining was "a high price" and a "lost opportunity for Salvadorans."

We followed these elections in the media and felt the exuberance of our Salvadoran friends and neighbors in the Washington, DC, area. Glued to computer screens, many stared in disbelief at first and then were elated as decades of right-wing death-squad rule finally came to an end. To our Salvadoran friends and those in the United States who had been deeply involved in denouncing US intervention in El Salvador's civil war, the 2009 election seemed like a watershed denoting that democracy had at last returned to El Salvador.

Pac Rim was not the only mining company in El Salvador also watching the March election campaign closely. Funes had announced his opposition to new mining licenses. Mining executives hoped that this was all a propaganda move—to match the anti-mining rhetoric that President Saca was spewing on behalf of ARENA. They hoped that a more rational, pro-mining view would settle in once Funes realized the full extent of El Salvador's economic woes.

To Pac Rim's chagrin, Funes's rhetoric did not change after his election. Just weeks after the election, Pac Rim filed an official "notice of arbitration" for a lawsuit against the government of El Salvador in the little-known tribunal housed at the sprawling World Bank Group headquarters in Washington, DC, the International Centre for Settlement of Investment Disputes. Tom Shrake's campaign to mine in El Salvador, which he had waged for years primarily inside El Salvador, had gone global.

We would not know the intimate, firsthand machinations of this lawsuit had it not been for our own unlikely friendship with El Salvador's lead lawyer on this case, Luis Parada. And the fact that Luis became El Salvador's lawyer during the Funes presidency was perhaps even more unlikely, given his background.

Luis was born and raised in a lower-middle-class neighborhood of San Salvador. He attended a nearby Baptist private school. In 1978, Luis was one of just over a dozen students of two hundred applicants from El Salvador selected to attend high school for a year in another country. Soon he was living with a family in an Oregon town of five hundred people and going to school in Lincoln City, population five thousand.

Six months after finishing his senior year at that school in Oregon and returning to El Salvador, Luis joined the Salvadoran Military Academy. In an interview with a Lincoln City newspaper one year earlier, Luis had explained: "Going to the academy will give me a big opportunity to help my country and I want to do as much as I can."

And his atypical path would continue. The US government has a long history of inviting a small number of candidates from allied countries to apply to West Point. Luis was among the chosen. Four years later, he had earned a prestigious West Point degree. Along the way, he met his future wife, a fellow cadet from the United States. Within a few years, she joined him in El Salvador, where they started a family. "A proud Salvadoran," as Luis put it, he served as a platoon leader in a paratrooper battalion, as a company commander in one of the most remote areas of the country, as a military intelligence officer, and as a military attaché in Washington during the civil war.

But Luis witnessed things he did not like during that brutal civil war. As a result, he testified in 1991 as a witness in a criminal case that convicted a senior officer. And, two years later, he voluntarily met with the UN Truth Commission for El Salvador. He presented recommendations to improve the military's record on human rights—recommendations that were included in the landmark commission's 1993 final report. As a result of his truth telling, Luis became well respected in the broader human rights community.

Luis became less respected in other circles. His testimony in the criminal trial led to warnings that he would, in his words, be killed "at the first opportunity." To avoid this fate, he extended his time as a military attaché in Washington by two years and earned a master's degree in government from Georgetown University. Luis's testimony—and his overall feeling of alienation from the military—pretty much ended his military career. When he deemed it safe enough to return to El Salvador, he found himself in what he feared was a dead-end job working in the security field. That job brought him to a security workshop at the Federal Aviation Administration Academy in Oklahoma City. By fate or serendipity, one of the interpreters passed Luis an extra application to Georgetown Law School—due a week hence. Luis submitted the application, took the LSATs, and was admitted.

As Luis began practicing law, he started to make a name for himself in a very specialized field. He climbed the ranks of the lawyers known for skill in the arenas where corporations sue governments, claiming that they have not been treated fairly. Here, however, Luis took a stance as he built his reputation   accepting only governments and not corporations as his clients.

As Luis dived into this international arbitration arena, he began representing El Salvador. The law firms where Luis worked were hired by four different Salvadoran attorneys general for cases spanning four different presidential administrations. One day, after victories in two cases and with another pending case already en route to victory, Luis was invited to dinner at an Italian restaurant near the San Salvador Sheraton by the legal adviser to Mauricio Funes, president at the time. The legal adviser handed Luis a large white envelope with a colorful presidential seal in one corner. According to Luis, his face glowing, the legal adviser conveyed this message: "The President of the Republic wants to know if you will agree to be El Salvador's lawyer for ICSID [International Centre for Settlement of Investment Disputes] arbitration." That day, Luis says, "was the best day of my professional life."

So continued the tradition of strange bedfellows in the Salvadoran war on mining. Many of those ICSID outsiders who followed the ins and outs of the Pac Rim lawsuit had Luis to thank. He encouraged the government to make the documents from the legal proceedings public, specifically asking the Ministry of the Economy to post the documents on its website.

Thanks to Luis, we also learned that Pac Rim had been planning its lawsuit for some time. Luis knew this because in 2007 Pac Rim's lawyers had tried to hire him to work on this very case, which they were already preparing. By letting it be known that it was preparing a lawsuit, Pac Rim had hoped to leverage the Saca government to take the company seriously and approve the concession. Some might call this legal blackmail or legal extortion. It is nonetheless a central element of the structural advantage the global legal system has created for corporations. A more than insignificant number of ICSID cases are settled out of court, typically in favor of the corporation. Shrake admitted as much: "I'm not of the opinion this arbitration will proceed to the end. In my opinion we will settle with El Salvador. I think settling will be moving industry and the gold mine forward."

In this tradition, Pac Rim hoped to get the Saca government to give in and either grant it the mining concession or pay it for costs incurred and future profits foregone. Yes, upping the ante by claiming profits foregone, not just compensation for original investments, is a key move in this game of global extortion.

In 2009, the Republic of El Salvador, through its attorney general, hired Luis for two such cases. The first was that of Pac Rim—which filed its lawsuit on April 30, just over a month after the Funes victory.

The second case for Luis started only two months later and involved the old Butters mine, then owned by a US firm called Commerce Group. Commerce Group's charge: the Saca government had wrongly revoked its mining license three years earlier when the Ministry of Environment concluded that Commerce Group failed to meet the requirements of its environmental permit. Earlier that year, a Salvadoran research group had tested those shockingly colored waters below the mine. The test revealed dangerous levels of toxic chemicals, including cyanide. Not surprisingly, high levels of iron explained the water's rusty orange color.

Just as Pac Rim launched its suit, the Institute for Policy Studies reached out to leaders of La Mesa to inform them that they had been selected for the prestigious Letelier-Moffitt Human Rights Award. The IPS invited La Mesa to send one or two of its leaders to Washington in October to receive the award. The invitation to bring their story to the United States thrilled Vidalina, Marcelo, Antonio, and the other water defender leaders: it was the first global recognition they had received for their work. Moreover, they had just learned that Pac Rim had filed its lawsuit in Washington, and they were trying to understand not only how such an investor-state case worked but also how they could possibly fight back. They knew they would need assistance from abroad for that.

La Mesa immediately asked to send five representatives instead of the originally invited two. Its leaders also wanted more than the one audience in Washington DC. They respectfully but firmly asked the IPS to help set up speaking tours for the five elsewhere in the United States and in Canada.

La Mesa addressed its requests to the IPS point person on Central America, Manuel Pérez-Rocha. Manuel, a Mexican-born researcher and activist with a graduate degree from the Netherlands, had worked in various parts of Central America for Oxfam before coming to the institute. And, prior to that, while still in Mexico, he had served with the Mexican coalition that fought against the North American Free Trade Agreement (NAFTA). Manuel and his colleagues' work revealed that this first big regional trade agreement between the US, Mexico, and Canada would give corporations virtually unchecked powers over communities, workers, and the environment.

In a nutshell, Manuel knew the region, the issues, and at least one of the key people in La Mesa. Hence, La Mesa's requests made sense to Manuel. And he knew exactly which groups he could rely on in Washington, DC, and elsewhere in the United States and Canada to help organize the tour for the Mesa Five. He extended La Mesa's request to groups that had worked in or on El Salvador for decades—human rights groups, religious groups, development groups, solidarity groups, and others. Among them were the Washington Office on Latin America, Oxfam, the Committee in Solidarity with the People of El Salvador (CISPES), US–El Salvador Sister Cities, the American Jewish World Service, and the Maryknoll missionaries. As these groups learned about the work of La Mesa and started to circulate the word, the excitement about the upcoming tour spread. With the groups' financial and logistical help, the tour of the Mesa Five became possible.

As the Institute for Policy Studies reached out to this broad set of allies, we learned of the Pac Rim lawsuit. The institute—and especially John and Manuel—had been involved for close to two decades in fighting the trade and investment agreements that facilitate corporations suing governments. And so the enthusiasm around hosting La Mesa leaders grew as the organizers asked the obvious questions: Should not the Salvadoran government be rewarded, not punished, for putting its people and its environment first? How could a corporation that does not yet have a mining license sue? It was not as if the Salvadoran government seized a working factory or mine. Even if it had, the compensation should at most equal the value of the expropriated property. But Pac Rim did not have a permit for such a working mine. How could such a corporation possibly sue for the fuzzy concept of future profits foregone?

In retrospect, La Mesa's request and Manuel's outreach would prove crucial for the global battle ahead. Years later, former Oxfam staffer Andrés McKinley would tell us that, in his view, the Letelier-Moffitt Human Rights Award had proved a game changer. As Pac Rim had gone global with its lawsuit, La Mesa needed to go global with its side. The IPS award became the vehicle to initiate that. The award enabled the water defenders to forge ties with allies in North America and made what might seem like a vague faraway battle specific and intimate, affecting the lives of people that the North Americans now knew.

Then terror struck.

For nearly two weeks, Marcelo's family—and the numerous volunteers who called themselves Marcelo's Search Committee—could not find him. They frantically implored the police and other authorities to search the area, to no avail. And then, on June 29, 2009, the family received an anonymous call telling them that a body could be found in an abandoned well just south of San Isidro. It was near where Marcelo had last been seen, getting off the bus twelve days earlier at a turnoff to the capital city.

We did not learn of the disappearance until the body was found. We did not read about it in the newspapers or hear about it in the news. After all, one missing person in El Salvador, even one later found dead and hor-rifically tortured, is not typically national news, never mind global news.

After the anonymous tip to Marcelo's family, they and volunteers se-cured the area around the well. Only then did the police act. They ex-tracted the human remains out of the dry, thirty-meter deep well—really a hole in the ground, almost invisible amid cornfields. The disfigurement was so extensive that the body was unrecognizable. Chillingly, the signs of torture were distinctly similar to those found on victims of right-wing death squads during El Salvador's civil war.

Marcelo Rivera had become the first water defender to be assassinated in the modern fight over mining in El Salvador.

We tried to help from Washington, DC. But given what we know now, we confess that from afar, from the relative safety of the United States, no matter how haunted we were by the news from San Isidro, we did not grasp the extent of the horror. We did not know the details—beyond the mere fact of Marcelo's disappearance, death, and discovery—that con-fronted the Rivera family and water defender friends on the ground in San Isidro. Even as they tried to begin to process their grief. And even as they began their mourning.

First, the family was told that, given the degree of the torture, DNA tests had to be done to confirm Marcelo's identity before his body could come home. Such DNA testing, they were informed, would take some days. Then, when Miguel and other relatives traveled, in their anguish and shock, to San Salvador to meet with the relevant officials to get permission to retrieve the body, they were told they were too late. Marcelo had al-ready been buried in a common grave elsewhere. In total bewilderment, as Miguel recollected to us, he called El Salvador's Human Rights Ombuds-man, well-respected lawyer Oscar Luna, who was by this point following the case, for assistance. The Ombudsman expressed astonishment at the news, saying, in Miguel's words, "I didn't know about this and I'm the one who can authorize this."

Who, then, ordered the common burial, and why?

Miguel appeared weary as he recounted the story to us some years later. "We had to initiate another process to try to exhume Marcelo's body. We even had to pay for the exhuming. We searched for Marcelo for twelve days and then it was another eleven days until we were able to recover his body."

Finally, in mid-July 2009, Marcelo's body lay in his beloved cultural center—the very place that, as young boys, the Rivera brothers had cleaned and transformed into a library—for, as Miguel put it, "final good-byes."

Following the funeral ceremony, hundreds of mourners clogged the streets. Old people, young people, women, men, water defenders from Cabañas, and others from outside Cabañas hoisted large cloth banners and huge photos of Marcelo. They took turns carrying Marcelo's casket as the procession passed the house he had been fixing up just around the corner from the cultural center, toward the headquarters of the organization where he had begun his nonprofit work, past the mayor's office, and past the spot where Miguel had saved his brother from the swerving car six months earlier.

Tears streamed down some cheeks. Other faces contorted with anger. One person fainted under the blazing sun. A young girl called out "Cipitio!" When you look at the photos of the people filling the streets with their banners, you could mistake the funeral procession for a protest.

In our imaginations we envision Marcelo in his Cipitio costume dancing through those streets, as if leading the procession, directing his mourners to the cemetery. We see Marcelo and Miguel's mother, the one who allowed those two youngest of her sons to transform the family living room into a lending library, barely making it to those gates. She would die by year's end.

July 2009 held still more terror. In the weeks following Marcelo's assassination and funeral, death threats escalated in number and tone, particularly targeting the staff of Radio Victoria. This youth-run radio station, started by ADES under Antonio's watch, played a key role in transmitting news of the water defenders and of Pac Rim to the far-flung homes of Cabañas.

The death threats to the water defenders and Radio Victoria staff had begun as early as March 2006 with this text: "We know where you live, we know who you are, we know your family, we know what time you leave the radio and if you don't shut up we are going to kill you." But the threats really took off after Marcelo's funeral in July 2009.

Some of the death threats arrived the old-fashioned way, via notes slipped under doors. But most arrived via anonymous cell-phone texts, texts that sent chills up spines. Many of those sent in the wake of Marcelo's assassination warned recipients that they would be joining Marcelo soon: "The same thing that happened to Marcelo is going to happen to you."

On July 23, 2009, a threat was pushed under the door at a Radio Victoria reporter's home. Earlier death threats to him had been texted to his phone. This one read: "You like to talk too much, be careful, you are also on the list. You spoke too much in San Isidro [at Marcelo's wake] and it will be for nothing because you see how . . . [Cipitio] appeared, ha, soon it will happen to you and no one will be able to save you, son of a bitch."

After such threats, the radio station moved three of its employees out of Cabañas to undisclosed locations for their safety. As July dragged on, the water defenders complained to local and provincial officials, to the office of Oscar Luna (who seemed to be using his limited powers to try to help), to the attorney general (who seemed not to be trying to help), and all the way up to President Funes himself.

On July 27, Luna convened a press conference and issued a resolution demanding that the National Civilian Police and the attorney general report back within seventy-two hours regarding what steps they had taken in investigating the threats against the three Radio Victoria correspondents who had been moved to safer undisclosed locations. Luna called on the director of the police and the attorney general to "guarantee the life and physical integrity of the youth" and their families. He directed these authorities to "urgently investigate in an impartial, exhaustive, and effective manner the threats against [the youth] to the effect of finding those responsible and making them face justice." But, as Luna reminded us when we met with him two years later in his San Salvador office, the human rights ombudsman in El Salvador—as with human rights commissioners in many other countries—has no real power, just a bully pulpit from which to urge action by others.

The threats continued. On July 29, 2009, one came via a note posted on the gate of a colleague of ADES director Antonio Pacheco, the man who brought in Robert Moran and made unlikely allies of Minister Barrera and Archbishop Sáenz Lacalle: "The hour has come . . . [Pacheco] for the bomb in your own house and of your pals, now is the hour you pay for what you did. . . . [You are] the next like Marcelo Rivera."

The following day, the female head of the Radio Victoria news team received a phone call just after everyone else had left the station that night: "Oh, you're all alone, mama[c]ita. Well, we came to visit you last night, but we didn't have luck, tonight we will have more luck. We saw you in Sensuntepeque today and know everywhere you went."

And, as if to demonstrate the omniscient spying abilities of those texting, that same day a threat somehow found its way to one of those who had left Cabañas for his own safety: "Why are you hiding, why don't you come back to Cabañas, we are waiting for you."

Yet another text, on July 30, warned: "You are dead, now you are in the mouth of the wolf, you goddamn dog."

Throughout this period of intimidation and surreptitious surveillance, the price of gold continued its historic climb, reaching $951.69 per ounce by month's end.

As July turned into August, the threats not only continued but escalated into actual violence. After a threat emailed to Radio Victoria staff on August 7 declared "Today, you dogs, yes we are going to carry out the objective, we are being pressured from above to carry out actions," someone shot Ramiro Rivera eight times as he walked out to milk his cow. Ramiro, no relation to Marcelo and Miguel, was a water defender from the village of Trinidad, an area north of San Isidro where Pac Rim also hoped to mine. Ramiro survived the eight bullet wounds to his back and legs. "Miraculous," the doctors termed Ramiro's survival of this first attempt on his life.

As with the car aiming for Marcelo, Ramiro recognized his would-be assassin. By week's end, the man was in jail. According to one account:

"Interestingly, this man . . . who has little financial resources, benefited from the legal counsel of three high-profiled lawyers." He would be free within half a year.

The water defenders were being terrorized. One of their own had been brutally tortured and murdered, and their tormenters were doing their best to keep them in a state of extreme distress. When we visited Cabañas for the first time a little under two years later, the reality of that terror sank in even more strongly for us. We realized that the local population still lived in constant fear. They looked over their shoulders. They arrived at destinations before dark. We got a sense of it too from the frequent phone calls from Miguel's wife to his cell phone when we were with him.

The question of how to protect one's self and one's family was always with them. Was police protection the solution? There was no easy answer. Bodyguards could—would—be killed. And police protection could make one even more of a target, even more vulnerable. Miguel, Vidalina, and Antonio said no to police protection, even as Vidalina walked the dirt road to her family's remote home. Others said yes—among them Ramiro, the man who had been shot eight times.

But who killed Marcelo? The water defenders had an answer right away. To them, all signs pointed to some combination of Pac Rim and the mayor's office.

Pac Rim's response was to offer condolences but simultaneously deny any connection and express outrage at the suggestion of any company involvement. "We've been cast as demons, responsible for violence, when in reality we are the victims of the violence," Shrake would testify in 2010.

This question of who killed Marcelo started to haunt us in 2009. And it haunted us even more so once the prosecutor's office and local police reported the crime solved. Allegedly, Marcelo's murder resulted from gang activity or drunken arguments or both: "a case of common delinquency" because he "chatted with a group of gang members who then killed him after a heated discussion." Yet Marcelo, like Miguel, did not drink, an aftereffect of growing up with an alcoholic father. Nor was there any indication that he had hung out with gang members. And what about the January attempt on his life? Or the hasty burial in a common grave, without the required orders from the national government? Why the evidence of torture?

Still, within days of finding Marcelo's body, the national police captured several gang members and named another person already in prison, saying they were suspects in the crime. It was reported that cellmates of these men said the arrestees spoke of having been hired to kill Marcelo in exchange for weapons and large sums of money. These may or may not have been the direct killers, the ones who pulled the trigger. It is always easy to point fingers at gang members looking for money. More difficult and more important is to find the "intellectual authors"—the ones who ordered the killing. Such orders can be done directly or indirectly, as in the mayor or someone with economic or political power suggesting "if only we did not have to deal with Marcelo Rivera."

This much we knew: Most towns that sit above gold deposits are economically poor. Their mayors struggle to raise funds for modest budgets. As is typical in many countries, the local government was slated to get 1 percent of Pac Rim's revenues once its El Dorado mine was up and running, with another 1 percent going to the federal government. For a local mayor, that 1 percent would be a bonanza. While Pac Rim waited for a yes from the government, it poured money into local projects, mostly pet projects of Mayor Bautista. Pac Rim also contributed money to local schools for activities including a curriculum touting the benefits of mining. Invariably this kind of money brings significant conflict, if only because such largesse offers local actors who stand to benefit enormous incentive to do damage to those who oppose mining.

A 2010 report on mining in El Salvador by the globally respected International Union for the Conservation of Nature put it this way: Pac Rim "played a significant role in destabilizing the region. . . . Mine opponents consider the mayors to function more as activists for the mine." Exactly how this worked would become even clearer over the next decade as our search for answers continued.

The delegation of five that La Mesa sent to Washington for the award ceremony in October 2009 included Miguel, Vidalina, and three other water defenders. Miguel took the place of his brother.

What does one say to people whose brother or colleague has recently been brutally murdered? How does the celebratory part of an award ceremony continue? But continue it did. Hundreds heard Vidalina at the National Press Club in Washington, DC, on that misty night in October. Hundreds saw the four other water defenders standing behind her, accepting the award with her on behalf of all the water defenders. Hundreds heard her dedicate the award to "the defenders of human rights and the environment, especially . . . Marcelo Rivera."

But something else was evident beyond their pain: The Mesa Five wanted to be there in Washington, DC. They wanted to tell their story, to tell Marcelo's story, and to find allies for the fight ahead.

Vidalina urged the audience to follow the related legal case unfolding just four blocks west of the National Press Club, just past the White House, at the World Bank tribunal. As Vidalina explained, Pac Rim had filed a lawsuit arguing that El Salvador had to allow it to mine or else pay it millions of dollars in compensation for costs and foregone profits. She ended her speech by invoking the "upside-down" world described by Uruguayan writer Eduardo Galeano, asking why it was not El Salvador that was suing Pac Rim as it threatened the water and well-being of her country.

Members of the Mesa Five delegation then packed their bags for trips to Philadelphia, New York, and elsewhere in the United States and Canada. The story of Marcelo and the water defenders began to spread.

That October night in 2009, as we huddled with Miguel after the ceremony, he sent us on our quest for more information about the Pac Rim lawsuit. And the two of us, along with our colleague Manuel, dug deep into the tribunal. The main venue for what is called "investor-state dispute settlement"—when foreign investors claim they are owed compensation from countries in which they have invested—is the World Bank Group's International Centre for Settlement of Investment Disputes (ICSID). At that point, ICSID was probably the least known of the five entities that comprise the World Bank Group. Robin had written her PhD dissertation and her first book about the World Bank. She had worked as World Bank program officer at the US Treasury Department in the mid-1980s, but she had barely heard of ICSID before the Pac Rim lawsuit.

Our research unearthed a drama dating to nearly a half-century earlier. Unbeknown to the Salvadoran government or really almost anyone else we conversed with, ICSID was created by the World Bank in a sea of controversy. At the 1964 Tokyo World Bank annual meetings, twenty-one developing countries—including El Salvador—voted no to the convention to set up this new part of the World Bank Group. They voted no to allowing foreign corporations to sue governments in a global venue. Such bypassing of domestic courts, they argued, would dramatically erode local democratic control over important political and economic decisions. The twenty-one that voted no included *all* of the nineteen Latin American countries attending as well as the Philippines and Iraq. So historic was this vote that it earned a name: the Tokyo No.

In 1964, speaking on behalf of the Latin American countries and the Tokyo No vote, Félix Ruiz, then representative of Chile, said: "The new system . . . would give the foreign investor, by virtue of the fact that he is a foreigner, the right to sue a sovereign state outside its national territory, dispensing with the courts of law. This provision . . . would confer a privilege on the foreign investor, placing the nationals of the country concerned in a position of inferiority." In other words, those voting no believed that the new investor-state dispute settlement system was both unnecessary and unfair.

In the upside-down world that bestows more power to the votes and voice of certain countries, the creation of ICSID was approved, despite the no votes. Initially ICSID was small and largely irrelevant. Its first case was filed in 1972, and just over two dozen cases had been filed by 1988. However, by the mid-1990s, ICSID moved center stage. Its power was upgraded thanks to the corporate-friendly clauses in bilateral and multilateral trade and investment agreements, starting in the 1990s with the North American Free Trade Agreement. In 2012 alone, forty-eight new cases were added to ICSID's docket. All of the forty-eight were filed against governments of developing countries, and more than one-third related to mining and other extractive industries.

As the number of cases brought before ICSID by corporations ballooned, so too did the critiques—mainly by human rights activists, environmentalists, and governments, but also by trade lawyers and others. Critics note that ICSID rulings fall largely into two categories of bias. First, the rulings are biased in favor of corporate investors over governments and therefore highly anti-democratic, as presaged by the Tokyo No's concerns. Second, critics contend that the rulings are too narrow in their focus on "commercial" rights—that is, of the private foreign investor—over broader social and environmental issues.

As of mid-2009, the fate of the water defenders—and El Salvador's water—seemed to be in the hands of ICSID.

The year 2009 is mainly remembered around the world as the year of global recession, which pushed hundreds of millions of people from the middle class into poverty. Many, especially in the United States, know it also as the first year of the presidency of Barack Obama, a big shift after eight years of George W. Bush.

In the midst of this global crisis, it would have been easy to miss an event that hit newspapers in the period between Marcelo's disappearance and the discovery of his disfigured body in the well. But that event would have huge implications for mining in Central America.

Just across the Lempa River to the north of the water defenders, Honduras had been experiencing three years of democratic rule under the presidency of Manuel Zelaya, a man from the elite who had begun to challenge the authoritarian ways of the Honduran government. But then, on June 28, 2009, a coup ousted the democratically elected Zelaya from the presidency. Among Zelaya's "crimes" precipitating the coup was a proposed anti-mining bill slated for congressional review in August that year. The still relatively new Obama government, through actions of Secretary of State Hillary Clinton, did not waste much time before announcing support for the coup government.

With the 2009 coup, Honduras was about to become, once again, a haven for Big Gold. In six years, almost one thousand new mining sites would enter the exploration stage in the country, and many were in the Lempa River watershed, a stark reminder that mining contamination does not respect national boundaries. Honduras was, according to the well-respected organization Global Witness, soon to become "the most dangerous country in the world to be an environmentalist."

Back in Cabañas, December and Christmas season could not come fast enough for those seeking a respite from the terror of 2009. As in many Catholic countries, the celebration is long and joyous. City dwellers return to their provincial bases, as do many Salvadorans who now live in the United States and elsewhere.

Planning and preparations begin far in advance, as does the holiday cheer. By late November, fireworks stands sprout up. Some folks save their money in anticipation, hoping to amass enough to afford more than just sparklers. So too for planning one's holiday clothes—at least pondering whether to wear red underwear for love or yellow for money.

And there are questions of food. For the traditional Christmas Eve sandwich feast, *pan con chumpe*—turkey sandwiches—if one could afford it. *Pan con pollo*—chicken sandwiches—for those who could not but could afford something besides the usual corn and beans. Plus, for dessert, *budin*, bread pudding with raisins. To drink, *horchata*, the beverage to which a Pac Rim official once pretended to add cyanide to show Marcelo and others that cyanide was safe. And, for sure in Cabañas, *atol de elote*—a cornmeal drink.

For the water defenders of Cabañas, the 2009 holiday preparations and celebrations came to an unexpected and abrupt halt on December 20. On that day, terror struck again—this time north of El Dorado, at Santa Rita, La Trinidad, where Pac Rim planned to open a second Cabañas mine.

Ramiro Rivera—who had "miraculously" survived those eight bullets just months before—was driving up a windy mountain road. Ramiro and his car were well known along these roads. He often offered his car as an ambulance for those in desperate need to get to a hospital, whether or not they could pay for gas. He was that kind of guy. Accompanying Ramiro to ensure his safety on this trip were two pistol-bearing bodyguards, assigned by the attorney general after that first assassination attempt.

Farther up the road, just around a sharp curve, three men hid. At least one of the three carried an M16 rifle. Before any of Ramiro's bodyguards could react, bullets from that M16 struck Ramiro.

On this trip, Ramiro's car once again served as an ambulance, carrying him to the hospital. He died along the way.

Six days later, on December 26, Ramiro's friend Dora Alicia Recinos Sorto trudged up a small dirt path from the creek where she had hand-washed her family's clothes. On her head, she carried her clean laundry and in her right arm, her eighteen-month-old toddler. Dora was eight months pregnant. Out of nowhere, shots felled her, also hitting her child in the leg. Dora's unborn baby died with her.

In their grief and as part of their mourning, Miguel and a large contingent of water defenders harvested the family's corn and sorghum crops for her widower. But such was the terror that her husband almost immediately fled the area with the wounded toddler.

Dora's fatal crime, like Ramiro's, was being against Pac Rim while also being a supporter of ARENA. Indeed, Ramiro had served as the local ARENA mayor's right-hand man and, according to a cousin, as "the president of the community board that was set up to support the mayor." But Ramiro was not an ideologue. "He had this quality that he wasn't closed-minded," a local community leader recounted to us. "The mayor realized he was losing the pillar of support [provided by Ramiro]. Ramiro was supposed to be the person who—in the mayor's eyes—sold the Pac Rim project to the community." But "they realized Ramiro's heart and his thoughts had been won over by the resistance, by the water defenders. Imagine what an obstacle he had become for the right-wing and for Pac Rim. . . . That's why they killed him."

Ramiro and Dora—in life and death—were also statements of the political diversity and widening reach of the water defenders. Both FMLN and ARENA supporters, as well as some who were not loyal to either major party, chose water over gold.

The photos of Ramiro and Dora would join those of Marcelo, the three environmental martyrs of Cabañas. Dora's photo is particularly haunting—showing her, Madonna-like, gazing down with innocence and love at the young child nursing in her arms.

Simple wooden crosses mark the spots where Ramiro and Dora were fatally shot. From the winding road where the cross marks the spot of Ramiro's shooting, the view of the Lempa River is stunning.

CHAPTER 5

With a Fat Cat and Sun Tzu, the Resistance Goes Global (2010–2015)

"There's a hole in the Fat Cat, and it's leaking air," John said, standing in the shade of the eighteen-foot-tall inflatable. The orange feline wore a royal blue business suit and clutched a fat brown cigar in its left paw. It was September 15, 2014, five years after Marcelo's assassination and after Pac Rim had launched its global lawsuit against the government of El Salvador.

On this day, the action had shifted from countering the "white men in suits" in El Salvador to stabilizing an orange cat in a blue suit in Washington, DC. But John was careful not to worry loud enough to be overheard by those assembled here with us. We were gathered outside the expansive World Bank headquarters in a high-rent, posh area of Washington that locals call the Golden Triangle. The irony was not lost on us, and there was more irony. This day marked the 193rd anniversary of Salvadoran independence from Spain. And today the Fat Cat with its cigar stood in as Pac Rim.

Inside, up on the fourth floor, the legal teams representing Pac Rim and the government of El Salvador and their witnesses convened for a hearing on a new phase in the Pac Rim lawsuit. That is what had brought us here, but the immediate problem for us and the other organizers of this outdoor event was the leaking Fat Cat. John hurried off to find the man from the Teamsters, the large US union that owned the prop. The man had just hooked up the gasoline-powered generator that was pumping air into the giant inflatable. We had been told that this man had driven the Fat Cat to rallies against corporations all across the United States and that he truly knew what made it purr. We wished it were as easy to figure out what made the ICSID tribunal purr.

About ten of us had arrived hours earlier at the World Bank's massive central building—as we had more than a dozen times during the preceding five years. Our pre-8 a.m. arrival was timed to beat the morning rush hour of the Bank's staff from all over the world. We positioned ourselves near the four big entrances around the building, which we had come to know well. With courteous smiles, we handed out more than one thousand leaflets to Bank officials and staff alike. Our leaflet alerted people about the unjust water-versus-gold corporate lawsuit against El Salvador and invited them to the demonstration set to start outside at noon: "Join us in telling the World Bank that cyanide poisoning of El Salvador's drinking water will increase poverty, not eradicate it. Join us in telling the mining company to drop its suit."

Around 9 a.m., the lawyers of Pac Rim filed past us. Just minutes later, the lawyers of El Salvador followed. The Pac Rim team wheeled in cardboard file boxes of testimony and background documents for the week's hearing. John politely offered them leaflets. The Pac Rim lawyers wore their game faces, poised for the first day of legal battle. They had no interest in our leaflets. We did not see Luis Parada, El Salvador's senior attorney for this case, among the government's suited lawyers. We knew he had entered much earlier, as had his boxes. But we recognized a senior member of the Salvadoran team from our annual visits since 2011 to El Salvador's Ministry of Economy to get the latest update and share what we knew. This man had always been friendly but professional to us. But that day in Washington, September 15, 2014, he seemed like an old buddy. He winked as he marched by. Apparently he felt the same way toward us.

At noon, duct tape along the armpit of the Fat Cat had slowed the leak. Still, he wobbled in the wind. Our prop had appeared huge earlier, but now, like us, it seemed dwarfed by the towering glass façade of the World Bank headquarters. How appropriate it was that we could not see in but instead saw the reflected images of those assembling outside. Franciscan priests from local churches with Salvadoran congregants arrived, their long flowing brown robes cinched by white ropes. The brown garb joined the brightly colored T-shirts of dozens of Salvadoran Americans. Red shirts of day laborers proclaimed "CASA," the name of a well-known national immigrant rights organization. Others proudly wore T-shirts that were light blue and white, El Salvador's national colors. A Salvadoran woman wrapped in a red, white, and blue US flag held up the light blue and white Salvadoran flag. Some of Robin's students, including a young woman from Guatemala, joined.

There was no dress code at this rally. Some came in jeans. Others, maybe on their lunch break, wore business suits. ID-wearing World Bank employees, maybe sympathetic and maybe just curious, watched from the main entrance as security guards paced back and forth to make sure we did not get too close. We spotted an official from the Salvadoran embassy, standing in the background, watching events unfold. By noon, we had grown to a couple hundred people squeezed into the small triangular park just across the street from the Bank's main entrance.

If you had been just walking by, perhaps going to lunch in one of the upscale restaurants of Washington's Golden Triangle, you might have thought it a multicultural social gathering, perhaps a parade of some sort. But our posters said otherwise: "EL SALVADOR IS NOT FOR SALE." "WATER IS WORTH MORE THAN GOLD." "WORLD BANK'S ICSID IS A KANGAROO COURT."

The five years since Pac Rim had launched its lawsuit had been a long, slow, frustrating time for our friends in Cabañas, for La Mesa, for the government of El Salvador, for us, and undoubtedly also for Tom Shrake and Pac Rim. But that week's multi-day hearing on the fourth floor showcased the crucial "merits phase" of the case. And that day, September 15, both sides would present the substance of their arguments and try to poke holes in the other side's justifications.

It would be something akin to a trial in court, albeit with ICSID's unique rules. To begin with, the ICSID hearing had not been publicized. We would not have known about it had it not been for Luis Parada. "What can we do that will help on the day of this hearing?" we had asked ourselves after Luis told us of the date. We knew we could not go inside. This was an invitation-only hearing between the Salvadoran government and Pac Rim—lawyers from both sides, each side's witnesses, and the three ICSID arbitrators who would eventually decide winner and loser. For the record, the arbitrators were each paid $3,000 a day. The water defenders from northern El Salvador had not received invitations—not Miguel to bear witness for his dead brother Marcelo, not Vidalina, not Antonio, and not any others. Like Luis and our friends in El Salvador, we had hoped that the case would not come to this. We had hoped that it would be dismissed.

We asked ourselves what we as allies could do to help from our outsider position. We concluded that the best thing would be to put together a demonstration outside the World Bank building to coincide with the start of the hearing, a gathering to let the arbitrators know that the world outside that building was watching. We figured we would need at least two hundred people to be noticed. That number would also be good for the media coverage we were hoping for.

It felt like we were in uncharted territory. Yes, demonstrators had gathered outside the World Bank Group for decades to protest the social and environmental devastation of World Bank-funded projects and to amplify the concerns of affected communities. In one instance, a Greenpeace protestor had even scaled a World Bank building to unfurl a banner beseeching the Bank not to cut down rainforests. But ICSID, the World Bank Group's lawsuit venue, was largely off the radar screen.

There we were, about two hundred of us plus the onlookers. As television cameras zoomed in on our makeshift stage at the feet of the stabilized Fat Cat, a leader from the corporate watchdog group Public Citizen warmed up the crowd with anticorporate, pro-water chants. Then speaker after speaker displayed the diversity of our side: The director of international affairs of the largest labor federation in the United States, the AFL-CIO. A red-shirted Salvadoran-born leader of CASA. A speaker from Friends of the Earth and another from the Sierra Club, two of the larger US environmental groups. A spokeswoman from the Committee in Solidarity with the People of El Salvador. One of the brown-robed priests. As their speeches mingled with songs and chants, the crowd grew louder, shouting up at the fourth floor. In the shade under the trees, a *Washington Post* reporter interviewed Robin. A Univision TV crew interviewed Manuel from the Institute for Policy Studies in his native Spanish.

Was our presence noticed on the fourth floor? We did not have a clue. But the next day Luis would tell us: "Of course we heard you. People were talking about it."

We coordinated our protest closely with parallel events in other parts of the world where the mining company had a presence. Our strategy was to amplify the water defenders' voices so that those deciding the fate of San Isidro would know that they were being watched. La Mesa convened a press conference in San Salvador. In Australia, allies held one of their monthly demonstrations outside the corporate office of the firm. And protestors converged on the company's Canadian headquarters.

We wondered then: even if we were covered by media worldwide, even if the resistance to Pac Rim and ICSID had greatly increased globally, would this matter to those three judges?

"Your coalition of US and other groups coordinating with La Mesa in El Salvador may be a great idea," a sympathetic foundation director had told us in 2011. "But it won't work if you don't have muscle." By "muscle" she meant the clout of large unions and other organizations with massive numbers of members.

Here is what we did have—what we had built up since the first tour of the Mesa Five back in 2009, just months after Marcelo's murder. For starters, we had Manuel Pérez-Rocha, who had worked at the Institute for Policy Studies for only two years at the time he coordinated the first visit of Vidalina, Miguel, and the others. But Manuel seemed destined for this work as he had mobilized groups against the corporate bias of trade agreements in Central America. He knew water defenders in El Salvador and other Central American countries, and he had earned their trust.

The two of us and Manuel entered the campaign against Pac Rim and ICSID already understanding the wide abuses of corporate power around the world and knowing about some of the rules rigged by corporations to give themselves an edge over governments and ordinary people. Between the three of us, we also had connections with a good array of groups from our decades of international work. Using the momentum from the 2009 human rights award to La Mesa, we began meeting and talking with likely allies. Looking back to 2009 some years later, Manuel explained the logic: "In those early months, we reached out to three streams of organizations. First were the groups that had campaigned against corporate trade agreements: the Council of Canadians, the Center for International Environmental Law, Public Citizen, unions, environmental groups, farm groups. Second were the groups that worked in El Salvador and Central America: faith-based groups, solidarity groups, community development groups. Groups including US-El Salvador Sister Cities, Maryknoll, Sisters of Mercy, Washington Ethical Society, SHARE, and CISPES—some of which had roots in El Salvador dating back to the civil war in the 1980s. And, third, groups with expertise on mining, notably MiningWatch Canada and Oxfam, which had long been working with communities trying to halt mining destruction in countries from Canada to Peru." This third group knew the nitty-gritty details of mining's environmental, social, and economic threats inside and out.

The members of these three sets of groups became the core. Yet we quickly learned that we needed to reach out beyond that core to grow "muscle," as that sympathetic foundation director had termed it. We certainly made mistakes. At one point we reached out to the big unions in the United States, institutions with significant muscle. Their representatives asked us where the Salvadoran unions stood in the mining fight. It was, to say the least, a logical question. Truth be told, we had no idea. Would we bump up against the Hinds report and Pac Rim's job-creating myths? Fortunately, perhaps because there was no active commercial mining in El Salvador at that moment, the Salvador unions responded that they were not opposed to the anti-mining activities of La Mesa. That opened the door for US and international unions, including the AFL-CIO, the

Communications Workers of America, and the Teamsters with their Fat Cat, to join in.

By 2011, the IPS and MiningWatch Canada decided to turn this array of groups and individuals into a more formal network called International Allies Against Mining in El Salvador. Two coordinators stood at the center: Manuel of IPS and MiningWatch Canada's Jen Moore, a journalist fresh from Ecuador with deep knowledge of mining in Latin America. Just as La Mesa coordinated its work through monthly meetings in San Salvador, the inner core of International Allies groups coordinated through monthly phone calls. Smaller working groups focused on specific tasks based on individual and group interests and expertise.

The International Allies had researchers, writers, activists, and lawyers. Insiders joined outsiders (and inside-outsiders like Robin with her academic credentials). Some focused on the old Butters mine and its subsequent US owners. Others concentrated on Pac Rim and Cabañas. Still others zeroed in on the World Bank tribunal. Religious groups made sure no one forgot the moral arguments at the center of the campaign. In Washington, DC, members of the Washington Ethical Society could be counted on for leafleting and demonstrations. Unlike La Mesa, we defined ourselves as a loose coalition. There was no pledge to make, no form to sign. Those who hopped aboard simply made a commitment to work together with guidance from La Mesa in El Salvador.

The International Allies was clear that we had no intent to duplicate La Mesa's work in El Salvador. From the start, we worked out distinct and logical lines of responsibility. La Mesa focused on stalling any new mining licenses in El Salvador while educating and advocating for a government ban on mining. The International Allies focused on pressure against the lawsuit and the global mining corporations, especially Pac Rim, while using media and other venues to spread the word about how global corporations unfairly sue sovereign nations like El Salvador.

The International Allies respected the expertise and domain of La Mesa and the Salvadoran water defenders, and vice versa. Vidalina and other Mesa representatives toured the United States, Canada, and Australia several times, and Manuel, Jen, the two of us coauthors, and other

International Allies members visited El Salvador regularly. Whatever the ease and immediacy of cyberspace connections, such face-to-face interactions proved vital to building trust.

While International Allies included Oxfam, which provided funding to some groups in El Salvador, that was the exception. Indeed, we understood that financial dependence could interfere with what was a budding relationship of coordination and trust. Still, we came to the realization that the International Allies needed an El Salvador–based representative so as not to overtax an already overburdened La Mesa secretariat and its members. So, in 2012, the work entered a vital new stage. The foundation director who had asked about "muscle" funded an International Allies liaison based in El Salvador. We hired Jan Morrill, a young woman originally from Maine who had worked in El Salvador for over three years at US–El Salvador Sister Cities, hosting sister city delegations. Jan was known for her knowledge of mining, her deep cultural sensitivity, her already-strong relationships to La Mesa, and her energy, as well as her driving skills along San Salvador's streets and the hills of Cabañas. The liaison post proved key to a constant and honest dialogue with La Mesa.

Just as the water defenders nurtured unexpected allies as they built networks and power, the International Allies had Luis Parada. We had been wary of getting too close to a government lawyer with a military background and with no ties that we knew of to La Mesa. And we could not imagine that such a person would be at all interested in us.

But in 2011, Manuel and John found themselves with Luis at an El Salvador meeting at the Oxfam office in Washington, and Luis struck up a conversation. The three ended up walking to the Institute for Policy Studies headquarters for a more in-depth exchange. Not long after this, Robin met Luis through a mutually trusted friend who arranged an odd and in retrospect somewhat comical dinner. The host almost immediately disappeared, leaving Robin and Luis alone in an Italian restaurant in a far-flung suburb of DC on something akin to a blind date.

Pretty quickly, our conversations with Luis became less guarded, even fun. Within months we were meeting regularly and quietly to exchange what we knew about Pac Rim and about the lawsuit. We spent a lot of time keeping Luis updated about the latest assaults of Pac Rim on the water defenders. Luis wanted to know everything happening on the ground. We wanted to know everything related to the tribunal. We two became laws students of a sort, trying to learn as much as we could from this legal master.

It turned out that Luis, from his West Point days, was a long-time disciple of a Chinese military strategist from 2,500 years ago, Sun Tzu, and his book *The Art of War*. Sun Tzu quotes and "strategies for battle" peppered Luis's words and moves, and he would constantly counsel us, "Know thy adversary"—be "one step" ahead of them. So too, he would quickly add, know your possible allies: "Befriend a distant state while attacking a neighbor." As we pondered our budding relationship with Luis, we realized that Luis might well be employing Sun Tzu tactics concerning cooperation with us.

As we strove to know our adversary, we would try out on Luis the talking points we were using in our International Allies work. We in the International Allies were getting quite good at pulling ordinary people in to take part in conversations about Pac Rim versus the water defenders. Simple sound bites proved effective: "Water, not gold." "People over corporate profits." "Corporate lawsuits versus a government listening to its people."

Likewise, as new people got involved in this work, and in questioning the rules at the heart of ICSID, we got better at explaining the existing global rules to protect consumers, workers, and the environment from corporate greed. We cited examples at a global level—such as the conventions in the International Labour Organization that lift up worker rights, and international environmental treaties to protect the ozone layer and to push governments to ban dangerous chemicals. A key problem was that these lacked the strong enforcement mechanisms of ICSID.

Luis did not disagree with our points. He was one of the few insiders in the investor-state dispute settlement world to publicly critique the system. He too wanted better rules and institutions with less bias in favor of corporations. But, given his job as El Salvador's lawyer, he had to focus on winning. And he constantly reminded us that to win at ICSID one needed

to master the rules of ICSID and the way that arbitration tribunals inter-
pret the international treaties that protect foreign investments, however
unjust. As we talked with Luis about social and environmental issues in
El Salvador, he reiterated that these issues had no bearing—"standing," in
legal terms—in the World Bank–based tribunal that would decide *Pac Rim
v. El Salvador.* "How can three people who have never been to San Isidro
decide our fate?," one of the water defenders had asked us, speaking of the
members of the tribunal. This was precisely how.

However frustrating this reality, we discovered that following Luis's
advice to learn the ways of our adversary helped us tell the story better.
Can you believe, we would say, that current global economic institutions
and rules protect corporate profits above all else? Can you believe that
these rules have far more teeth than the rules that advance consumer,
worker, and environmental rights and standards? Even more shocking,
how is it possible that the pressing consumer, worker, and environmental
issues of our times have no standing in this major international tribunal?

Luis liked our arguments. But he said bluntly, "Let me warn you, you
are not going to see a win with those arguments." In other words, allies
of the water defenders needed to operate on two very different battle-
grounds. One was the battlefield of public opinion, both in El Salvador
and around the world. The other was inside ICSID and the minds of those
three arbitrators. Sun Tzu said, "If you know yourself but not the enemy,
for every victory gained you will also suffer a defeat." In the early years of
our work, he would have been disappointed in us. Our early sound bites
demonstrated that we knew ourselves and allies, even our unexpected
allies—but not that we knew ICSID.

To learn more, we dove into the work of perhaps the best known
of ICSID's DC-based insider critics: lawyer George Kahale, the chair of
one of the very few law firms that defend only governments—not corporations—in such suits. Kahale described these tribunals as the "Wild,
Wild West of international practice," saying, "There really are no hard
and fast rules. . . . Speculation and shoddy reporting in newspapers passes
as evidence." Kahale continued, "Misrepresentations of fact and gross
miscitations of authorities are rampant and, when discovered, usually go

unpunished." Kahale included among the numerous deficiencies of this system "the way tribunals are formed; the lack of meaningful arbitrator qualifications or serious standards for arbitrator disqualification; the inherent bias in the system against states, . . . and the relatively unchecked powers of arbitral tribunals."

The more we learned, the more we realized that the Wild West rules of ICSID resembled in some ways the Wild West of Cabañas. Justice was scarce, and it tilted toward the powerful.

From our first encounter with Luis in 2011, he began preparing us for a key tribunal ruling, a ruling that he hoped would throw the Pac Rim case out.

That ruling was finally announced in early June 2012, on a day that found John and Vidalina in Vancouver, getting ready to speak at a major gathering of pro-water, anti-mining forces convened by the Council of Canadians. The council, a member of the International Allies, had energized tens of thousands of Canadians into creative advocacy to protect water, fight unfair trade and investment agreements, and protect ordinary people. It was no surprise that Vidalina stood as a featured speaker in the opening plenary. By 2012, she had emerged as a global spokesperson of the Salvadoran water defenders, her combination of authenticity, power, and humility captivating audiences. The June 2012 gathering pulled in Vidalina and other water defenders from Latin America, a few of us from the International Allies, including MiningWatch Canada, and a range of Canadian indigenous leaders, environmentalists, and workers.

About fifteen minutes before the session was to start, Luis informed us that the tribunal had reached a verdict on the "jurisdiction phase," the decision on whether the Pac Rim case would go forward or be dismissed.

Over the years, Luis had laid out clearly for us what parameters the arbitrators would likely be pondering in making their decision. Pac Rim was headquartered in Canada, a mining-friendly country with hundreds of mining firms listed in its stock exchanges. "Pacific Rim El Salvador" was the name of the corporation's venture in El Salvador. Yet the legal entity that filed the lawsuit in Washington was Pac Rim Cayman. And Tom Shrake worked out of Nevada.

As Luis had explained, this game of geography had intent. The Cayman Islands is British territory that is well-known as being a tax shelter for thousands of companies. In most cases, those subsidiaries are "shell" companies, consisting of little more than a post office box. In terms of the ICSID case, having a shell company as the claimant served as more than a tax advantage. If El Salvador eventually prevailed, the entity losing would only be Pac Rim Cayman—an entity that has no actual physical presence, no actual bank account, indeed no actual money. "Not even a chair or a desk," Luis had stressed. Pacific Rim overall would have no legal duty whatsoever to pay any ICSID financial rulings against Pac Rim Cayman. Score one for the adversary—choosing a clever entity from which to launch a lawsuit.

Luis had explained this and other moves by Pac Rim and its lawyers to set up their lawsuit to their maximum advantage, moves that global corporations routinely use to get the upper hand over governments and communities. Case in point: why did Shrake work out of Nevada? Here too Luis knew his adversary and the logic behind the move. When Pacific Rim began to contemplate a lawsuit against El Salvador, the company wanted to ensure the strongest support base for its lawsuit. How to do this? Sue from the Cayman Islands for the reasons above? Or sue from the United States? Or how about trying both?

Suing through a US subsidiary could take advantage of the strong leverage the United States had in El Salvador. The Central America Free Trade Agreement (known as CAFTA), then recently signed by the United States and countries in Central America including El Salvador, was seen as a treaty likely to intimidate El Salvador. The catch for Pac Rim in 2009 was that only corporations from Central America, the Dominican Republic, and the United States could sue under CAFTA; Canada and the Cayman Islands were not a part of the agreement. So Pac Rim had shifted the nationality of its "shell" subsidiary from the Cayman Islands to Nevada in the United States. And—poof, just like that—Pac Rim Cayman could claim itself as a US entity and sue under the Central America agreement as well. "Treaty shopping" is the term for this search for the best options for entities or venues under which to sue. And such treaty shopping is absolutely legal—as long as it takes place before a dispute exists or is foreseeable. Score another one for the adversary.

We felt prepared for the jurisdictional decision, but it turned out we certainly were not. As Luis detailed, with this decision, El Salvador won, but it also lost. Pac Rim lost, but it also won. But the final result was a win for Pac Rim. Confusing indeed. Luis explained that the three judges would not let the case go forward under CAFTA because the tribunal understood that Pac Rim did not have the necessary substantial activity in the United States. Clearly a win for El Salvador. But the tribunal ruled that the case could go forward anyway, because Pac Rim had also filed the case under El Salvador's 1999 investment law that was written with advice from the World Bank. That law contained a clause that allowed foreign corporations that have a dispute with El Salvador to skip El Salvador's domestic courts and rather file charges directly in international tribunals. We knew little about this law, but Pac Rim lawyers clearly did.

That was not what we expected to be the crux of the jurisdictional decision. Luis had also told us that he thought, if the arbitrators were following the details, he could get the case tossed out at this stage because Pac Rim was basing its entire case on misinformation. Pac Rim argued that it had been led to believe that it would get a Salvadoran mining concession and that it had learned about the government deciding to halt new mining licenses only in 2008. However, as you may recall, Pac Rim's law firm tried to hire Luis for this case in 2007. Luis had submitted evidence that Pac Rim knew the government had halted mining licenses before 2008. That, Luis had felt confident, would be reason enough to toss out the case. Yet, without any justification, the three arbitrators chose to ignore this discrepancy at this point.

In Vancouver, John and Vidalina shared a moment of stunned silence as they digested this news. This was not the first time, nor would it be the last, that we would be dumbfounded by a decision by one of these global institutions. How could the three arbitrators have ignored Luis's firsthand evidence? How could they have not seen through what certainly seemed like a faulty accounting of events by Pac Rim and its lawyers? At that moment in 2012, we felt powerless, stung, and scared. How could we—or anyone else on the water defenders' side—help set matters right?

Still, Vidalina's speech at the Council of Canadians gathering had to proceed as scheduled. The woman often referred to as "Canada's Ralph Nader," Council of Canadians national chair Maude Barlow, invited Vidalina to the stage. As she did, John recalled a comment by Vidalina's boss, Antonio Pacheco: "Vidalina is humble and quiet. She looks like she won't hurt a fly. But when she takes the microphone, she shines with a different light." Sure enough, Vidalina onstage appeared as a confident spokeswoman for La Mesa. She relayed their story, sharing the long and deadly fight of the Salvadoran water defenders, pausing a moment to pay respect to the environmental "martyrs." She impressed upon her audience the injustice of Pac Rim's lawsuit. She conveyed outrage that the company was demanding $300 million, the majority of that not for compensation for its past exploration investments but for future profits foregone. She repeated those words: "future profits foregone." As always, that phrase elicited gasps. She brought her audience to its feet in indignation as she shared what we had just learned: the tribunal had chosen to let Pac Rim's lawsuit against the government of El Salvador proceed to the next stage.

As a rally, one could not have asked for anything better. But neither Vidalina nor John slept well that night in Vancouver. The next day, during the lunch hour of the anti-mining conference, John and Vidalina joined hundreds in a march through the streets of Vancouver to the corporate headquarters of Pac Rim. It was a Saturday. Shoppers packed the streets. Some stopped to watch and listen. Vidalina led the crowd in chants, vowing to fight Pac Rim until justice was won. The doors of the building where Pac Rim had an upstairs suite were locked. The demonstrators slipped dozens of handmade signs under the glass front door of the building.

Would janitors toss the signs in the trash or the recycling? Did the International Allies and La Mesa, coordinating with the likes of Luis, have muscle? Were we one step ahead of our adversary? The jurisdictional verdict certainly did not suggest so. We did not query each other aloud about this.

We on the water defenders' side certainly had reason to be worried. But we also had reason for hope.

As shocked as La Mesa and the International Allies were in 2012 by Pac Rim winning the right to advance its case, we were soon buoyed by good news in the other lawsuit against El Salvador in the World Bank Group's investor-state court. This other mining firm, Commerce Group of Wisconsin, had also sued El Salvador in 2009. But Commerce Group lost its case in 2011 and lost its appeal (an "annulment," in ICSID lingo) in 2013. Commerce Group was the firm that had mined the old Butters mine in eastern El Salvador, where the toxic orange-red waters emerged from the foot of the mountain. Once again, Luis was El Salvador's lead lawyer.

As we learned of Commerce Group's loss, we felt cheered. But again we found ourselves jolted by the tribunal's narrow boundaries, by those two distinctly separate "battlefields" we faced. Like La Mesa, we had focused on outrage at Commerce Group's toxic wastes and resulting environmental destruction. And we had applauded the Salvadoran Environment Ministry's testing of the waters and its subsequent decision to close the mine in 2006. But this was not the battlefield on which ICSID made its decisions. Rather, as Luis had counseled us, ICSID governs based on its own set of rules. And the key one here had nothing to do with poisoned waters and lands or destruction of livelihoods for generations to come. In this case, the tribunal ruled that Commerce Group was wrong in jumping directly to the World Bank–based tribunal from El Salvador's domestic courts before those courts had made a final ruling. As one of El Salvador's lawyers put it, Commerce Group was trying to get "two bites at the apple."

The ICSID verdict against Commerce Group revolved around a legal detail, a "technicality," as some in the International Allies termed it.

It infuriated Luis when any of our allies used the term "technicality" to describe his win in the Commerce Group case. "You win and lose these cases based on the law, based on what you are tossing aside as technical issues," he fumed. His acumen allowed him to build—and win—cases based on such details. "The ICSID charter says nothing about the environment. Maybe it should, but that is beside the point." He assured us that he knew that we, as new students of Sun Tzu, would already be wise enough not to demean the win over Commerce Group as having been based on a technicality.

Luis confided his assessment: "[The Commerce Group fight was] one of the finest examples of legal strategy and execution I have been involved in, which delivered the desired results (elimination of the threat of a $100 million award) with the least expense and risk." Luis again quoted his "old friend" Sun Tzu: "To fight and conquer in all our battles is not supreme excellence; supreme excellence consists in breaking the enemy's resistance without fighting."

Luis's point on the narrow terrain of ICSID reminded us of what we had known all along. The target of our anger could not be exclusively ICSID or the tribunal members but also had to include the people, mainly men, from rich countries who had written these biased international conventions and rules, and the unequal power arrangements they codified.

Commerce Group was now finished, but Pac Rim was charging ahead. However, it still had to contend with the water defenders of El Salvador, now joined by the International Allies, which was seeding global media coverage framed in the seemingly effective "water versus gold" soundbite.

Pac Rim had assumed that a charm offensive in Cabañas—combined with cozying up to key leaders and the pressures of the global lawsuit—would do the trick. But it had not worked thus far. So Pac Rim went to the global airways.

This new stage of Pac Rim's campaign came across starkly in a twenty-eight-minute Canadian Broadcast Corporation radio show that aired in January 2013, called "High Stakes Poker" (from a Tom Shrake quote). Shrake appeared prominently in this documentary, along with his boss, Pac Rim board chair Catherine McLeod-Seltzer, a third-generation mining executive with a business degree and expertise in mining finance. On air, Shrake's boss claimed that the murders of Marcelo, Dora, and Ramiro were due to general violence and lawlessness in Cabañas: "The three people who were killed have nothing to do with mining. I mean, these are Hatfield and McCoy areas, right?" she said, laughing. "I mean, people carry long grudges and they have access to firearms. And, you know, you come on my land, I'm going to shoot you. A very long leap was made to say that, you know, this is an anti-mining murder. It wasn't."

Pac Rim's problem, McLeod-Seltzer explained, was "rogue" groups and "factions." More specifically, "anti-development NGOs fomented anti-mining by spreading lies." When the CBC commentator asked for specifics, Pac Rim's board chair named Oxfam, adding, "I don't think they control their people on the ground. I think these are probably rogues who seize upon an opportunity." Outside of such "rogue" elements, McLeod-Seltzer asserted, the local communities absolutely wanted Pac Rim to mine: "I mean, they subsist on beans and corn." In her view, there could be no other logical explanation for opposition beyond those "rogue" elements: "[They] purport to be environmentalists. They're not. . . . If they were, they would support this mine."

Shrake put on an air of bravado for the CBC audience: "This is going to be mined. I mean, these things are too precious to the country and to people in the country to sit here. Eventually we'll get a permit."

The bluster and the name-calling were unnerving to La Mesa and unsettling for the International Allies. But, summoning up Sun Tzu, we wondered if we could turn Pac Rim's media assault and faulty claims to the water defenders' advantage. As Sun Tzu had admonished, "Force [your enemy] to reveal himself, so as to find out his vulnerable spots."

Back in San Isidro, Miguel devised a way to identify and take on those "vulnerable spots." Driving with us over the mountainous roads of northern El Salvador one afternoon soon after the CBC program aired, Miguel and an ADES colleague started listing the spurious claims of the company. To wit: The company had met all the regulatory requirements. The mine would not negatively affect water supplies or quality. The mine would bring jobs and an economic boost. Pac Rim's global lawsuit was just. Pac Rim had a global reputation as a socially and environmentally responsible company. "Could International Allies do a report exposing the lies of Pac Rim?," Miguel asked as we pulled into San Isidro. "Let's work on it together," Robin replied.

The result became *Debunking Eight Falsehoods by Pacific Rim Mining/ OceanaGold in El Salvador*, a 2014 report by an eight-person International Allies team led by MiningWatch Canada's Jen Moore, building on input from Miguel and others in El Salvador. The report scrutinized and discredited eight of the on-the-record statements of Pac Rim officials, as Miguel had suggested. A carefully fact-checked document with eighty-three endnotes, the "Falsehoods" report—available in both English and Spanish—became a valuable part of our outreach and media tool kit.

This report is one example of the work that the International Allies did on behalf of—and with input from—the water defenders of El Salvador. In addition to reports, members wrote popular articles, briefer opinion pieces in newspapers around the world, and amicus legal briefs to bring the voices of the Salvadoran communities into ICSID. They leafleted and protested outside and raised questions inside at the company's annual shareholders' meetings. With La Mesa, they organized delegations of allies and would-be allies to travel to El Salvador, including one with nearly fifty people from twelve countries in 2013. International Allies orchestrated even more tours by La Mesa leaders through Canada, the United States, and Australia, and in one trip these leaders testified before the US Congress. International Allies circulated letters to the company and others to the tribunal signed by hundreds of organizations representing millions of people. Those to the company demanded: "Drop the suit." Those to the tribunal demanded: "Dismiss the case against El Salvador." All focused on freeing El Salvador from this ICSID challenge. Whatever the venue, all aimed to expand the outrage beyond Pac Rim and El Salvador to make this one lawsuit represent all that was wrong with ICSID and investor-state rules.

By 2013, Pac Rim had more than an image problem. It had a money problem.

This was not what the mining companies had expected. Remember how the game was supposed to play out. Pac Rim, as a junior exploratory mining company, was in El Salvador not for the long run but rather, once the lucrativeness of its gold vein was confirmed, to get a license to mine the El Dorado concession. And then, as with junior mining companies the world over, Pac Rim intended to sell that for a tidy sum to a major mining company with the expertise to do the actual mining.

But, by late 2012, Pac Rim seemed to be running out of money even for the tribunal suit. Lawyers' fees were mounting, and tribunal fees were falling due. To Pac Rim's rescue came a much larger, senior Canadian-Australian mining company, OceanaGold. Melbourne-headquartered OceanaGold had gold mines in New Zealand and the Philippines, and it would soon acquire rights to a large mine in South Carolina. The top echelons of international mining corporations are a small and tight-knit world, and so, unsurprisingly, OceanaGold had a director who also sat on the Pacific Rim board. In 2012, OceanaGold provided financial support to Pacific Rim—what is called "third-party financing." OceanaGold's infusion of cash granted it a one-fifth stake in Pacific Rim.

But that infusion proved insufficient for Pac Rim to continue its lawsuit and public relations campaign. In November 2013, OceanaGold shareholders approved an outright purchase of Pacific Rim, injecting vital new finances. OceanaGold was gambling—just as Pac Rim had been doing. It was exactly as Tom Shrake had phrased it in that CBC radio show, a game of "high stakes poker." OceanaGold was betting that its relatively small investment in a company, one whose primary asset was hoped-for mining concessions in El Salvador, would turn into a winning hand, yielding a healthy profit. As a result, Pac Rim became a wholly owned subsidiary of OceanaGold, with more money to pursue the case at the tribunal.

There was yet another interesting twist here in terms of "knowing thy adversary" and the game of geography and ICSID's pro-corporate bias. OceanaGold now owned Pac Rim and was financing the ICSID case. But the claimant in ICSID case ARB/09/12 remained Pac Rim Cayman. And while Pac Rim now had an infusion of cash from its new owner OceanaGold, there would be no assurance that OceanaGold would pay El Salvador should Pac Rim lose its ICSID gamble.

We could follow these changes in corporate identity through our computers—notably when the Pacific Rim website disappeared entirely. We could also follow them during our trips to Cabañas by the large sign at the entrance to the El Dorado mine. On our first trip in 2011, the sign had said "PACIFIC RIM" in big bold letters, along with relevant contact information. In May 2013, we found exactly the same sign. But in 2014, white paint covered the sign—leaving a blank slate except for small print at the bottom with two phone numbers, a fax number, and a local address. These, we discovered, were the very same address, fax number, and one of the phone numbers as before. At some point thereafter, the words "Fundación El Dorado"—OceanaGold's social responsibility arm that donated funds to community projects—filled the space where Pac Rim had once announced its presence.

OceanaGold's bailout of Pacific Rim reminded us that Big Gold could ensure that at least some corporate lawsuits against recalcitrant governments would be well funded for years to come. But no such funding, no such bailout, existed for El Salvador and other countries that were victims of these lawsuits.

If this had been a play, Tom Shrake would then have moved from center stage to the wings, to reappear onstage only as needed for ICSID proceedings. In his place entered OceanaGold managing director and CEO Mick Wilkes.

International Allies met Mick Wilkes in May 2015—less than a year after the Fat Cat event—at the World Bank Group in Washington. Our rendezvous with Wilkes occurred not at the building where ICSID was housed but rather at the private-sector lending arm of the World Bank, which hosted a two-day seminar on socially responsible mining. CEOs of several mining firms attended, including Wilkes. Robin, as a professor, got an invitation to join the seminar. But Wilkes's first in-person encounter with International Allies was when he took a leaflet from Manuel, who was with several International Allies protesting outside.

Once inside that first day, Wilkes stood to the side, busy with his phone, not particularly dashing or attention-grabbing. He was short but not too short, a bit stocky but not too stocky. His bland glasses lent a nerdy demeanor. Other attendees walked past him without stopping. He did not seem a known member of the big boys' club here. In contrast, one could imagine Tom Shrake or Robert Johansing holding court, announcing deal-making goals with pithy phrases.

When another attendee approached Wilkes on the first morning, he displayed a bit of unexpected bravado as he shared the International Allies' leaflet he had taken from Manuel, the final line of which read: "the World Bank Group should not be hosting Wilkes, but rather should be siding with the affected communities and government of El Salvador." He appeared to be comfortable being the center of attention of the day's protest.

According the program, joining Wilkes in the formal part of the two-day event was a long and impressive slate of speakers from or allied with Big Gold, Big Oil, and Big Gas companies Rio Tinto Zinc, Roxbold, Shell, China Gas, and Eco Oro, which would later sue Colombia at ICSID when Colombia halted mining in its highlands, its key water source. The executive director of the Prospectors & Developers Association of Canada, at whose convention Shrake had learned of the El Dorado mine more than a decade earlier, was on the list. A few big nonprofits, notably Oxfam, made the cut. But there was no one on the program from grassroots community-based groups—no Miguels or Vidalinas—and no one from a religious group. Nor were there even any ministers of environment.

Overall, the topics of the main panels zeroed in on the increase in conflict in poorer regions where these mining companies now found themselves, and on the need to build "trust"—notably the trust of the community. Wilkes seemed to have come at least in part to share his optimism about all of this. His physical appearance alone may not have exuded swagger, but he certainly conveyed this. He was the man, and OceanaGold was the company for the task at hand in El Salvador. Maybe Pac Rim and Tom Shrake were not up to the challenge, but Wilkes had faced similarly tricky situations with anti-mining groups in Laos, Australia, the Philippines, and Papua New Guinea, where many water defenders were killed before he had come on the scene. The mines that now existed in these places proved his prowess.

Over these two days, Wilkes displayed enormous confidence in his ability to use OceanaGold's corporate social responsibility foundation, formerly run by Pac Rim, to win over the people of El Salvador. He was not the kind of guy to mine where the local people say no. And he was not the kind of guy to sue governments at ICSID; that had been Pac Rim's doing.

Yes, he had kept the lawsuit going—with the belief that surely the government would reach a settlement with OceanaGold before long. He knew he would convince Salvadorans to say yes as he had done elsewhere. He would turn the community in El Salvador around, as he had done in the Philippines, which had a highly lucrative working mine at that time, another participant reiterated on the side. Wilkes would not repeat Pac Rim's mistakes.

One could not help but wonder if Mick Wilkes, too, was a fan of Sun Tzu.

During a break in the seminar, the head of a junior mining exploration company, another man who had tried to find gold in El Salvador, privately shared his thoughts on El Salvador and Wilkes. This CEO's bio in the program revealed: "Following the moratorium of all mining in El Salvador in 2008, [he] successfully repositioned the company in Nicaragua, acquiring 100% of eight concessions." In other words, he had reversed Butters's move from Nicaragua to El Salvador a century earlier. He asserted that it was not worth staying in El Salvador and trying. His advice to any other company interested in El Salvador besides OceanaGold: get out as soon as you can. On OceanaGold, the man added without hesitation, "It's a punt. If it wins, it wins big. If it loses, small change." He concluded that chances were good that Wilkes would win in El Salvador.

The worlds of the Golden Triangle of Washington, DC, and the gold veins of Cabañas, El Salvador, could not be more different. For Mick Wilkes, as it was for Tom Shrake, it was a poker game, a gamble.

So too was it a gamble for the water defenders in El Salvador, but the stakes in Cabañas were of an entirely different kind. College student Juan Francisco Duran disappeared a day after he was seen putting up posters in Cabañas against a consultation on mining in 2011. He was murdered for posting flyers.

And when we met Miguel at ADES in 2014, we found him distraught about the safety of his family. It took some time, but we finally got him to explain the cause: three of the men arrested for being involved in Marcelo's murder had been released from jail. Even more distressing, Miguel continued, soon thereafter a neighbor had seen someone intently watching Miguel's house and recognized the loiterer to be one of the newly released men. Miguel's reality—the threat of violence in the present and the memory of the terrible death Marcelo had suffered—seemed to exist in a different universe from the legal wars of Tom Shrake and Mick Wilkes and the posh offices of the World Bank tribunal and the three arbitrators who would decide the fate of El Salvador's mines and waters. Yet these worlds were intertwined.

CHAPTER 6

Judgment Day at the Kangaroo Court

"El Salvador Always Loses" (2016)

O ur host pointed to a wall filled with framed photos, each featuring the same young guerrilla fighter. One need not have spent long in El Salvador to know the historical moment: El Salvador's civil war. Framed on the facing wall were poems authored by that same combatant, Oscar Ortiz.

It was mid-2016, and we were standing with Ortiz in the Casa del Vicepresidente, located in a posh neighborhood of San Salvador. His days in the mountains with the FMLN were long gone. Since 2014, he had served as the country's vice president under President Salvador Sánchez Cerén, himself a former guerrilla comandante. Ortiz's fatigues, also long gone, had been replaced by the traditional men's double-pleated *guayabera* shirt.

We were with Manuel, and on this hot July 2016 evening the three of us engaged in chitchat with Ortiz, now playing the role of charming host. We had never expected to find ourselves here with El Salvador's vice president. But Ortiz had invited to dinner dozens of international solidarity activists from the civil war days. The delegation of activists had come to El Salvador for events celebrating a quarter century of bearing witness and offering support to the Salvadoran Left. One of our La Mesa friends had helped to organize the delegation, and he graciously invited us to the dinner.

We had arrived a half hour early, driving from Cabañas and worried about the prospects of a long security line at the Casa's gates. Instead, we arrived first, and the security guard whisked us in. Ortiz introduced us to his wife and some family members. A staff member appeared, offering drinks. Ortiz then summoned a photographer to snap photos of us with him and his wife. The TV was on in the living room. We felt like intimate guests, friends of the family.

After our tour and having seen the walls of photos and poems, we sat in a quiet corner of the expansive patio—alone with Ortiz as we sipped tamarind fruit juice. The buses carrying the solidarity delegation were still en route.

"Tell me what is on your mind," Ortiz began. Okay. We knew that part of the traditional job description of Salvadoran vice presidents is to attract foreign investment into the country. We wondered if that applied to a former guerrilla poet. After saying how much we loved the north of El Salvador, we decided to dive right in: "What do you think about mining?" we asked.

Ortiz launched into tales from his meetings with the top leaders of Nicaragua, Venezuela, and Ecuador, noting how much faster their economies had grown thanks to mining, oil, and natural gas. Somewhere along the way, he added Costa Rica and Bolivia. Our minds flashed back to that Robert Johansing memo—the one we thought perhaps the most astute of all we read from El Salvador's wannabe mining executives. In that memo, as he had processed his frustrations with his failure to mine in the country, Johansing had predicted that there would be mining whether the Right or the Left won in the 2009 Salvadoran election.

Ortiz continued, noting that the rest of Central America was mining, as was much of Latin America. El Salvador on the other hand, by not mining, was being left behind. "Why not mine now?" Ortiz mused aloud, with the clear implication that, with the additional revenues, the government could easily fix the environmental damages later. The problem, he clarified, was that the government demanded too small a percentage of total revenues—only 2 percent—from mining corporations like Pac Rim.

Realizing that this was a brief opportunity with a key player, we pushed back. Not all Central America is going full steam ahead with mining, we told him. In fact, we offered, long-term environmental dangers inherent in industrial mining had led governments in Costa Rica, Panama, and Argentina to place limits on mining. To try to bring our conversation back to the choices confronting El Salvador, we shared our firsthand accounts of the dismal environmental, social, and job-creation records of Pac Rim's owner, OceanaGold, in the Philippines—problems that could not be solved simply by increasing the mining tax.

Our host seemed surprised but not convinced. We realized that he had likely heard the purported positive jobs and economic growth side of the mining story but had focused less on the overblown economic promises, the violence, and the ecological costs. A good half hour of exchange ensued, brought to a close by the arrival of the buses carrying the solidarity delegation.

Over the next few hours, plentiful food and drink commingled with laughter and speeches. The keynote, of course, belonged to Ortiz. He wooed the crowd—some of whom he knew by name—by reading from his poems, as he urged those in the delegation to continue their support for the FMLN government. We looked for an opening to share with him more details on the dangers of mining and more on the mining resistance by his former comrades in the north. Our moment came as we said our good-byes. Robin thanked Ortiz for his hospitality, remarking on how moved she had been by one of his poems about the beauty of what he saw when he lived as a guerrilla fighter in El Salvador's mountains. "All that natural beauty can be destroyed by mining," Robin warned. It was bolder than etiquette probably deemed appropriate, but it felt like a one-time chance.

Our tête-à-tête with El Salvador's vice president definitely worried and disheartened us. However, we kept reminding ourselves, the vice president's job included wooing foreign investment.

Alas, the dinner with the vice president was not the only ill omen during 2016. Manuel and the two of us had set the date of this trip to El Salvador in early 2016 as we sensed the endgame coming in the legal case in the World Bank–based tribunal. We knew that the average ICSID case dragged on for three to five years, and we were approaching the end of year seven. All of our intelligence, all we had dug up, suggested that the three-person tribunal at ICSID would release its decision in the spring of 2016. So we three had planned to travel to El Salvador in July to confer with La Mesa on next steps for International Allies work, which would be based on the tribunal's decision.

But in the months before our scheduled departure, we witnessed a series of delays that might have been comical were the stakes not so high. At one point, an insider confidentially reported that the English version of the decision had been finalized and the required Spanish translation was in the works. When we asked Luis about this stage of the process, he told us that such translations typically take less than a month. The Spanish translation of *Pac Rim Cayman LLC v. The Republic of El Salvador*, however, inexplicably dragged on. And dragged on further. Could that reflect a difficult translation job given the unusual technical details? Or could the translator's job be growing more difficult due to changes in the English version? Or might OceanaGold or its lawyers be the ones slowing things down, trying to make a deal with the Salvadoran government behind the scenes? Or was someone on the three-person panel purposely delaying completion of the final decision, the so-called award?

We knew well that corporations either win most of their ICSID cases or convince governments to settle out of court. One study of investor-state suits against countries in Latin America and the Caribbean found that more than twice as many cases were won by corporations or settled out of court than were won by governments. In other words, past experience provided good reason to worry about delays in the award.

In March 2016, right in the middle of the delays, dreadful news came from north of the Lempa River of another assassination—the savage killing of Berta Cáceres, Honduras's most prominent water defender. To the water defenders of Cabañas, Berta was one of their own. Indeed, she and ADES were in the midst of a project together—a video on women defenders of the environment in El Salvador and Honduras. (ADES would finish this after her murder.) Her assassination hit hard. How could one not help but feel that the water defenders' chances for justice in this fight were slipping away? How could one not help but feel that the forces were further aligning with the powerful mining corporations and global institutions like ICSID that have historically served their interests?

In Washington, as the tribunal delays dragged on with no end in sight, we pondered with Manuel what to do with our already-purchased plane tickets to El Salvador for July 2016. We decided to go ahead with the trip—to use the visit to check in with La Mesa and others. We could share updates and possibly figure out more about what lurked behind the ICSID delays. Our timing overlapped with one of Luis's more frequent trips to check in with the government and provide his own updates.

Upon arrival, we encountered frustration and anxiety among our allies—both expected and unexpected allies. Friends in La Mesa described the desperate financial crisis that was plaguing El Salvador, with public employees on the verge of not being paid as the government scrounged for cash. One night over dinner, the Ministry of Economy official who had winked at us on the Fat Cat day, put it bluntly, "The government of El Salvador is broke." Revenues from gold, he mused aloud to us, would look awfully tempting to many in government at a time like this.

Such temptation must be exposed and countered. Among La Mesa's collective talents was their skill at using the occasion of an International Allies visit to garner media attention and remind Salvadorans about the ICSID suit and the dangers of mining. Indeed, soon after we arrived, La Mesa convened a standing-room-only press conference at an upscale hotel to comment on the upcoming ICSID decision. John was given a specific role. OceanaGold had been bragging about its superb environmental record at its gold and copper mine in the Philippines, a giant open pit mine that the two of us visited in 2013. So John used his allocated five minutes to describe the environmental ruin, the destruction of land and water, that we had witnessed near the Philippine mine.

Luis Parada spoke after John. He promptly introduced more drama. As the government's lawyer, he explained, he believed that the government's silence up until that time had been "prudent." But enough was enough, he continued. The public needed to know what was going on behind closed doors. In terms of banning mining, "Not just seven years of lawsuit, but El Salvador has had seven years of having a knife at its throat and not being able to move forward." The cameras really started clicking as Luis asserted that OceanaGold was attempting to cajole certain government officials to settle the case and seal a deal allowing OceanaGold to mine.

How could Luis know all this? Chalk it up to the swanky Sheraton Hotel. Luis had long ago told us that the Sheraton's first floor—with its red leather chairs in the bar, intimate seating areas in the lobby's nooks and crannies, and comfortable chairs overlooking the pool—offered some of the best intelligence in El Salvador. After the press conference, Luis reminded us that he had been shuttling back and forth to and from El Salvador all spring. He had spent a good deal of time walking around the Sheraton. And, in both planned and unplanned encounters, he had bumped into people in the know from both business and government.

So, for the rest of our San Salvador stay, we two hung around the Sheraton and nearby tony restaurants. And we asked well-connected friends and friends of friends about who was plotting with OceanaGold and about what. As we learned, OceanaGold had indeed been meeting with a range of top—very top—government officials. According to various sources, these included our new friend, the poet vice president. We were told by more than one person that these meetings also involved the president's technical secretary, the head of the state energy corporation, and the foreign minister (who, in the 2019 elections, would run and lose as the FMLN's presidential candidate).

Thanks to the Sheraton, we uncovered more about OceanaGold's intense efforts to make a deal if the government agreed to ask the World Bank to drop the case. This was an interesting twist given that Pac Rim, not the government, had initiated the ICSID case and that OceanaGold had purchased Pac Rim knowing that the lawsuit stood as its primary asset. Plus, we were told that there had been an attempt to sweeten the deal by offering the government partial ownership of the mine, with OceanaGold running the actual mining operation.

Little remained secret for long in San Salvador. Another option discussed, we were informed, involved splitting El Salvador into two parts— one part with mining and the other without. This proposal would have taken a country the size of Massachusetts, with already overtaxed ecosystems, and cut it into two. The proposal reflected bravado and a total lack of understanding of how watersheds operate. Still, we found ourselves pondering the absurd. Which way could they possibly have proposed to split the country? John thought it would have been a north-south split. Robin thought east and west. We had to stop ourselves from contemplating such nonsense. There was no way to isolate the negative effects of mining in northern El Salvador, no way to ensure that the poisoned water and land could be quarantined.

As much as the stories depressed us, the behind-the-scenes jockeying did not surprise us. History stands replete with examples of big corporations from the United States and other countries wooing governments. A US Senate Subcommittee on Multinationals spent years in the 1970s investigating the "foreign corrupt practices" of US corporations. The dirt dug up fills seventeen riveting volumes. Since then, corrupt dealmaking by transnational companies has only become more prevalent. This kind of corruption invariably lines the pockets of top government officials in poorer countries, providing an incentive for them to privilege corporate interests over the welfare of their citizens and ecosystems. Such deals at times have involved corporations dropping their legal cases or their threats of a legal case in exchange for a green light to operate. Needless to say, few corporations have ever listened to the concerns of ordinary people—the Miguels and Vidalinas—whose lives and livelihoods might be affected.

None of the shenanigans we heard about in 2016 involved Lina Pohl, El Salvador's minister of environment and natural resources. So, on the final day of our trip, we sat down with her. We had first met Pohl in 2014 soon after she had assumed her post. We knew that any and all mining licenses required the signature of the minister. And, of course, we recalled that almost a decade before Pohl's tenure, Minister Barrera had held tough against signing off on Pac Rim's El Dorado claim and become one of the water defenders' most unlikely allies. We wanted to know much more about Pohl. And we wanted to know whether Pac Rim before 2014, or OceanaGold since, had ever knocked on her door.

She happily regaled us with her own story over breakfast. Pohl's father, a professor of architecture and admirer of socialist Chilean president

Salvador Allende, had moved the family to Chile in the early 1970s to witness Allende's experiment in socialism firsthand. Pohl had attended elementary school there. Young as she was, she told us, "[The Chilean experience] had an impact on me. I understood very young that the world is big. . . . And that you can dream, and that you can live those dreams."

Just before the violent coup that launched the brutal dictatorship of Chilean general Augusto Pinochet in 1973, Pohl's parents moved the family to Costa Rica. There her parents threw Pohl and her brothers into classical music lessons. "We became the *Sound of Music* family," she joked.

Later Pohl studied sociology in Spain and Mexico, earning a master's degree in "social economics" and another "in social movements with alternative development models in Latin America." Partway through a doctoral program in Mexico, she received the first of a series of job offers that she could not resist. She returned home to become the El Salvador–based representative of the German Green Party foundation, the Heinrich Böll Foundation, from 1996 to 2009. Our colleague Manuel was then working out of Mexico on Central America issues, and they met and bonded as colleagues and friends as they strived to stop the Central America Free Trade Agreement.

Working for the German foundation influenced her deeply, Pohl explained to us. During this period, she became tougher. "I'm told I'm strong. I guess that is from my experience with the German people. They are so direct." And Pohl liked that. "I can say 'this is bullshit,' if it is."

Then Pohl—totally out of the blue, she stressed—got the call to join the environment ministry as vice minister when the FMLN won the presidency in 2009 with candidate Mauricio Funes. And, again unexpectedly, newly elected President Sánchez Cerén tapped her to become minister of environment in 2014. Pohl knew the science of mining and water contamination well. As vice minister, she had commissioned national water-quality studies, including one of the San Sebastian River at the old Butters mine. That test of the discolored waters had confirmed the off-the-charts levels of toxic substances and reinforced her concerns about mining: cyanide at about ten times the acceptable level and iron at one thousand times the acceptable level. But what she saw in a subsequent trip to the old Butters mine still shocked her: "We saw a cow lying down, dead. We saw the awful colors and impacts of the acid mine drainage in the streams firsthand."

Over that 2016 breakfast with us, Pohl was clear that neither Pac Rim nor OceanaGold had ever approached her. Perhaps it was no surprise. Pohl exuded the message "do not mess with me," from her actions to her facial expressions to her choice of words.

At that point, in July 2016, OceanaGold's lawsuit and the ICSID delay had become "nonsense" that "annoyed" Pohl. She launched into a tirade about how the seven-year Pac Rim lawsuit was a gag order on her and Sánchez Cerén's government. We knew that Luis Parada had been adamant in his advice to top government officials that they not move ahead with any kind of formal mining restrictions until the ICSID case was over. Luis knew all too well that such action could add to Pac Rim's case or provoke another ICSID case. Presumably, Luis's advice had been shared by the attorney general's office with the various ministers, including Pohl.

Pohl understood but explained the frustration that such a straitjacket imposed. She would love to act to restrict mining, she said. But "[because of the legal case] the minister of economy and the president have been saying to me: 'Please, Lina, be quiet about mining. Don't say anything about mining. . . .' It was very difficult as, all the time, civil society was criticizing us for not talking about mining."

When we shared with Pohl the news about OceanaGold seeking to broker a deal with other top government officials, she looked disgusted. She seemed surprised too but did not share any details about what she did or did not already know. Rather, her reply focused on her absolute unwavering commitment to not approve any mining license that should reach her desk for the necessary approval. She extended that unwavering commitment to President Sánchez Cerén, for whom her admiration stood strong. She knew that some in La Mesa were annoyed not only with her but also with the president, who publicly appeared to be on the sidelines of the mining wars. La Mesa wanted the president to come out forcefully against mining.

Pohl stressed that she had told the president numerous times that she would never sign off on mining and that she would resign should he, as her boss, ask her to approve any license. "And he replied, 'don't worry. That decision is not going to happen.'" Pohl continued, without naming names: "Others said to me, 'Mining will be fantastic for us. Look twenty years in the future.' I said to them, 'Talk to the president to ask for my resignation. Because I'm not going to sign any mining licenses.'"

Our conversation with Pohl continued for longer than expected. She took a few more minutes to reassure us that the president would stand with the water defenders and would not agree to mining. She just knew him, she stressed: "I am his conscience. . . . It [our relationship] feels personal. He likes me. He trusts me. He laughs at my jokes. Nobody laughs at my jokes."

Before Pohl departed, she made two more points: First, she told us that she would inform the president about the supposedly secret OceanaGold meetings to woo top government officials. Second, she would recommend that he meet with La Mesa.

On hearing Pohl's praise for Sánchez Cerén, our minds flashed back to our encounters over the years with Ángel Ibarra, one of El Salvador's most venerated environmental and health experts. We first met Ibarra in 2011, when he headed the Salvadoran Ecological Unit (UNES), a key environmental group that was part of La Mesa. Ibarra never envisioned himself leaving that world and joining the Salvadoran government. But mid-2014 found him sitting in his government office as the newly appointed vice minister to Pohl. As he explained to us, he took the job because President Sánchez Cerén had asked him to join the ministry: "I have a lot of respect and affection for the president. . . . I trust him. He's a very honorable man. . . . I also support his vision. Even before he became president, he had a long-term vision of a new paradigm for El Salvador—not a model based on aggregate economic growth for the few but a paradigm of sustainability, based on health, jobs, and water. In Latin America, we call this paradigm *buen vivir,* or living well." As Ibarra told us, Sánchez Cerén had even authored a monograph titled *Buen Vivir.*

We wanted to believe in Pohl's and Ibarra's optimism. We wanted to believe this government had grappled with redefining progress. But at least two people told us they were worried about the resolve of President Sánchez Cerén. One confided that he and others had met with the president to share the results of a 2015 University of Central America poll. Nearly four out of five Salvadorans opposed mining—a decided jump from the

already impressive 62 percent in the 2007 UCA poll. Opposition to mining had soared, they showed the president. According to our source, the
president listened patiently and then startled them by replying succinctly
that the government was desperate for revenues. On another occasion, we
were told that "one guy"—a water defender supporter—had said "we're
fucked" after being a part of a meeting with the president where mining
was discussed.

Overall, our meeting with Lina Pohl energized us. But Vice President Ortiz still haunted us, as did the government's palpable desperation
for new revenues. And, of course, the executive branch was not alone in
determining El Salvador's mining policy. The unicameral Legislative Assembly would presumably play the key role in any new mining legislation.

We hoped for less equivocal news in our visit to the national legislature. At
this point in 2016, we knew well its hallways with their cacophony of red
posters bearing photos of FMLN legislators competing with office doors
adorned with red posters of the leading opposition party, ARENA.

The FMLN had chaired the legislature's Committee on Environment
and Climate Change for years now. We had met with that committee's
chair regularly over the years—starting with the staunchly anti-mining,
purple-framed-eyeglass-wearing Lourdes Palacios in 2011. We set up another meeting with the 2016 committee chair, the FMLN's Dr. Guillermo Mata, a pediatrician by training. With his crisp tailored suit and
well-groomed mustache and sideburns, Mata very much looked the part
of a respected senior legislator. A younger FMLN representative, Estela
Hernández, joined the meeting. Hernández was an unlikely member of
the national legislature: a community organizer, environmentalist, and
lawyer, first in her family to go to college, someone who had helped re-
store the ecosystems in the area where the Lempa flows into the Pacific.
Given Mata's concern for health and Hernández's community roots and
environmental expertise, we entered the committee room hopeful.

We chitchatted with them about changes in their government since
the 2014 elections and the upcoming 2016 US elections. We attempted
to explain the unexpected popularity of the brash real-estate tycoon and

reality TV star Donald Trump with segments of the US population. We then proceeded to inquire about their sense of the possibilities of legislative action on mining. Specifically, could they imagine their committee and then the full legislature passing a bill to ban industrial mining?

At least one of them sighed. Both reminded us of the math. In 2010, a new conservative party had split off from ARENA: the Grand Alliance for National Unity (GANA). ARENA and GANA controlled the majority of seats in the legislature. Plus, Hernández explained, "It is equally complicated even just within the Environment Committee, where FMLN has only three of ten seats." She warned us that even bringing up a mining ban for discussion might well backfire, opening the door to "neoliberal counterproposals." She added that rumors were circulating that northern El Salvador held even more gold than originally thought. Neither did Dr. Mata equivocate. "No," he said. La Mesa's hoped-for mining ban would not move forward in this session of the Legislative Assembly.

Almost every step of our July 2016 trip depressed us. The vice president, the legislature, would-be secret meetings discussing outrageous deals, deals that should have been unthinkable: almost every interaction reduced our sense of favorable possibilities. We left the country with a deeper understanding of why translating the English version of the ICSID decision into Spanish might have been taking so long. And we left dreading the months to come.

As July turned into August and the ICSID award was still elusive, the water defenders and their allies were feeling increasingly frustrated. Hearing frustration in the voice of Luis Parada no longer surprised us. But Luis's exasperation reached a crescendo on August 24, 2016, after our return from El Salvador. That day, he and another lawyer on his team received an emailed letter from OceanaGold's lawyers informing them that OceanaGold "propose[d] to initiate private and confidential amicable discussions with" the government of El Salvador. The letter further stated that OceanaGold proposed that ICSID delay any announcement of their award "for thirty (30) days during these discussions," which would "be subject to a confidentiality agreement."

Earlier that day, before sending the communication to Luis, Oceana-Gold's lawyers dispatched a one-paragraph letter to the three tribunal members. This note, a copy of which was attached to the communication to Luis, formally asked for a thirty-day delay in the award beyond what it claimed was "expected to occur in mid-September." As Luis read the two messages, he feared betrayal. In his view, the letter to the tribunal members implied that someone in the government had agreed to such "amicable" meetings. Luis well knew, even better than we, that at the highest levels of the Salvadoran government some wanted mining. Could this communication indicate that those pro-mining factions in El Salvador were getting ready to seal a deal with OceanaGold?

Livid, Luis moved quickly, contacting the attorney general's office asking for "immediate instructions to reject this request." In El Salvador, the Legislative Assembly appoints the attorney general. In this sense, the attorney general serves like a fourth branch of government, with more independence than someone appointed by the president, for example, would have. Luis waited only two hours for the attorney general's response—but it seemed like much longer to him as he fumed over the treachery. To his relief, he was informed that the attorney general had no knowledge of any such talks. Therefore, Luis was instructed to reject the request for an extension. Luis's emotions shifted quickly. Instead of feeling betrayed, he "felt really good" with the rapid response and decisive answer from the attorney general, as he told us later that day when he walked the ten minutes from his office to the Institute for Policy Studies office to recount the events of August 24, 2016.

The final of that day's volley of emails on the subject was a five-sentence letter from Luis to the members of the tribunal. The terse communication made El Salvador's no-negotiation position vis-à-vis discussions with OceanaGold crystal clear: "The Attorney General of El Salvador instructed us to communicate to the Tribunal, on behalf of the Republic of El Salvador, that El Salvador does not consent to Claimant's request to delay the dispatch of the Award. On the contrary, El Salvador hopes that the Award is issued as soon as possible."

We could not help but wonder: Would another legal team or attorney general or minister of environment have stood as vigilant? Would they have stood so firmly if the water defenders had not been so persistent? What if OceanaGold had been given those thirty days to entice more government officials? We felt that the water defenders had yet again averted disaster. But the need for vigilance was exhausting.

In our weariness we were heartened to hear that behind the scenes, Environment Minister Pohl had followed through and informed President Sánchez Cerén about OceanaGold's clandestine maneuverings. Further, the president had met with representatives from La Mesa on August 25. We heard that at that meeting, he had assured them that there would be no mining in El Salvador.

September 2016 came and went, and still there was no ICSID award.

In early October, the Salvadoran government finally received word from the ICSID secretariat that the ruling would be announced in mid-October. From our research on ICSID's controversial history, we knew this to be around the date of the fiftieth anniversary of ICSID opening its doors. We found the timing rather curious and contemplated whether Sun Tzu might have read the coincidence as a good sign. But when we mentioned the possibly auspicious timing to Luis, he dismissed it as a decidedly "weak" reason for hope. Still, we managed to register online for the ICSID anniversary cocktail event set for Friday, October 14, as did Luis and Manuel.

As those of us in the International Allies continued our long ICSID vigil, we felt we were as prepared as we possibly could be for the award. Since the merit hearings in September 2014, when we had wheeled out the Teamsters' Fat Cat, the International Allies had been coordinating with La Mesa around the possible outcomes. So too had we been coordinating about what to do and say when what we had come to think of as Judgment Day finally arrived.

Judgment Day would, in the view of the International Allies, bring one of four possible scenarios. We delineated these four carefully in an insider memo for the International Allies and La Mesa. Manuel translated this into Spanish, and we spent much of 2016 refining the scenarios with La Mesa. As mid-October approached, we culled the list, reducing it to the most likely two. Based on those, the International Allies drafted two different press releases, in both English and Spanish. Among ourselves, we informally called them "best case win" and "most likely loss."

It was so easy to lapse into the "win" and "lose" terminology. But each time we did, Manuel reminded us—and we all agreed—that if the decision was in El Salvador's favor, we should never use the terms "win" or "victory." Pac Rim could win or lose. But El Salvador, Manuel repeated whenever anyone in the International Allies got sloppy and lapsed into "win" and "lose," had suffered over seven years from this case. The cash-strapped government had been forced to spend roughly $13 million defending itself during a period of financial crisis. Top government officials such as Lina Pohl had endured the paralysis of not being able to speak out or take action to regulate mining for fear of retribution. The academic literature might have termed this "regulatory chill," but it was even more than that—not a chill but a freeze, a literal halt in democratic processes. So too was it a halt in normal life for frontline water defenders, given the threats and murders.

Judgment Day creeped closer. And, although we never admitted it publicly, it felt more and more inconceivable that "the simple people" (in the words of mining executive Robert Johansing) could win—or, rather, not lose—in this global court. As we waited for a decision and became privy to the behind-the-scenes maneuverings of the tribunal, its pro-corporate bias became clearer and clearer.

We now had a list of many of these biases from all we had learned from Luis and from the writings of the Wild, Wild West lawyer, George Kahale. To that list, *Pac Rim v. El Salvador* had taught us that there were no set time limits or deadlines for a given stage of a case and no clear rules for responding to the government or its lawyers. Rather, ICSID seemed to be allowed to ignore evidence from lawyers defending the governments being sued. Luis more than once had told us that that the tribunal had never replied to a formal request he had made to submit a new, "smoking gun" document. This document proved that Pac Rim knew the government was not allowing mining as early as 2007, despite Pac Rim's legal claims that it had learned this only in 2008. Why no answer to a request to submit supplemental documentation that might prove critical to the case?

As we all awaited a decision, we were feeling increasingly uneasy about the pattern of the tea leaves.

Later we would ask a wide range of water defender allies in El Salvador what they were thinking in those final days as they awaited the ICSID decision. Salvadoran legislator Estela Hernández confided: "I think we were all in the negative space."

As for Lina Pohl, while unwavering in her certainty that President Sánchez Cerén would not cave in and allow a deal, she admitted to being almost certain that El Salvador would lose the ICSID case. One had only to look at El Salvador's past history, she expounded: "El Salvador always loses. Our country has never been very good at defending itself." Why would ICSID be any different?

In mid-2019, we would learn that El Salvador's Catholic archbishop, José Luis Escobar Alas, had carefully followed the ICSID proceedings. He smiled a sad smile when we asked him what he had expected back in October 2016: "I was convinced that the resolution was going to be negative." He shrugged his shoulders as if to say: "How could it be anything else?" He quickly added: "I asked the Divine Savior to please do not allow [the World Bank tribunal] to make a sentence against El Salvador." Could the archbishop's prayer be El Salvador's best hope?

Judgment Day finally arrived. And, propitious or not, the date indeed coincided with ICSID's fiftieth anniversary celebration on Friday, October 14, 2016. Dawn broke at 7:17 a.m. in Washington, DC. Most in the United States surely missed the ICSID ruling amid the day's headlines in major papers: "Trump Calls Groping Allegations 'Pure Fiction.'" "Judge Says Bridgegate Misconduct Case Can Proceed Against Christie." "Dodgers Beat Nationals to Advance to National League Championship Against Cubs."

We were at our posts, as were Manuel and Jen. Manuel was ensconced in Luis's law office. John was at the IPS office, ready to adapt the press release. Robin in Washington and Jen in Ottawa were ready to speak to media. Jen's MiningWatch Canada had raised funds to get help on press coverage of the decision, whichever way it went. Various International Allies and La Mesa members stood on alert in their countries. Our goal: to get the decision to the media as quickly as possible.

El Salvador's attorney general, who had flown to Washington the day before, was also in Luis's office. Did this mean Luis was feeling confident? Or was this pro forma? We did not dare ask him.

Luis, also understanding the historical significance of the day, had asked ICSID to hand the award to the attorney general in person. Those who joined Luis to walk the few blocks from his office to the ICSID offices at the World Bank included the attorney general, the deputy attorney general, El Salvador's ambassador to the United States, the attorney general's lawyer, two members of Luis's team, and a reporter. They were to be met by ICSID secretary general Meg Kinnear, but the meeting and handoff could not take place until after ICSID had emailed the decision to the legal offices of both OceanaGold and El Salvador. As a result, while Luis and his entourage awaited the ICSID secretary general, Luis's office received an email with the official copy of the verdict. Before the attorney general was handed the hard copy, Luis received a text from his office with a photo of his staff with their arms raised high in victory. Victory for El Salvador! Or, more correctly, defeat for OceanaGold!

Manuel moved into action, phoning us and Pohl. We received the award, with its 224 pages filled with legalese to read and process. As we had learned to do from Luis's how–ICSID–works lessons, we flipped immediately to the end. There it was, just before the three signatures: "For the reasons set out and incorporated above, the Tribunal . . . dismisses on their merits all the Claimant's pleaded claims for damages and interest in this third [merit] phase of the arbitration."

The international tribunal in Washington, DC, stunned even insiders with this unanimous decision against OceanaGold. Even the Pac Rim–chosen arbitrator concurred with the decision.

Even more unexpected was this: the tribunal "orders the Claimant to pay to the Respondent the total sum of United States Dollars 8 million." This was not enough to cover El Salvador's near $13 million costs in the arbitration, but to order corporations to pay any amount in these cases is unusual. Typically governments are ordered to pay their own way or are required to pay for at least part of the legal and ICSID expenses of the suing corporation.

Our best-case scenario had been a 2-to-1 vote against OceanaGold, with the arbitrator chosen by the company siding with the company, plus the costs being split equally. Instead the reality was a unanimous decision against OceanaGold, with the company ordered to pay El Salvador millions of dollars. As a result, we realized, we had no press release ready to send out. John quickly revised the best-case release, still careful not to call this a "win" for El Salvador.

After Luis read through the full award, he explained to us the bottom-line rationale for the decision: "The Tribunal had lots of reasons to reject the claim [of Pac Rim]. They picked only one, the easiest one, which we had laid out in 2010." The tribunal had used "the very same arguments: Pac Rim hadn't met the requirement regarding ownership of the land." We flashed back to over a decade earlier, the 2006 forum where Hugo Barrera, then minister of environment, had informed hundreds of water defenders of this legal requirement.

We viewed that logic for ourselves as we plowed through the 224 pages. Even with the loss for Pac Rim, the logic of those pages and the bottom-line rationale seemed faulty. Why did a panel of three well-paid ICSID arbitrators—who, as the award revealed, collectively made over $1.2 million in fees (excluding expenses) on the case—get to decide whether El Salvador's mining law, with its requirements for land ownership or permission to mine, was legal? Why should a panel of three de facto judges from other countries, using a biased set of rules, get to decide whether a sovereign nation's laws were legal? We found this completely wrong, completely outrageous. And we knew that there were hundreds of such biased rules and policies of international importance, with equally unjust, equally anti-democratic provisions, written by corporate lobbyists.

However, as Luis kept reminding us, countries agreed to create and continued to maintain this system; they agreed to sign bilateral and multilateral trade and investment treaties giving power to these tribunals. But, in turn, we reminded Luis that all of Latin America had voted against ICSID's creation in the infamous Tokyo No vote of 1964.

Of course, across the International Allies and La Mesa we were elated with the OceanaGold loss, as were Luis and his legal team. At the same time, we were frustrated. So too was Luis: "I thought 'really?' Did we have to go through this additional six to seven years?" Why couldn't the tribunal have made this decision in 2010? And given the additional half-dozen years, why did the tribunal ask the company to pay only $8 million—just over three-fifths—of El Salvador's total costs? "Why didn't they punish Pac Rim with the full amount?"

Regardless of all of that, we had to focus on getting the word out. Dozens of press calls needed to be placed. Dozens of interviews needed to be completed that Friday and during the days that followed.

The surreal world in which we found ourselves on October 14, 2016, did not end with our media work. That evening, Luis, Manuel, and the two of us attended the reception at the World Bank for the fiftieth anniversary of ICSID. We were hoping for a celebratory party of some kind, maybe a reception like that hosted by Vice President Ortiz. Instead, the event turned out to be a book launch with a panel of contributing authors, all celebrating the fifty years of ICSID.

Before the panel commenced, we mingled as best we could. Luis pointed out to us one of the three arbitrators on the El Salvador case. Moving closer, we overheard this arbitrator telling another attendee words to this effect: "We know the case has been followed internationally. They even had protests here at the World Bank. I took a leaflet from the protestors in 2014." We also learned that at least one of the arbitrators had found a leaflet calling ICSID a "kangaroo court" to be insulting. Later, as we processed this, we would chuckle. The "kangaroo court" language in the International Allies leaflet had been meant to pique the interest of as many people as possible. Little did we know that it would pique the ire of at least one of the arbitrators. In the view of another reception attendee sympathetic to the water defenders, the leaflets, protests, and the media work "made them [the three arbitrators] pay attention to the case" and made them more careful with their verdict.

Luis needed to stay for the entire event, before joining his legal team, Manuel, and El Salvador's attorney general for a dinner celebration at a restaurant a block away from the World Bank. But we two found it too unsettling to listen to chapter-by-chapter summaries of ICSID's vaunted history, and we quietly ducked out.

We confessed to one another that we were in a state of shock. Of disbelief. As we mulled over our reactions more analytically, we realized that we, like others, had not simply been expecting the worst-case outcome. Rather, we had also been expecting what seemed the most likely outcome given the empirical evidence of past corporate wins in these investor-state dispute settlement cases. We knew that ICSID Case Number ARB/09/12 would go down in history as a huge loss for Big Gold. At the same time we were disappointed that it was not more of a loss and that the ICSID party celebrating its fifty years could proceed.

In El Salvador, the water defenders and their allies celebrated Judgment Day. As Lina Pohl would recollect: "Manuel called me, and he said, 'congratulations.' And I replied, 'Come on, Manuel, I can't believe it.' Yes, I was very surprised. . . . This is the first thing we won at a global level." She added: "It was fantastic. It was the first time that I really believed that anything could be possible about mining." Unlike us in Washington, Pohl partied. In El Salvador she celebrated late into the night, a rare treat for a no-nonsense person like her in this country of defeats.

A few years later, we asked Vidalina about her reaction to the news on that Judgment Day. She laughed an uncharacteristically hearty laugh. "Well, I was out of the country. But in La Mesa, we have a WhatsApp group. It was through that app that I read the information of the ICSID decision. But I really didn't believe what I read. I thought 'this can't be happening.' I even had to call La Mesa coordinator Rodolfo Calles to make sure that someone wasn't pulling our hair [that the message was not a prank]."

Archbishop Escobar recalled without hesitation: "I thought this was a miracle."

In the days that followed Judgment Day, the media work of La Mesa, the International Allies, and Luis paid off. The news of the corporate loss spread around the globe. It blanketed El Salvador. It reached Spain, Germany, New Zealand, Venezuela, Cuba, and even Romania, a country suffering from the environmental and social effects of gold mining. "El Salvador Wins Dispute over Denying a Mining Permit," the *New York*

Times headline read. Likewise: "World Bank Hands El Salvador Win in Case Lodged by Miner" (*Financial Times*) and "World Bank Tribunal Dismisses Mining Firm's $250m Claim Against El Salvador" (*Guardian*). Lina Pohl, Andrés McKinley, and various International Allies members were prominently featured in the English-language press.

It was a rare moment of celebration—for the win of El Salvador's water defenders over Big Gold, of David over Goliath, of the common good over corporate profit. After more than seven excruciating years, including more than two years since the merits hearing, finally the ICSID panel had ruled on the merits of the case. OceanaGold had lost the high-stakes poker hand it had purchased when it bought Pac Rim.

But Judgment Day resolved only one mystery. At the end of 2016, two mysteries still haunted us: Who had ordered the killing of Marcelo Rivera? And what impact, if any, would the "kangaroo court" decision in Washington, DC, have on the water defenders' quest to ban mining?

CHAPTER 7

Decision Time

Water for Life or Water for Gold? (2017)

While Minister Lina Pohl was partying, someone at OceanaGold was busy composing a press release. It read like Donald Trump bragging at a rally—all spin and no facts. The company congratulated itself for being a "world class producer" with a "proven track record for environmental management and community and social engagement." As proof of this, OceanaGold's press release noted its "flagship operation" in the Philippines and its "sustainable and ethical" track record.

Had not OceanaGold just resoundingly lost its case against El Salvador in a unanimous 3–0 decision with an order to pay El Salvador $8 million? On that, the company admitted to being "disappointed." Then the press release proceeded to lecture El Salvador about why the country needed mining: "The Company believes that a modern resource industry that operates in a safe and sustainable manner and within internationally recognized best practices"—that is, OceanaGold—"has the potential to unlock a sustainable and multi-decade development opportunity for the Republic of El Salvador." It continued as if ICSID had chastised El Salvador rather than ruling against OceanaGold: "[T]he Company recognises that the Government will need to take positive and definitive steps towards establishing a stable business environment if it wishes to attract foreign investment." In other words, it said in effect, "El Salvador, grow up."

The press release was clearly geared toward reassuring OceanaGold's shareholders. It offered no clues on whether the company intended to pay the $8 million that the ICSID tribunal had ordered its "indirect subsidiary company" (in the press release's terminology) Pac Rim Cayman to pay. Here ICSID rules are clear. Payment is due immediately—unless the losing party asks for and obtains an extension while it pursues further ICSID action.

The possibility of OceanaGold initiating further action at ICSID was why the water defenders, the International Allies, Lina Pohl, and others stopped partying soon after October 14. It was possible that OceanaGold would try for an ICSID oddity called "annulment." If you lose in a normal court, you can appeal the decision with a clear set of rules. However, ICSID tribunals are not subject to appeal. Rather, one can request an "annulment" of the decision. In such cases, a new three-person ad hoc annulment committee has the power to decide "not to annul," even if an error has been found. Once again, welcome to what ICSID insider lawyer George Kahale dubbed "the Wild, Wild West." Annulment proceedings can add another two or more years before a final decision, clearly favoring the party with the deepest pockets. And if OceanaGold were to ultimately win in the annulment stage, the company could then file *another* ICSID case.

Manuel, Jen, and others in the International Allies strategized with water defenders in El Salvador. The International Allies tried to keep its message positively focused on October 14, 2016, and on the rare and stunning corporate defeat. But we knew we had to try to reduce OceanaGold's chances of asking for annulment. We were outraged that OceanaGold remained in El Salvador, its foundation continuing to operate in San Isidro, trying to win hearts and minds. We feared a behind-the-scenes deal as OceanaGold continued its propaganda about how workers, communities, and the environment supposedly had benefited from its mining operation in the Philippines. Both of us knew OceanaGold's Philippine mine very well, and we knew the propaganda for what it was. But how does one convey the reality of something that is literally on the other side of the globe?

Grappling with this, those of us in the International Allies thought back to where we had muscle. And to what we had learned about our clout from the Fat Cat demonstration at ICSID.

The result was an International Allies "OceanaGold: Pay Up and Pack Up" campaign demanding that OceanaGold pay the $8 million and leave El Salvador. International Allies launched this less than two months after the tribunal's award, reaching out to unions, environmental groups, and other allies, asking them to sign on as organizations. In addition to the "pay up and pack up" demand, our petition demanded that OceanaGold "not seek an annulment" and that the company "cooperate fully in a full, impartial investigation into the murders [of Marcelo and the others]." To put more pressure on OceanaGold, Luis Parada submitted a formal request to ICSID asking for a supplementary decision ordering OceanaGold to pay interest on the $8 million, from the date of the award until payment.

We all knew that we had to let OceanaGold—and its shareholders— understand that people all over the world were watching. If we needed two hundred individuals to show up at the Fat Cat demonstration, we needed at least that number of organizations signing and circulating the petition. It was a daunting challenge, to say the least. Yet, when the International Allies publicly released the petition in February 2017, 280 organizations representing over 180 million people had signed on, among them the massive International Trade Union Confederation. Attracting such significant trade union support for a set of largely environmental demands was no small feat. And it certainly demonstrated muscle.

But how could we ensure that our petition was widely read and that OceanaGold not only read it but felt obliged to reply? For that, we turned to the London-based Business and Human Rights Resource Centre, a nonprofit set up to facilitate dialogue between local communities and global corporations around allegations of corporate human rights abuses. In 75 percent of its attempts, the center had been effective in generating engagement with critiqued companies. Thus began a back-and-forth in which OceanaGold—or at least its public relations team—replied to criticisms and our side countered the company's arguments.

————

As the International Allies and Luis Parada and his legal team focused on OceanaGold and ICSID, the water defenders in El Salvador focused domestically. Government action to further restrict or end mining remained paramount in their minds. Recall that a decade earlier, La Mesa had emerged as a coalition around the demand for a legislative ban on mining. And recall that there had been a decade-long executive branch de facto moratorium on new mining licenses as the government studied mining's impact. The right-wing Saca administration had stopped all permitting of mining in mid-2006 as it agreed to launch a "strategic environmental review" of the sector—an initiative that was unusually farsighted in attempting to merge economic and environmental considerations. Conducting that review had fallen in 2009 to the Funes administration, which contracted the work to a Spanish consulting firm. The review included many activities, from workshops to public forums.

Plus, the Funes government established a prestigious international "blue ribbon committee" of three mining experts to provide external review and turn the Spanish firm's work into policy proposals. It selected geographer Anthony Bebbington, geochemist Ann Maest, and Robert Goodland, who in 1978 was the first full-time ecologist hired by the World Bank. All three were renowned in their fields, known worldwide for their mining knowledge and their fieldwork in poorer countries. Goodland, for example, by then retired, had been widely called the "conscience" of the World Bank. And, in terms of the task at hand, he had become a pioneer in work to define what might constitute "no-go zones," areas where governments should halt all mining. Goodland included among such areas indigenous peoples' lands, conflict zones, fragile watersheds, and special "hot spot" biodiversity habitats.

As the committee studied the Spanish consulting firm's reports and the ecosystems of El Salvador, with its extreme "environmental vulnerability" and its frequent earthquakes and tropical storms, the question emerged as to whether all of El Salvador should constitute a "no-go zone." Based on committee recommendations, the Ministry of the Environment stopped short of proposing a complete ban, instead recommending a complicated set of benchmarks that would need to be met in order to allow mining in a specific area.

All this had happened during the long ICSID suit. La Mesa had opposed this approach of benchmarks, fearing it allowed too many loopholes for powerful pro-mining interests. And the proposal never came up for a vote in the legislature. Instead, the de facto executive ban lasted through three administrations, right and left—those of Saca, Funes, and Sánchez Cerén.

But October 14, 2016, further increased the possibility of changing Salvadoran mining policy. Water defenders wondered at that point what should be done, with the legal noose no longer around El Salvador's neck. What should be done given that OceanaGold was making no move to acknowledge its loss of the lawsuit, never mind paying the $8 million?

La Mesa members wanted to use the momentum of Big Gold's loss at ICSID and OceanaGold's intransigence to force government action through the quickest means possible. For some, this meant an immediate executive branch ban on mining. Others preferred a legislative ban.

Across town from the La Mesa office, the never-say-no Andrés McKinley, by then working at the Jesuit University of Central America (UCA), also believed that the water defenders could use the momentum of the ICSID decision to secure government action. He and his UCA colleagues were adamant that the Salvadoran legislature should pass a new law banning mining. In fact, in preparation for a new push for legislative action, Andrés along with lawyers and other colleagues at UCA had been expanding La Mesa's earlier draft mining ban bill. In its place, they proposed a long, detailed draft bill of 150 articles covering mining of both metals and non-metals (such as quarrying rock and sand).

La Mesa and Andrés and his UCA team were not the only ones who sensed that the post–Judgment Day climate offered a rare opportunity for water defender action. So too did FMLN members of the environment committee and especially Representative Estela Hernández—she who had traded her jeans and her job as environmental activist and organizer in the lower Lempa River area for a more legislator-appropriate black pants and black jacket. In 2019, Hernández recalled it this way: "We took as much advantage of the ICSID decision as we could. It was not only a victory for El Salvador; it resonated around the world. It gave us confidence. We planned a meeting with La Mesa to talk about a future mining law."

Quickly a larger planning group coalesced to discuss options and co-ordinate political strategy. Hernández and the other two FMLN members of the legislature's environment committee joined with members from the UCA, church organizations, and some members of La Mesa. "It was an unprecedented group of people," Hernández explained to us in 2019, and the group's work required unprecedented resolve and coordination. Their task seemed daunting: How could the water defenders and their allies quickly unite in the post–October 2016 moment? And how could they do so effectively, knowing that OceanaGold, with its own allies—including some top FMLN leaders—had not given up its behind-the-scenes lobbying as it contemplated pursuing an annulment?

Those meetings of water defenders and allies became what one participant politely called "lively," starting with more disagreement than agreement. La Mesa members criticized the length of the bill that Andrés and the UCA had drafted. The UCA argued against those in La Mesa who proposed use of executive power instead of legislative power. A law by the legislature, it argued, would be more binding. FMLN representatives agreed but worried about opening a can of worms with a prolonged legislative debate. And FMLN members of the environment committee sought a winnable offering—a bill that had a shot at being passed by the committee and then the full Congress.

How could these disparate views come together? A key initial step was reaching agreement to slash the draft bill way back to a much simpler ban on metals mining—a mere eleven articles. With this move, La Mesa felt listened to, respected, and it felt ownership. Andrés and UCA also felt ownership. And FMLN representatives Mata and Hernández of the environment committee felt galvanized enough to contemplate moving forward. But getting agreement on a draft bill among this select group was just the beginning. For a legislative ban, the groups would need the FMLN fully on board, despite the pro-mining feelings and dealings of at least some of its leaders.

And even full FMLN support would not be enough since the FMLN held under two-fifths of the legislative seats. Of the other parties, two larger right-wing parties (ARENA and its breakaway, GANA) collectively held the majority in the legislature. The implication was clear to those

sitting around the table in these meetings. The water defenders needed
some new big names on board to get this bill through the legislature. One
potential game changer came to the minds of many in the group. But this
individual would need to be convinced to step out of his comfort zone.

The modest office of the Catholic archbishop of El Salvador sits on the
second floor of an unimposing two-story building tucked away in a San
Salvador neighborhood packed with hospitals and medical buildings. This
office already held history for the water defenders. Here, in 2007, Andrés
and other water defenders had transformed the chemist and Opus Dei
Archbishop Sáenz Lacalle into an unlikely anti-mining ally. All it had
taken was the word "cyanide." But Sáenz Lacalle had stepped down as
archbishop in 2008. In his place, the Vatican had named José Luis Escobar
Alas, a Salvadoran bishop at the time serving one of the country's seven
dioceses.

With a degree in philosophy, Escobar was a cautious man of thought,
hardly an activist cleric. Indeed, in 2013, Escobar had abruptly shuttered
the archdiocese's legal aid office—despite the office's ongoing cases (including ones related to war-time massacres) and its extensive archives doc-
umenting human rights abuses. The time had come, Escobar had claimed,
to put conflicts of the past behind. His action had led to condemnation in
multiple circles around the world.

But Escobar had long held unexpected and firm views on mining. As
the US embassy in San Salvador reported in a cable to Washington just after the archbishop assumed his new office in 2009: "In a highly publicized
move, Escobar used his inaugural message to call on the [government] to
reject mining operations in El Salvador. With high-level government officials in attendance, he further asserted that the [government] should not
allow mining because the cyanide used in mining harms people, plants,
and animals."

In the subsequent eight years, Archbishop Escobar had continued to
speak out against mining. Yet he remained a man of words, not a man of
action. The archbishop readily admitted as much to us, in retrospect, in
2019: "We [in the church] had a shy, weak way . . . a very passive way."

But, after the ICSID decision, those gathering to strategize next steps wondered if the archbishop could be convinced to up his game.

An archbishop is a busy man. Even getting in to see him required finesse. The obvious best candidates as messengers were Escobar's fellow Catholics from the UCA. So in the fall of 2016, Andrés and others from the UCA succeeded in gaining an audience and brought their most recent version of the bill to ban mining—those eleven articles fitting on less than two pages—to Archbishop Escobar. According to Andrés, "He read the bill. And it was like a hungry man getting food. He liked it. And immediately his discourse changed to active advocacy for the bill."

What exactly catalyzed the archbishop's transformation? We two met with the archbishop, a young-looking sixty, in his office in 2019. The office did not feel like Escobar's. Rather, the presence of assassinated Archbishop Romero—canonized as a saint in March 2018—dominated the room, from photographs and art to commemorative medallions that held miniscule pieces of Romero's clothing. In comparison, Escobar almost seemed to will himself to disappear. Against his simple dark clerical pants and shirt, our eyes could not help but focus on the large silver cross dangling from a long chain below his white clerical collar.

The archbishop warmed up as we told him about the International Allies and asked him about the mining bill. He recalled that 2016 meeting vividly: "The Jesuits [of the UCA] came to this very room and they discussed the bill they had prepared with their lawyers. . . . I am so close to the Jesuits. I studied with them so there is a level of closeness and friendship. . . . The law they presented to me was brilliant. . . . I was astonished at how well written it was." It was "concise," he said, and "logical" and "authentic."

The local Jesuits were not the only ones who deserved praise, the archbishop reminded us: "Pope Francis, with his encyclical on the environment, *Laudato Si'*, was key to our [the archbishop's] shift in strategy." With that 2015 encyclical, Pope Francis had laid out a bold argument and agenda for protecting the planet. In early 2017, the archbishop met with the pope: "I asked him to pray for the bill, and he said he would." However, Pope Francis and his encyclical did not call for prayer alone. He urged priests to take to the streets to defend the environment. As the archbishop continued: "This helped us shift from a passive, intellectual position to more decisive support [for the water defenders' demands]."

The archbishop was eager to tell us about a moment of such "decisive support" and action: "On February 6, 2017, I brought the proposed law to the legislature." According to numerous people, this marked the first time that an archbishop had brought a draft law to the Salvadoran legislature. In El Salvador as in the United States, it is rare to have members of different political parties gather together publicly to greet a religious leader bearing a draft bill. Yet members of the environment committee from the different parties represented in the legislature met the archbishop on that day to receive the proposed bill. Presumably their constituents would expect no less. The archbishop leaned forward in his chair, his dangling cross reflecting the sun's rays, as he recollected this encounter for us: "They said they would study it." And, in his recollection, they committed to bringing it before the legislature and approving it.

As Andrés explained, "So now Archbishop Escobar had shifted from denouncing mining to demanding a new law to ban it. This was vital." But just how significant and for how long? Remember that the water defenders' allies did not control the legislature. It was one thing to get all parties to greet the archbishop. It would be another to corral the FMLN legislators fully behind a ban. And it would be yet another to shift years of opposition to a mining ban in either of the larger right-wing parties.

Among those legislators who greeted the archbishop at the legislature that early February day in 2017 was the right-wing ARENA party's lead person on the environment committee—a young first-term deputy, John Wright Sol.

The Wrights and Sols have long occupied top spots on that list of families dominating El Salvador's economy, El Salvador's one-percenters, if you will. And John Wright Sol's father—a Wright—was one of nation's largest sugar mill owners. Yet John Wright Sol's name and lineage hid his own personal story—and his growing passion for the environment. Still in his thirties, "Johnny," as he insisted we call him as he drove us across San Salvador to the Legislative Assembly in 2019, was born in Miami, "like many wealthy Salvadorans." He grew up in both the United States and El Salvador, a citizen of both who "loved both." He graduated from George Washington University in Washington, DC. Then, in an unlikely career move for a Wright or a Sol, he became a firefighter in suburban Virginia for several years. After that, he chose a more likely career move: an MBA in Spain.

Wright returned to El Salvador in 2012. Somewhere along the way, he decided to run for legislative office. To no one's surprise, given his family's deep and long-standing relationship with ARENA, he ran under that party's banner. And of course he won. The family name did not hurt, nor did his tall, chiseled features and charisma. Handsome but not aloof, Wright was like a combination of JFK and Bill Clinton: Salvadoran royalty with a common touch. It was especially noticeable when he leaned in to listen intently to what we had to say. Articulate, smart, and friendly, Wright also reminded us—as he undoubtedly reminded voters—that he had held a workingman's job: "My years as a firefighter were like an MA in public service."

But why in the world did he request the environment committee upon his election in 2015? That would not have been a prime choice for most ARENA deputies. Part of the answer may have been, as some assumed, that the Wright family's vast sugar holdings needed water. But Wright instead offered a deeper response when we queried: "My interest in the environment goes back to being a kid and learning about my great, great uncle on the Wright side." George Melendez Wright, a wealthy US biologist who married into a wealthy Salvadoran family of some repute, conducted the first scientific survey of fauna for the US National Park Service. Melendez Wright funded his own research and that of his team—converting his Buick sedan into an expedition vehicle. He then died young, barely into his thirties, in a car accident.

If the environment committee was on John Wright's radar screen at the start of his legislative career, mining was not. But, when mining became a key issue, Wright became the knowledge-thirsty student again. Rather than rely on ARENA advisors, he "turned to universities, civil society, think tanks." One in particular was especially important to Wright—an educational forum at San Salvador's InterContinental Hotel "sponsored by the UCA or La Mesa." "I went. I was the only legislator there." The speakers included Andrés McKinley, Luis Parada, and UCA researcher Laura Andrade speaking on the 2015 poll. "I learned from McKinley that our gold was micro-powder. The amount of water you needed in the mining process literally required moving mountains." He learned from Parada that OceanaGold had less than high "ethical and moral standards." And he learned from Andrade that the public was overwhelmingly opposed to mining.

As Wright spent the following months learning more about mining and about the country's water crisis, his opposition to mining in El Salvador solidified. Armed with his new knowledge, he felt ready to reach out to his fellow ARENA legislators. "One on one, I started building allies." He began with his two ARENA colleagues on the committee. That proved easy: "I was fortunate. My colleagues always followed my lead."

But moving beyond those two was more difficult. "I struggled more with party staff," he told us. "Initially, I was seen as a bit of a rebel, not afraid to have a dissenting view." They thought he was "weird" for trying to cross the aisle on what ARENA traditionally viewed as an issue of the Left. Wright also noted, "Consensus is hard to come by in these halls. We are used to a very polarized situation. Cut-and-dried, with no gray areas, no middle ground."

As he reached out to ARENA colleagues, Wright reflected on the evolution of his own thought processes: "I came to understand the environmental costs, but I also knew that my cell phone has gold in it." He carefully laid this out as an ARENA-friendly approach, circumventing a larger global debate about gold and other metals. "I didn't want to turn it into 'mining companies are the devil.'" Rather, he chose to ground his proselytizing in the reality of El Salvador's ecosystems: "Every citizen in this country must have access to clean running water." With this approach, Wright felt somewhat confident, at least for the moment, with ARENA.

Across the aisle, FMLN members of the committee such as chair Dr. Mata and Representative Hernández found Wright a surprisingly sympathetic colleague, a transparent player. But how were Hernández and Mata doing with their own FMLN colleagues? In 2019, Hernández recalled the heated debates in the FMLN on mining when she entered the legislature.

"Many said, 'We are in financial crisis, yet we have gold beneath our soil. How can we not use it?'"

In this post–ICSID award honeymoon, seeing it as a brief opportunity, neither Hernández nor Mata wanted to return to that debate. Like Wright, they aimed to keep the topic narrow. Hernández told us, "We reminded our FMLN colleagues of the party's proud history on this issue, starting with FMLN leadership in an anti-mining march in 2006. We reminded them that from that period on, the FMLN became the environmental voice and conscience of the legislature. It led the environment committee, and it led on many environmental issues. We talked to everyone in the party, including President Sánchez Cerén, Vice President Ortiz." She mentioned these names casually to us—but we knew with whom Oceana-Gold had been meeting. "We reminded them that the FMLN party had no choice." By the time that Archbishop Escobar brought the draft mining bill to the legislature in February 2017, the FMLN was behind a mining ban—or so its leaders said and so Mata and Hernández hoped. One never could be totally sure with OceanaGold's secret wooing.

The weeks rolled on in February without any legislative action on the bill. Archbishop Escobar was getting testy, annoyed. Now that he had dipped his toes into the waters of political advocacy, he as the archbishop clearly expected immediate action. Some of the ad hoc group of water defenders who had been meeting on the bill, reflecting back on their dozen years of waiting and pushing and waiting some more, found Escobar's impatience humorous but also an endearing and welcome change. They thought they might as well lend their voices to the archbishop's expressions of outrage after one month of no action from the legislature.

The question became how to up the ante to provoke the legislature to move the bill. One idea pushed by the archbishop was a huge march to the Legislative Assembly to demand passage of the bill. At that moment, the archbishop later confessed to the two of us, he did not see himself as part of the actual march. But he again turned to Pope Francis's strong admonitions to his disciples. "Pope Francis had instructed us to march, to take to the streets." Escobar took that instruction literally—and agreed to march.

He also agreed to act in advance of the event and called on local parishes to mobilize thousands to join the march. And he called on them to get tens of thousands across El Salvador to sign a petition supporting the bill. On one single Sunday, in Masses around the country, over thirty thousand people signed the petition.

On March 9, 2017—a mere four weeks after the archbishop's presentation of the draft bill to the legislature—thousands from local parishes gathered with students, water defenders from Cabañas and elsewhere, other members of La Mesa, and other social movement groups at a central plaza in San Salvador. The archbishop did not plan to lead the march, but others urged him to the front. It was impossible to miss him—there under a dark umbrella to shield himself from the sun, in his dark clothes and white collar, large cross dangling—leading the march. Bishops, authorities of the UCA, and other leaders of El Salvador's Catholic and Protestant churches surrounded him.

The official greeting party at the Legislative Assembly suggested that all the political parties understood that the stakes had been raised. Not only key legislators but also the heads of each party awaited the archbishop and the thousands of marchers. As journalists took notes and photos, the archbishop warned those assembled that the threat was grave and that the legislature's action was needed urgently and immediately. The president of the legislature committed to reviewing the bill and acting within two weeks. *Not a chance,* Andrés later recalled thinking at that moment.

As the archbishop and the church increased the pressure, John Wright conveyed the increased stakes to his ARENA colleagues. "I said we have a very motivated church base, and every Sunday they go to church, and priests are saying 'call your congressperson' to support the mining ban. My proposal is that we stand with the ban." He warned, "If you want to go against the current on this one, go ahead but. . . ." He knew that transcending partisan politics was easier said than done. Think Democrats and Republicans in the contemporary United States. For decades, ARENA had voted against anything that might be deemed an FMLN victory—and vice versa.

Meanwhile, OceanaGold held on to El Salvador's $8 million. As if pretending that it had not lost that ICSID battle, OceanaGold continued privately to try to make a deal with top government officials, a deal to allow it to mine. And, while it had not—so far, at least—filed for an annulment of the ICSID award, its lawyers misleadingly wrote in a private communication that "our client's claims have not been finally resolved by the still-pending ICSID processes." The company pressed forward with its public relations campaign, holding a conference in February on the benefits of "green mining." And on March 23, OceanaGold's El Salvador foundation organized a pro-mining protest. Each person who attended from Cabañas was compensated with a free lunch and seven dollars.

That same day, OceanaGold lawyers wrote to Luis and others, with a copy to the president of the legislature, Guillermo Gallegos, who would preside over any legislative vote: "We understand from press reports that some members of the Salvadoran legislature may be considering enactment of [a] statutory metallic mining ban. In our view, the consequences would be regrettable."

And always, OceanaGold warned the Salvadoran government against depriving the poor people of El Salvador of the "long-term opportunities for the Salvadoran economy," the progress that responsible mining had brought other countries. Again, the heart of OceanaGold's claims in this regard focused on its mine in the northern Philippines. That Philippine mine, OceanaGold stressed, brought well-paid, plentiful jobs for the locals. The company advertised sparkling clean waterways and verdant trees, even more trees than before thanks to OceanaGold's reforestation efforts. This line of argument clearly struck a chord with some members of the legislature. What if OceanaGold's mine in the Philippines was indeed a showcase of so-called responsible mining in economic, social, and environmental terms? How could a Salvadoran legislator without any firsthand knowledge of OceanaGold's mining in the Philippines, even someone leaning to support the eleven-article ban bill, be sure that OceanaGold was not El Salvador's answer to its long-term quest for poverty-ending growth, for progress?

———

Three guinea fowl waddled by in V-formation around the lush outdoor area of the Sheraton Hotel on the last Sunday in March 2017. With their fat bodies, black with white spots and red wattles, they were reminiscent of free-range turkeys. They wandered past Representative Alberto Romero, ARENA party leader in the Legislative Assembly, who sat with his wife at a poolside table on this sunny afternoon. The fowl continued in a circuitous path, past nooks and crannies where OceanaGold may well have conducted some of its wooing sessions. They waddled toward the hotel restaurant, passing the outdoor table where Carlos Padilla, governor of the Philippine province where OceanaGold had its mine, sat huddled deep in conversation with his companions.

If the birds typically found in Africa appeared unlikely guests at this five-star hotel in San Salvador, the Philippine governor was perhaps even more unlikely. Padilla rubbed his eyes as he watched them, as if trying to sort out jetlag-induced hallucination from reality. He and his provincial planner had journeyed from the other side of the globe, traveling back across fourteen time zones, so that the day was night and the night was day. The governor loved to travel. But he had never imagined being invited to work on such an important mission in such a faraway place. He had never imagined being so tired at such a historical moment.

Nor could OceanaGold officials likely have imagined the entrance of this player to its Salvadoran scene. Governor Padilla was the water defenders' March 2017 surprise. He was the answer to the conundrum of how to bring the reality of OceanaGold's remote Philippine mine to El Salvador, to expose the misinformation about the mine in his province. It had taken some thought and time, fund-raising, complicated logistics, and meticulous planning by the UCA. But Andrés had linked up with MiningWatch Canada's Philippine expert Catherine Coumans and the two of us, so that we three could deploy our decades-long Philippine connections to find this credible-beyond-the-shadow-of-a-doubt witness to counteract OceanaGold's false claims.

The governor fit many profiles. He was the elected leader of the Philippine province where OceanaGold had an extremely profitable mine. As a former congressman, he knew how to work that world. As a farmer, he possessed great love for the land and water. He was a man with a zest for storytelling. And, finally, he know how to be assertive but in an unassuming and avuncular manner. Padilla had insisted on bringing along his right-hand man, his provincial planner, knowing that between the two of them they could answer just about any question. Both were perfectionists, willing to stay up late into the night to redo PowerPoint slides, reframe talks, and iron the appropriate Philippine dress shirt for the next day's events.

At Sheraton poolside with Padilla and his provincial planner (both in informal polo shirts this first afternoon) were Andrés, Luis Parada and his wife, and Robin. The group had gathered to review the full itinerary organized by Andrés and his UCA colleagues and to brief Padilla on what to expect. The itinerary was challenging. The work was to start bright and early the next day with the first of many press conferences and public forums with various of the water defenders' likely and unlikely allies—among them Lina Pohl, John Wright, Dr. Mata, and El Salvador's human rights ombudsman. TV and radio appearances were scheduled for each day, some beginning in the wee hours.

If all went well, Tuesday would include a critical meeting with the Committee on Environment, chaired by FMLN's Mata, with ARE-NA's John Wright as vice chair. On Wednesday, Padilla was slated to address Environment Minister Pohl's regular gathering of top government, private-sector, and civil society groups. Andrés, in his never-say-no fashion, had somehow managed to set up a meeting with President Sánchez Cerén for Wednesday afternoon. And it was hoped that, toward the end of the week, Padilla would travel to Cabañas, where this story began. Andrés ended by sharing a rumor that the legislature might move to a vote on the mining ban bill that very week.

The jet-lagged Philippine governor said yes to it all—simply asking for feedback on how best to frame his remarks at each event. And, he confided to Robin, he needed advice on which Philippine attire would work best for each occasion.

The next day, Monday, Padilla's performances commenced. He tailored his mix of folksy stories, Philippine-style corny jokes, impeccable data, and photos to best reach each of his audiences. "I traveled nine thousand miles," he would typically begin, "because our countries have three things in common: We were colonized by Spain. We border the Pacific

Ocean. And . . ." He paused before stating the third thing in common: "OceanaGold."

Then Padilla showed a series of riveting slides, including one depicting a lush Philippine landscape with a small mountain. In a subsequent slide showing the same location, the mountain and adjacent land totally disappeared, replaced by OceanaGold's gigantic open-pit mine and underground tunnels. More slides showed the waste and water emptying into OceanaGold's long, murky, gray, waste-filled "tailings pond" and its ghostly dead trees. Key slides were carefully labeled "before" and "after" in Spanish. Audiences never failed to gasp at the "after" pictures. "Responsible mining?," Padilla would ask.

The presentations wove scientific evidence with storytelling. The audiences learned how the surrounding rivers and streams had become contaminated and toxic. "Even our water buffalos won't wade in," Padilla told them. They learned how Padilla's beloved province—"one of the Philippines' top rice-producing areas, a big vegetable supplier" and also the country's citrus capital—found itself facing a challenging agricultural future. "Because of the mine, the water table has sunk. Now our springs and rivers are drying up." As a result, communities near the mine were especially hurt, with "no access to water for drinking or for irrigation." And, given that Padilla's province was the watershed of the northern Philippines, the impacts were starting to be felt downstream. Dead fish were washing up on riverbanks.

Padilla anticipated questions about better development paths and alternatives to mining before they were asked: "Our agriculture could thrive for thousands of years. Compare that to mining, which will only be here ten to twenty years, with all these problems." To be even more clear, he added, "No amount of money can compensate for the destruction." He had come to El Salvador, he explained, because of his concern for future generations: "Foremost in my mind, will my grandchildren say, 'Grandpa, why did you do this, why did you allow mining?'"

With Dr. Mata and former fireman Wright at his side, and community organizer Hernández and the rest of the committee listening and watching intently, Padilla spent a full hour making a version of the presentation to the Environment Committee. He patiently answered questions, including some that seemed to indicate that not all parties or members were onboard, that they were considering amendments or a no vote should the bill get to the floor. Like a careful academic, he refuted OceanaGold's claims of responsible mining on environmental, social, and economic grounds. As a former congressman himself, Padilla took care not to overstep what he viewed as his appropriate roles: witness to reality and visitor. "It is not my place to tell you in El Salvador what to do," he stressed. "But I wish my country and my province had known [the reality of OceanaGold's so-called responsible mining] before we allowed it in."

Hours later, we learned that the committee had voted unanimously to send the mining ban bill on to the full legislature. And Andrés's prediction of congressional action that week was becoming a reality: the bill was to come before the full legislature for a vote the very next day.

March 29 began earlier than usual for Vidalina. She woke at 3:00 a.m. and made her family's usual daily supply of tortillas. She donned her white La Mesa T-shirt with its "No a la Minería" message, a skirt, and her usual flat shoes. Vidalina's bus—one of the two she had arranged to get herself, Antonio, Miguel, and about 130 other people from Cabañas and Chalatenango to the Legislative Assembly early that morning—left at 5:00 a.m. from her hometown to be sure to arrive in time for a 9:00 a.m. La Mesa press conference. There they would be joined by hundreds of others. "We were told that the mining vote would be one of the last on the legislative agenda that day. So, since I do logistics, I also had to figure out how to get tamales delivered for our delegation for the early afternoon."

Representative Wright did not get much sleep either. His workday kicked off at 7:00 a.m. with a breakfast meeting with ARENA party colleagues before the legislative session. "The Environment Committee meeting had gone well the day before and we'd passed the mining ban bill. . . . But, I walked into the breakfast meeting without full ARENA approval on the ban." Wright made his pitch, but he could not pretend to know how the vote later in the day would go. Would his colleagues show up for that day's legislative session? If they did show up, would they rudely walk out before the vote—a tactic used in the past? Would they vote against the bill simply to deny their age-old enemy, the FMLN, a victory?

Representative Hernández put on black pants, black shirt, and a bright red-orange jacket with black trim—an outfit to project the confidence that she lacked. She did feel buoyed by the Philippine governor's testimony to the committee the day before. She thought Padilla was especially important for the right-wing legislators. She tried to stay focused on that rather than the various things that could go awry. Would the president of the legislature, Gallegos, who was neither FMLN nor ARENA, actually call the vote? She and her FMLN colleagues had emphasized to him what a coup passing the mining ban would be for him, in terms of leadership and legacy—without reminding him that his party had never supported a ban.

As always, the main legislative assembly hall was decorated with portraits of Salvadoran politicians, flags of allied countries, and two statues of lions. An air of seriousness, of decorum, prevailed. Front and center in the hall and facing the entry doors, elevated dark wooden tables and leather chairs provided seating for the fourteen officers of the legislature, with that of legislative president Gallegos in the middle. The remaining members of the eighty-four-person legislature faced front, sitting across four rows of elegant wooden desks. Just behind these four rows, separated by a gold-colored bar, was a VIP observers' section. Seals from each province decorated the back wall. Above the seals, a large balcony was split into three areas. The balcony's two sides were reserved for the media. That left a large middle area of the balcony with one hundred or so seats for the non-VIP public, a section referred to as "behind the glass" given the transparent barrier separating it from the rest of the hall.

On that day, most FMLN members had La Mesa's red, orange, yellow, and white banners hanging in front of their desks, emblazoned with the slogan: "*No a la Minería, Si a la Vida*"—No to Mining, Yes to Life. Had the main hall of the legislative assembly ever looked so colorful, so festive?

Water defenders, among them Vidalina and Miguel, quickly filled the public area of the balcony. Vidalina's team had brought some of the same banners along with photos of Marcelo and the other martyrs of this long struggle. Antonio stayed outside with others from La Mesa to help rally the hundreds of water defenders, with their banners and placards. The banners suggested festivity, but that was not what Antonio and others were feeling. Rather, waves of anxiety swept through the crowd as people agonized over whether the ban would pass or not. According to Antonio, "We knew that we had some ARENA deputies but not others."

Guillermo Gallegos, as president of the legislature—he who had received the archbishop and his petitions just over two weeks earlier and who had been sent a copy of OceanaGold's communique just days earlier—called the session to order. Sitting at her desk bedecked with a banner, Hernández had never felt more nervous in a legislative session than on this day, particularly with the vote scheduled so late. Once the session finally began, every time Gallegos got a phone call, she feared he would call off the vote. She and others expected some kind of OceanaGold intervention, some last-minute maneuver. After all, it still had not paid the $8 million, the amount creeping upward as interest on the unpaid bill accumulated. Plus, in this upside-down world, nothing happened in El Salvador without some kind of intrusion from more powerful countries or powerful corporations.

There was palpable impatience among some legislators, VIPs, and those behind the glass. About an hour into the session, as legislators felt the pressure of the crowd, a motion was made—and passed—to move the mining issue up to the very next item. And, with that, John Wright found himself with "the distinct honor" of standing up in front and reading the bill aloud word for word, article by article. At the end of each article, he could hear cheers from behind the glass.

As Wright continued to read the bill, a call arose from behind the glass that could be heard clearly on the floor. "*Voten! Voten! Voten!*" the water defenders chanted. One after another, legislators rose to speak. Dr. Mata spoke for the FMLN. Then came Wright again. Both gave credit to the social movements, stressing that this was the result of their activism. Both included mention of those who had lost their lives in the fight against mining. Mata pronounced: "This law is not any law; this regulation is bathed in blood. . . . Marcelo Rivera, Ramiro Rivera, Dora Sorto . . . Juan Francisco Duran." The crowd in the balcony chanted louder. "*Voten! Voten! Voten!*"

There was much chatter back and forth among the representatives and the few guests on the floor. Luis Parada was there, invited by another member of the legislature, to be in easy reach should his legal view of any possible amendments be needed. At least one congressman admitted to another his nervousness about limiting El Salvador's economic growth options by banning mining. "Remember what the Philippine governor said," came the response from his colleague.

"*Voten! Voten! Voten!*" Hernández looked up to those behind the glass, grateful for their chants.

Would the vote ever be called?

By now, Environment Minister Pohl could be seen in the front of the VIP section. She had started the day with her long-ago scheduled meeting with government, business, and civil society leaders, a meeting that featured Governor Padilla talking about mining. With the vote pushed earlier, she rushed from that meeting to the legislature. She got a seat for Andrés as well. A former FMLN legislator had ushered Vidalina down from behind the glass to the VIP section. She now stood directly behind Pohl, proudly holding up a "*No a la Minería, Si a la Vida*" banner that matched her T-shirt.

Later, in 2019, as Vidalina recalled those agonizing moments, her voice would shake. "I remember feeling, *This is it*. I can't express what I felt. I remember looking straight at Johnny Wright Sol as he read the articles. And then later, when he said the names of our martyrs. And when he said he would vote for the articles. Then all the talking was a blur."

Finally the vote was announced. Hernández later explained the process to us: "There was an electronic screen that tallies the votes, and displays the votes by each seat of the 84 members. We knew we needed 43 votes to win." A simple majority.

That day, that moment, Hernández willed herself to watch the electronic vote tally, expecting the worst. Very quickly, the numbers appeared on the screen: "Si: 69, No: 0, ABST: 0." She later recalled, "I could not believe what I was seeing." Subsequently, one more registered a yes—making the final yes tally 70. Fourteen did not vote. Nobody voted against the bill.

Vidalina felt dizzy. She thought she was going to faint. "I remember yelling at the top of my lungs: '*Sí, se puede!*' [Yes, we can!] Everyone started hugging. Many of us started to cry. The first thing I thought was: how many had to die for us to achieve this? We all rushed out to the plaza outside to join the others. That is where the celebration began. We had the La Mesa sound equipment. I took the microphone. I had my heart in my

throat. I was still crying." Miguel too was crying. Hernández and other
key FMLN legislators joined them outside, proudly displaying their No a
la Minería banners.

For John Wright, the vote was a high point for El Salvador: "Of all
the laws we passed in that legislature, the one item that made it feel like a
truly democratic process was that moment. No other piece of legislation
had such organized and large social support. . . . This day, water won
[over] gold."

That afternoon, as planned weeks earlier, the Philippine governor—with
his entourage that included Andrés, UCA vice rector Omar Serrano, and
Robin—proceeded to the Casa Presidencial. President Sánchez Cerén
and his entourage, including Lina Pohl (straight from the celebration at
the legislative assembly) and various other ministers and deputy ministers
awaited them. More than once before entering, Padilla had warned Robin
that this meeting had to be kept brief—protocol deemed it inappropri-
ate for a mere Philippine provincial governor to meet with a country's
president.

But Sánchez Cerén had other ideas. He welcomed Padilla and his entourage warmly. He asked for remarks from the governor and Andrés and
peppered the governor with questions. Then Sánchez Cerén spoke without
notes: "We are so pleased with the passage of this law, which was passed
due to the efforts of the environmental defenders, and of the Church."
Thanks also were due to the efforts of Minister Pohl, he added, looking
at her seated to his side. He then quoted the words of Pope Francis, in his
famous encyclical "*Laudato Si'*": "to protect our common home." "All of
this helped us stay strong. I will sign this bill when it comes to my desk.
We will write the regulations to support it."

The next day, Robin accompanied Governor Padilla, Andrés, and Luis
over the dusty roads to Cabañas. They stopped first for an already planned
forum, moderated by two of the brave young adults of Radio Victoria,
those community radio reporters who had stood fast against those chilling
death threats over the years since 2009. About a thousand people were
packed into the standing-room-only hall. Baseball caps, sombreros, and

T-shirts mingled with Sunday go-to-church dresses and long-sleeved collared shirts. Vidalina spoke, as did Andrés, Luis, and the Cabañas governor. The crowd roared and many rose to their feet when "the governor from the Philippines" showed his slides. Phones flashed and clicked as photos were taken of the "before" and "after" slides. Someone loudly uttered what many were thinking: "This could have been us."

Then Padilla's entourage traveled onward to ADES, over the very same roads on which Miguel had driven us on our first trip to El Salvador nearly half a dozen years earlier. These were the same roads that the mining executives Johansing and Shrake had traversed years before our travels— and that Vidalina traveled regularly for La Mesa meetings after making sure her family had enough tortillas for the day. As always on these roads headed toward San Isidro, Robin looked to the right when passing the turnoff that led to the old dry well where Marcelo's mangled body was found. As always, she looked to the left when passing the entrance to the Pac Rim/OceanaGold mine site—or, rather, what would have been the mine site—where countless people from different parts of the globe had stood to let the men in suits know that the world was watching.

At ADES, where the strength-inducing amaranth had grown taller, Miguel was waiting. "Welcome home, Robin," Miguel said softly in English, "and thank you." He almost never tried to speak to us in English. His doing so at this moment was especially moving, as if he had been practicing, hoping. We knew this was going to be a bittersweet moment, the best-case scenario for March 2017. OceanaGold had lost. It had lost not once but twice. The world's first countrywide comprehensive metals mining ban had passed. But Miguel's beloved older brother lay in a tomb a few miles away. And the so-called intellectual authors of Marcelo's and the other murders remained at large. Miguel and Robin hugged each other, tears rolling down their cheeks. Vidalina and others were also crying. There was celebrating to be done. But first, as was appropriate, Cabañas had to mourn its martyrs.

The Vote Heard Around the World . . . but Who Killed Marcelo?

I n the summer of 2019, almost three years had passed since the lawsuit decision against OceanaGold and over two years since El Salvador's legislature banned metals mining. It had been a full decade since Marcelo's tortured body was found in that dry well.

On July 19, hundreds of water defenders gathered at San Isidro's central square—just outside the Marcelo Rivera Cultural Center—to commemorate their beloved Cipitio's life and work. Vidalina arrived in an immaculate white blouse with red embroidered flowers, a red skirt, her hair pulled up against the blazing sun. Antonio, as usual, sported formal dark pants, the leather shoes that he polished daily, and a long-sleeved white shirt that taunted the heat by retaining its ironed crispness. Others, including a handful of journalists, had traveled there from San Salvador. We two had made the journey from the United States. Standing out among the baseball hats and sombreros, jeans, and T-shirts were seven or so children, as young as six years old. The words "La Comenita"—Little Hive—were emblazoned in yellow across their black T-shirts. Yellow headbands with antennae completed their bumblebee costumes. The little bumblebees took turns carrying a large poster bearing a striking photograph of Marcelo.

From the square, we all marched toward the cemetery on the outskirts of town. We walked past an old Nissan truck with a broken back light, its bed filled with cows. We passed old adobe houses and newer cement ones, people watching from doorways. The procession slowed as we walked by some of the chipping murals that the youth of Cabañas had painted after Marcelo's murder. Once through the cemetery gate, we followed a winding dirt path. The path brought us past aboveground tombs, most just larger than a coffin, some painted blue, green, and assorted other bright colors. Several simple rusting metal crosses peeked out amid the tombs, crosses welded together from pieces of old scrap pipe. They marked the anonymous graves of men who had mined underground at the El Dorado site seven decades earlier.

Our destination was Marcelo's grave, at the far end of the cemetery. We two had been here a year before with Miguel—but never when Big Gold was around, never in the years of terror. Marcelo's tomb was wedged among several others. His grave was not the grandest but it stood out, with its gray and white tiles covering the aboveground tomb and its locked black metal enclosure with scrolling grillwork and a roof to protect the site.

We stationed ourselves with many others in the shade of the large tree that bends over Marcelo's grave. Others stood or sat on nearby tombs or along the path. The crowd quieted as several participants moved in to unlock the enclosure and sweep away the leaves and debris that had accumulated on the tiled surface. Others draped flowers on the grillwork. Someone placed a centerpiece of red roses with a yellow bow on the cleaned tiles, along with two white memorial candles. A black "*en memoria*" banner with a photo of Marcelo covered the back wall of the tomb. The members of the Little Hive took turns holding the poster—almost as tall as they—with the larger-than-life photo of Marcelo. In the photo, Marcelo raised his left hand to make a point. Below the photo, large print proclaimed: "*Amigo, Maestro, Defensor ambiental . . . Cuando las justicia calla, El pueblo alza su voz.*" Friend, Teacher, Defender of the environment . . . When justice is silenced, the people raise their voice.

A brief service featured the Marcelo Rivera Cultural Center director, who reminded us of the ideals and vision for which Marcelo lived and died. The procession then turned back toward the town square. Vidalina lingered at her friend's tomb, carving out a moment between the two of them before rejoining the rest of the group.

We had returned to El Salvador for this event and to see if we could gain any clarity on the final remaining mystery of this story: who ordered the killing of Marcelo Rivera?

We could not help but remember our naïveté a decade earlier in assuming this would be the easiest of the mysteries to solve. We now knew from the organization Global Witness that over 1,700 "environmental defenders," including Marcelo, Ramiro, and Dora, had been killed across fifty countries between 2002 and 2018. Another chilling figure in the 2019 Global Witness report further chastened us: only 10 percent—one out of ten—of the murders of environmentalists from 2002 to 2013 had ever resulted in a conviction, compared with 43 percent of known global homicide cases. Given this reality check, what was the chance for Marcelo's family and allies to find justice?

As we pursued that final mystery, we also checked on what had become of the main protagonists in this drama. Much had changed.

In 2019, the presidency of Salvador Sánchez Cerén ended, and Salvadoran voters pivoted in a new direction. For the first time since the civil war ended, neither ARENA nor the FMLN won the election. Rather, young and charismatic Nayib Bukele, a millennial of leather jackets and Twitter, triumphed by a large margin. Bukele had been expelled from the FMLN and had run as the GANA candidate, with an anti-corruption message. As of mid-2020, President Bukele had not announced his views on metals mining—but had made no move to change the Salvadoran law that banned it.

Just in case a future legislature or president should make such a move, members of La Mesa reminded us that in their years of work to stop mining in El Salvador, they had succeeded in getting several local municipalities to vote themselves "territories free of mining" through local referendums.

Johnny Wright Sol exited the Salvadoran legislature—and the ARENA party—in 2018 after one term in office. In 2019, he launched his own new political party, Nuestro Tiempo (Our Time). So too did FMLN congresswoman Estela Hernández depart the legislature in 2018. She returned to her life as a community organizer with an environmental and social justice organization based at the mouth of the Lempa River. When we met her there in 2019, she had traded in her black pants for jeans. She, like Vidalina, Antonio, Miguel, and other water defenders, remained laser-focused on protecting the anti-mining bill for future generations. As she explained: "Yes, there is pride to know we won a battle of such caliber. We've given a light to the world. It is now our responsibility to make sure the law and the light are not revoked."

The FMLN's Dr. Guillermo Mata, former chair of the legislature's Committee on Environment and Climate Change, returned to his career as a pediatrician.

As for Lina Pohl, the Environment Ministry she headed sent this tweet in the final days of the Sánchez Cerén administration in 2019: "Today ends 10 years of service of Lina Pohl, an official who broke the mold through her particular way of being, her commitment to work and leadership, who put the environment on the lips of everyone." She moved on to Mexico City as the UN Food and Agriculture Organization representative for Mexico.

Antonio, Vidalina, and Miguel remain at ADES. The water defenders of El Salvador—and especially the grassroots leaders in Cabañas—have become celebrities in other countries confronting Big Gold. They have been invited to Guatemala, Haiti, Peru, the Dominican Republic, Bolivia, Australia, Ecuador, Romania, and other countries where water defenders are anxious to learn the lessons of El Salvador's victories. Back in 2009, who could have imagined that one day you would be able to Google the name "Vidalina Morales" and get thousands of results?

Andrés McKinley continues as a researcher at UCA. With the mining ban in place, he, like many of El Salvador's water defenders, expanded his focus to stopping legislation that would privatize El Salvador's water.

International Allies and its member organizations continue to work with colleagues in El Salvador. They have also expanded their alliances with organizations in Guatemala, Peru, and the Philippines, where water defenders are engaging with governments to limit destructive mining activity. International Allies members are working with groups in Colombia, Guatemala, Peru, and Romania to help them fight Big Gold corporations that have filed investor-state lawsuits.

The small community where Vidalina lives worked with Engineers without Borders and the Washington Ethical Society (the International Allies participant whose members had been regulars at the World Bank protests), to build a community-controlled, solar-powered, water system. By 2019, water was being pumped up the hill to Vidalina's home and the homes of her neighbors. Vidalina still cooks dozens of tortillas for her family every morning when she is not traveling.

Miguel was out of the country around the time of the tenth anniversary of Marcelo's murder—for a much needed respite. Miguel and Margarita's daughter is following her dream and studying dentistry in San Salvador, and she wants to practice in San Isidro—which would have pleased her Uncle Marcelo. She gifted us with her very first wax model of a tooth.

Luis Parada briefly vied to be ARENA's candidate for president in the 2019 elections. He fairly quickly backed out after realizing that (in his words) "the ARENA party leaders—and their most important wealthy financiers" had already decided to back the son of a wealthy businessman, "someone who had shown clear sympathy toward mining." The son in fact became the ARENA candidate, only to lose badly against Bukele. Luis lives with his family outside of Washington, DC.

Presumably understanding that the ICSID panel's unanimous vote against it did not bode well, OceanaGold never requested an annulment in its legal case against El Salvador. OceanaGold paid the government of El Salvador $8,097,072—the $8 million plus interest due for the months of delay—in July 2017. With that, El Salvador and the El Dorado mine disappeared from OceanaGold's website. Its website instead boasts of its mining expansion in South Carolina and New Zealand.

After 2016, news of former Pac Rim president Tom Shrake has largely disappeared from the Internet.

As of August 2020, Robert Johansing—whose job Shrake took over when Pac Rim entered El Salvador in 2002—appears to be continuing to sniff out lucrative new deposits elsewhere as the president and CEO of Gold79 Mines Ltd. This company's website says it engages in minerals exploration and mining in Arizona, Nevada, Canada, and Mexico.

And what of Governor Carlos Padilla, who traveled to El Salvador in March 2017 and played such a pivotal role in cementing that historic El Salvador vote? Padilla returned to his Philippine home province of Nueva Vizcaya even more adamant in his opposition to the extremely profitable OceanaGold gold and copper mine there. He extended his educational efforts about mining's deleterious impacts to surrounding provinces. In September 2018, he convened a water summit of officials and community members from his and neighboring provinces, which concluded with an agreement "to reject the extension of large-scale mining operations in Nueva Vizcaya, including the approval of new applications for mining rights."

Padilla was reelected governor of Nueva Vizcaya in 2019—soon after which OceanaGold Philippines' twenty-five-year mining permit expired. Seemingly to the company's astonishment, the Office of the President of the Philippines did not routinely renew that permit for another twenty-five years. Instead, the Office of the President sent the application back to OceanaGold, saying that it was incomplete in terms of not demonstrating that the company had gained the legally required free, prior, and informed consent of the indigenous communities in the area.

Local mining opponents from the frontline communities around the OceanaGold mine—groups similar to ADES—set up roadblocks to ensure that OceanaGold did not mine without a permit. The two national anti-mining coalitions in the Philippines—groups similar to La Mesa—ramped up their work against OceanaGold in conjunction with these grassroots groups and with petitions and research support from the International Allies. In the face of popular protest combined with provincial government opposition and actions against the mine, OceanaGold found itself with no option but to suspend its operations in Nueva Vizcaya in the fall of 2019. OceanaGold's share prices plummeted. And, in March 2020, Mick Wilkes's tenure as OceanaGold president and CEO came to an abrupt end when his resignation—for "personal reasons"—was announced.

As of this writing (mid-2020), the Philippine government has not renewed OceanaGold's permit, and the frontline communities' blockade of the mine remains in place despite police harassment. OceanaGold has moved its fight into domestic courts there, courts that have so far backed the local and provincial anti-mining efforts. Given what we know from OceanaGold's El Salvador intrigue, we expect that the company has also moved its fight into the back rooms and corridors of power.

Thus, another incredible David-and-Goliath story unravels on the other side of the Pacific, although it is too soon to know its ending. While the story of Big Gold versus the Water Defenders in El Salvador is over for now, it continues in the Philippines and elsewhere.

While El Salvador may have been the forerunner—the first country to pass a total ban on metals mining—there were important victories against destructive mining in other countries over these same years. These wins were mostly led by frontline communities, often indigenous, that catalyzed their governments to take action to restrict mining. Costa Rica is notable in this regard. As early as 2002, the Costa Rican government first initiated an executive ban limiting mining. The policy specifically banned new open-pit mining and use of cyanide, the combination of which essentially banned any new mining operations. As in El Salvador, this policy change began as an executive branch decision but then was passed into law unanimously by Costa Rica's Congress in 2010. The Costa Rican Supreme Court subsequently upheld the decision.

As in El Salvador, water was center stage in other countries' actions to limit mining. In 2016, the Supreme Court of Colombia upheld laws that prohibit mining in the country's unique *páramos* uplands, a key source of water. So too did this lead to clashes with a wide range of mining companies, some of which initiated lawsuits at ICSID.

Water was also central in Argentina, where mining laws can be passed at both the provincial and federal level. As of 2020, nearly one-third of Argentina's provinces had either banned open-pit mining or banned the use of toxic chemicals like cyanide. That same year, the Supreme Court of

Argentina upheld the national law banning mining in glacier areas, ruling against a challenge from the mining giant Barrick Gold.

Across the globe, in almost every country where there is substantial mining activity, from Chile to Thailand, South Africa to New Zealand, Canada to the United States, there have been intense debates in frontline mining communities and also in legislatures over laws to restrict mining. In the United States, for example, Montana banned gold mining techniques that use cyanide, and Maine banned open-pit mines. Panama prohibited mining on indigenous lands covering one-tenth of the country, significant because indigenous communities' land often overlaps with veins of gold and other ores. In New Zealand there has been a contentious debate over initiatives to limit seabed mining while giving power to indigenous communities, noteworthy since seabed mining is a relatively new frontier for mining corporations. And, after the COVID-19 pandemic spread in 2020, over three hundred organizations around the world signed a statement of support for mining communities, indigenous peoples, and mine workers—all suffering as mining corporations sought to continue operations despite the obvious dangers.

When we traveled to communities near OceanaGold's mine in Nueva Vizcaya in the northern Philippines in 2017, just months after Governor Padilla's trip to El Salvador, Filipinos were heartened to hear of the victories of the water defenders in El Salvador. They wanted to know what lessons we could share from the El Salvador experience that might help them defeat OceanaGold there and avoid a global lawsuit. And, beyond that, some asked what lessons might help them end mining altogether in this country with over three dozen large operating mines.

We pondered these questions. We have come to believe that several factors came together to enable such an unlikely win for El Salvador. Had any single factor not been present, victory might not have been achieved. Undoubtedly, the most vital component of success was the determination and smarts of Vidalina, Marcelo, Miguel, Antonio, and their allies on the ground in poorer communities that depended on water. The fact that water defenders risked and lost lives made the importance of this struggle undeniable to others.

Yet other community-based movements had lost similar battles all over the world. So what else was critical? In El Salvador, the water defenders carried out concerted education campaigns on the science of mining and water, and they creatively spread the word through radio and television programs, community forums, church sermons, university-based events, fact sheets, and flyers at mass marches. The success of these efforts showed up in the 2007 and 2015 University of Central America polls, which revealed overwhelming public disapproval of mining.

Another factor—one that resonated deeply with Philippine groups opposed to mining—was the framing of the goal. El Salvador's water defenders did not see their fight as simply anti-mining and therefore did not portray their fight that way. Instead, they were "pro water, pro-life." *Agua es vida*, water is life. Some coalitions in other countries that address mining have names like the So-and-So Coalition against Mining. The Salvadoran story suggests that, whatever the name, campaigns should lead with the positive goal—expressing what the movements are *for* particularly if it is something as vital and popular as ensuring affordable and clean water for everyone. The terms "water defenders" and "water protectors" resonate broadly and effectively around the world.

The right kind of international alliances also played a major role. To the extent that the loose International Allies network was successful, it was because members of the network understood the global part of the fight— the corporate lawsuit against El Salvador—to be their own fight too, not just something done in solidarity with Salvadoran groups. And the International Allies members did not believe that they knew what was best for positive change within El Salvador. Instead, the global coalition respected La Mesa's lead on the domestic mining ban. The International Allies' creative media work also turned the El Salvador fight into a global story—the poster child calling attention to the upside-down rules that privilege corporations over people and the environment, gold over water in this particular case—and helped raise the profile of the struggle. In addition, La Mesa received international funding (not from International Allies', which was not a funding entity), valuable for keeping the coalition going. But when donors chose to favor different groups and individuals among the coalition, it often caused friction that weakened the overall coalition.

Among the most intriguing lessons entailed the Salvadoran water defenders' pursuit of unlikely allies. In this pursuit, individual water defenders recognized this to be less a contest of Right versus Left and more a contest of right versus wrong. Yes, the FMLN—and, strikingly, women from the FMLN in the executive branch and in the legislature—proved instrumental in getting the ban passed. But notable heroes emerged in the right-wing ARENA party as well. Allies in all the parties—all building on the grassroots social movement—proved necessary for the win.

Remember that in El Salvador, roughly seventy-five thousand people were killed in a brutal civil war that had polarized the country. Thus, it took enormous courage for the water defenders to reach out to ARENA ministers in the first years of the work and to reach "across the aisle" to an ARENA legislator from a rich family in the final stages. It took moxie to reach out to an ultraconservative archbishop early on and later an archbishop who had angered many of those allied with the water defenders by shutting down the archdiocese's legal aid office. Likewise, it took courage and smarts to form bonds with the lead lawyer who had been in the military on the government side during the civil war. So too did key water defenders demonstrate an ability to maintain a remarkable calm and perseverance when some likely allies high up in the left FMLN party were tempted by the inducements of Big Gold.

What the two of us have learned from the water defenders has transformed the way we think about unlikely allies in our US work. We are not certain what we would have thought or recommended more than a decade ago had we been part of the debate about reaching out to the likes of Minister Barrera. But we know this for sure: we now scour the landscape as we strategize campaigns against specific corporate abuses or rules that benefit the rich and powerful, expanding our sense of who might join a fight because of an unlikely common interest. In this vein, we applaud those in the United States who reached out to the millionaires who then joined the fight for fair taxation, even when it would mean paying higher taxes themselves.

A corollary of this unlikely ally lesson: some in the private sector can emerge as allies in a fight that many perceive as anti-corporate. The water defenders in El Salvador had an advantage over their counterparts in countries like Guatemala, Peru, and the Philippines, where multiple mining projects created webs of local corporate leaders who were intertwined with and enriched by mining. The Salvadoran civil war provided a clean break from mining, hence there were fewer elite families linked to it. Rather, domestic elites in tourism and agriculture depended on water, and some would, in their own fashion, become water defender allies—or at least would not actively support Big Gold. Reaching out creatively but carefully to unlikely business allies could be even more vital for communities fighting corporate encroachment elsewhere. Case in point in the United States are the legions of small business owners who have joined the battles against Walmart.

According to Archbishop Escobar, there was one final factor in El Salvador's wins, an X-factor from God. As Escobar retold the story of his battered country with its history of losing, the victories involved a miracle from on high. Whether you agree with this or not, any such miracle would not have occurred without the blood, sweat, tears, and doggedness of so many who had so much to lose.

As we attempted to articulate lessons for frontline communities, we also reflected on what we had learned about the questions we posed at the outset of this book. We realized that we were ending this journey with at least partial answers to many of the questions with which we began.

At the outset, we mentioned the pervasive myth that poorer people cannot afford to care as much for the environment as wealthier people. The evidence from northern El Salvador is to the contrary. It is the poor who often care most, in part because the precious land and water and natural resources that surround them are vital to their survival. The water defenders had many middle-class and some wealthy allies, but their core was rooted in poorer communities.

The debate over the question of what constitutes progress—shorter-term financial gains or longer-term preservation of communities and natural resources—is omnipresent around the world. It is central in thousands of community battles against the Amazon corporation, giant sports arenas, fracking companies, and pipelines. It is relevant to debates now happening in our small city in Maryland about whether the local cooperative grocery store is vital to our community. Let us hope that El Salvador's victories can inspire others with its longer-term definition of progress and its articulation of a *buen vivir* paradigm. We can also learn from the two public opinion polls that water defenders urged the University of Central America to carry out. Those widely publicized polls, which showed that the public overwhelmingly viewed protecting water over gold as progress, helped win over the politicians.

The tale of El Salvador's water defenders can also help us understand the root causes of conflict, violence, dislocation, and migration—and the need to address these causes rather than the symptoms. A number of factors stand out as root causes, starting with global corporations' and richer governments' support of right-wing political parties and coups. Another is "progress" that deepens poverty and inequality and, in so doing, pushes people off their land or destroys their sources of water. This faulty definition of "progress" exacerbates the climate catastrophe, which makes more countries even more water-scarce, which in turn drives even more people off their lands and out of their countries. Mining would have brought more conflict to Cabañas and sent more dispossessed people onto the roads leading north toward the United States. Ending mining in El Salvador has lessened these tensions as well as conflicts in communities in gold country.

As we pointed out in another of the big questions we raised at the outset of this book, our modern lifestyles depend on metals. We asked: Could we imagine being able to keep most of the minerals that remain unmined in the ground? Could we imagine being able to stop most new mining? During our 2017 trip to the Philippines, we spoke with dozens of college students about whether they could imagine a future without the metals that make up their phones, computers, kitchens, furniture, you name it. The answer was an unequivocal no. But—and this is key—they could imagine a future that upgraded today's technology to recycle most of the metal that is currently discarded in old factories, old cars, old refrigerators, old computers, and old phones. As of 2019, roughly 30 percent of discarded metals were recycled. Can we get that closer to 90 percent? And how do we manage the mining of minerals like lithium that are vital to rechargeable batteries and to other cleaner energy alternatives?

Part of the answer to the metals recycling question is that more will be recycled when more governments incentivize metals recycling and when metals prices rise. Prices go up when more countries follow El Salvador's lead and stop most or all mining. There are thousands of companies engaged in metal recycling all over the world, and the numbers are growing. And so, as we did in the Philippines, we need to turn this question around to ask students: can you imagine your generation taking the lead in carving out more careers recycling metals so that more minerals could be kept in the ground? Many Filipino students said yes.

Using less gold may prove easier than using some other metals since over half of new gold ends up in jewelry. Much of that jewelry is destined for two countries—China and India. There is more hopeful news: demand for jewelry in both countries dipped in 2019, in part due to higher prices but also due to shifting tastes away from gold jewelry, especially among younger generations.

Vidalina, back in 2009 when our paths first crossed, told the Washington, DC, audience that honored La Mesa with the Institute for Policy Studies Letelier-Moffitt Human Rights Award that she could imagine changing the current global economic rules that give corporations privileges and enable them to sue governments in international tribunals. We were less sure than she then, but we can imagine it more easily now. However, we remain cognizant of the power of the imbalanced, unjust rules. Over the last decade, we have learned more about two opposing dynamics at play in this regard. On the one hand, as more countries challenge mining, oil, and gas corporations, the number of lawsuits against governments has continued to rise. In Latin America alone since 2009, mining companies filed or threatened to file lawsuits against Bolivia, Colombia, Costa Rica, the Dominican Republic, Ecuador, Guatemala, Mexico, Panama, Peru, Uruguay, and Venezuela.

Such mining lawsuits affect not only Latin America. Thailand was hit by a lawsuit from an Australian mining corporation in 2018, when the government shut down its gold mining operations after urine and blood tests showed high levels of arsenic and manganese in people living near the mine. In 2019, ICSID ordered Pakistan to pay $5.8 billion to a copper company partially owned by the Big Gold mining giant Barrick Gold, an amount a whopping twenty-five times greater than the exploration costs of the mining firm. Unlike the El Salvador case, corporations still win most investor-state cases, whether via final decisions or through settlement agreements as governments get cold feet along the way or even by the mere threat of an investor-state dispute.

On the other hand, more and more governments are questioning the biased rules that facilitate the lawsuits. Even some richer countries have withdrawn from or rejected these rules in agreements, albeit in agreements with other richer countries. Australia refused to include these corporate rights in the 2005 Australia–US Free Trade Agreement. European Union countries have begun phasing out bilateral investment agreements among themselves. The 2020 US–Mexico–Canada free trade agreement eliminated these rules between the United States and Canada.

Likewise, some poorer nations have been taking steps to extricate themselves from these unjust rules and institutions. Several Latin American governments have challenged corporations' rights to sue them in international tribunals. Brazil has never accepted such rights in any international agreement but has still attracted abundant foreign investment. Bolivia, Venezuela, and Ecuador have withdrawn their membership from the ICSID tribunal. Several governments have gone on record supporting the creation of fairer regional or global mechanisms to ensure more balanced rules when settling disputes between corporations and governments. South Africa has canceled a number of bilateral investment agreements, instead requiring that disputes with corporations be resolved in South Africa's domestic courts. India, South Korea, and other large poorer nations have also taken steps in this direction. However, the pressures to attract foreign investment—whether that foreign investment actually contributes to real "development" or not—have led most governments of less powerful, poorer nations to continue to participate in venues like ICSID.

These initiatives to rewrite unjust corporate rules are critical. If the momentum of corporate-biased investment rules can be slowed or halted, the power of global corporations would be significantly curtailed. Let us be clear: no one should expect that the hundreds of pro-corporate rules written and strengthened over the course of decades can be dismantled overnight. But dismantling rules protecting global investors' rights is a key strategic front where forward movement is possible. The victory in the David-and-Goliath battle of El Salvador over Pac Rim and OceanaGold, of the water defenders over Big Gold, was huge. Both symbolically and substantively, that win shifted some momentum back toward the rights of people and toward the health of the environment they inhabit.

To end where we began: what about justice for Marcelo? Two days after the July 2019 ceremonies marking the tenth anniversary of Marcelo's death, we sat down over coffee in the ADES open-air dining area with Antonio and Vidalina to finally to ask them exactly what they had come to know about the people behind the murder.

Antonio and Vidalina started by focusing on the murders of Dora and Ramiro, each killed during Christmas week just half a year after Marcelo's murder. "Neither murder even got an official investigation," Antonio reported, sweeping his arm though the air in disgust. His face crumbled as he continued, explaining that he stayed in contact with Dora's husband: "Dora's husband and children still do not have a safe place to stay." They and other victims and their families are "totally psychologically destroyed." And, Antonio and Vidalina emphasized, there have been no reparations of any kind. Nor was there any compensation for those living at sites ruined by mining exploration or living near the old Butters mine, last owned by the US-based Commerce Group.

Marcelo's case received more attention. Antonio reminded us that the attorney general's office had classified Marcelo's killing as a "common gang crime." The circumstances surrounding the murder and the burial of his body, as you have read, suggested otherwise. Indeed, even El Salvador's Human Rights Ombudsman's Office believed that the murder was not a common gang crime. We knew from prior conversations with Miguel that soon after Marcelo's tortured body was found in July 2009, the police had arrested some gang members. With that, they closed the investigation. Over a year later, three of these men were convicted of the murder and sentenced to forty years in prison. Another three were found guilty of trying to cover up the murder. Whether the men who actually carried out the killing were among the ones arrested will probably never be known.

Antonio shifted the subject away from the question of who tortured and killed Marcelo. Rather, as he stressed, whoever the actual killers, the fundamental question in nearly all cases of political killings is who are its "intellectual authors"? That is, who ordered or suggested the killing? Were they identified and tried? Was there some measure of justice? As we discussed this with Antonio and Vidalina in the ADES compound over a din of chirping insects and birds, Antonio removed his glasses, rubbed his eyes, and sighed. "We pushed and pushed and pushed the police authorities. They kept saying they were investigating, but they did nothing. And they kept saying that Pac Rim had nothing to do with it." One man even warned Antonio that he was "pushing too much." The attorney general's office, Antonio continued, served as "a cover for the intellectual authors. It represented a wall of impunity. And the fact that the police wouldn't investigate could only mean there was a political order from higher up."

Over the years, water defenders voiced various theories on the identity of the intellectual authors behind the 2009 murders of Marcelo, Ramiro, and Dora. Most included some level of participation by Big Gold. Antonio reiterated one of the top theories: "Remember that, when the resistance to mining grew here"—and when Pac Rim was unable to get the legislature to pass a weaker mining bill—"sparks started flying out of their eyes." Pac Rim had hired high-profile Salvadorans: that was the period when the company had hired former ARENA minister Manuel Hinds, who argued that El Salvador had no sane option but to allow mining. In addition, Antonio reminded us, "Pac Rim hired a former presidential candidate as a legal advisor and his son Rodrigo Chávez Palacios as a vice president of Pacific Rim El Salvador, the local subsidiary."

As Antonio repeated the name "Rodrigo Chávez Palacios," his eyes narrowed in anger. We recognized the name immediately. In a case splashed across the Salvadoran media, this former vice president of Pacific Rim El Salvador had been found guilty of participating in the grisly murder of a municipal employee in a western suburb of San Salvador in 2014. The victim's body had been cut into pieces and those pieces distributed around San Salvador. Chávez Palacios was subsequently imprisoned for his role in this macabre murder. Miguel had formally requested that the attorney general investigate the possible involvement of Chávez Palacios in Marcelo's murder. "As usual," Antonio added, "no investigation was launched." *Nada*. Nothing.

Over their years of work, almost every time that La Mesa or the International Allies issued a statement or petition, they had called for a careful investigation into the "intellectual authors" of the murders of Marcelo, Ramiro, and Dora. They did so even as some water defenders and their families understandably expressed—as they continue to express—ongoing fears about whether such inquiries could further endanger their safety, could provoke new violence in this country where justice has remained so elusive. If you were a member of Marcelo's or Dora's or Ramiro's family or if you worked at Radio Victoria and had lived through those blood-curdling death-threat texts, would you not think twice? Would you not have concerns about the ramifications of asking authorities to pursue such investigations?

As this book goes to press, the question of who killed Marcelo Rivera remains unsolved. No higher-ups have been charged with a crime. No serious investigation has taken place. *Nada*. Nothing.

After the brief tenth anniversary ceremony at Marcelo's grave, the procession wove back through the narrow streets of San Isidro toward the central town square adjacent to the Marcelo Rivera Cultural Center. It passed Miguel's house, then the small house that Marcelo had been renovating. "Cipitío" Marcelo would have delighted in the theater of the march. Youngsters donning many varieties of scary and funny masks led the procession. The little bumblebees, close behind, held their Marcelo poster high. An ensemble of half a dozen or so school-age drummers followed and helped keep the beat for the marchers. Three youth dressed as clowns brought up the rear—one sporting a wig with a rainbow of colors and all towering over the rest of the crowd as they pranced nimbly on very tall stilts.

At the end of a morning filled with dance performances by the bumblebees and others, spoken tributes, and raps, Vidalina herself took the stage and the microphone, although as usual she did not really need it. Her voice was adamant and clear: "Marcelo was so much more than an environmental martyr. He was a seed who bore fruit, the fruit of this country banning mining. Today is a day of commitment against violence as we take a strong stand against those who kill environmental martyrs." Her voice quivered for a moment. "Death is not real death when your mission in life has been completed to the fullest. Marcelo did not die. He continues to walk with us and to guide us."

Seated with the audience, the young bumblebees listened. They had not even been born when Marcelo was killed. But a decade later, they marched and danced in his honor and then sat in attentive silence.

And we wonder: will they pass along to their children and their children's children the story of Cipitio and how the water defenders saved their country from corporate greed?

Will others?

ACKNOWLEDGMENTS

O ur work on this book spanned more than a decade of research, activism, and writing, and we owe thanks to innumerable people, a number of whom appear on the book's pages. Perhaps our major regret is that we could not include many others. Having said that, we want all those with whom we interacted to know how appreciative we are.

First and foremost: the members of La Mesa Nacional Frente a la Minería Metalica (the National Roundtable on Metals Mining) and the other Salvadoran water defenders are the key protagonists in this book and provided much of the interviews and background materials. This book tells a version of their story as actors in their own history, as we came to understand it by our participation, interactions, and observations. We are forever grateful—indeed honored—for their willingness to let us be a part of this drama as it unfolded after 2009 and to share with us details of other events before that date. Several provided feedback on drafts of the book.

Now we will try to give appropriate thanks to key individuals (with organizational affiliations from when we interviewed them).

In El Salvador, numerous individuals and organizations (including those that made up La Mesa) spent an enormous amount of time sharing their perspectives and history and analysis of this story. To begin in Cabañas: Antonio Pacheco, Vidalina Morales (and family), Miguel Rivera (and family), Jaime Sánchez, Alirio Napoleón Hernández, and the rest of the staff of ADES; Don Carlos Bonilla and other residents of Santa Marta; Don Alejandro Guevara from La Trinidad; Rina Navarrete and other members of ASIC; Ricardo Navarro of CESTA; Hector Berrios and

Zenayda Serrano of MUFRAS-32; Francisco Pineda and other members of CAC (Environmental Committee of Cabañas); Cristina Starr, Oscar Ramirez Beltran, and the rest of the staff of Radio Victoria; Elvis Zavala; and Lidia Urias.

Among La Mesa members based in San Salvador: Rodolfo Calles, then-coordinator of La Mesa; Alejandro Labrador; Luis Gonzales of UNES; Bernardo Belloso of CRIPDES; Sandra Carolina Ascencio and Fray Domingo Solís of the Franciscan Justice, Peace and the Integrity of Creation (JPIC); David Pereira and Edgardo Mira of CEICOM; and María Sylvia Guillen, Saúl Baños, and Luis López of FESPAD.

Others in San Salvador: Jan Morrill and Pedro Cabezas of the International Allies; Andrés McKinley, Omar Serrano, and Fr. José María Tojeira of the UCA; US-El Salvador Sister City staff; Archbishop José Luis Escobar; Susan Kandel of PRISMA; and Rafael Cartagena of PRISMA and then UCA.

In Chalatenango: Benigno Orellana, Augustin Bonilla, and Miriam Ayala of the Community Development Association of Chalatenango (CCR); Rufina Romero from Arcatao; Tobias Orellana of the municipal council of San José Las Flores; and Don Felipe Tobar from San José Las Flores.

In La Union, Fr. Lorenzo Cruz who brought us to the old Butters mine.

In the Salvadoran government: President Salvador Sánchez Cerén and Vice President Oscar Ortiz; in the Ministry of Environment (MARN), ministers Lina Pohl and her predecessor Herman Rosa Chávez, and vice minister Ángel Ibarra (formerly UNES), as well as Salvador Nieto (executive secretary of the Central American Commission on the Environment and Development, CCAD); in the Ministry of the Economy, Minister Salmon Tharsis, lawyer Daniel Rios, and Carlos Aquilino Duarte Funes and Maria Soledad in the Ministry's Bureau of Hydrocarbons and Mines; in the Human Rights Ombudsman's Office, Ombudsman Oscar Luna and deputy attorney Yanira Córtez; in the Ministry of Agriculture, Hugo Flores; and ambassadors of El Salvador to the United States, Francisco Altschul and Rubén Zamora.

In the Salvadoran legislature: Environment and Climate Change Committee chair Guillermo Mata, his predecessor Lourdes Palacios, committee members Estela Hernández and John Wright Sol, and other committee members and staff.

In the United States, Canada, and Europe (most of whom participated in International Allies): Ross Wells and Peggy Goetz of the Washington Ethical Society; Marcos Orellana and Amanda Kistler of CIEL; Vicky Gass, Stephanie Burgos, Sofia Vergara, and Keith Slack of Oxfam; Alexis Stoumbelis of CISPES; Cathy Feingold of the AFL-CIO; Melinda St. Louis and Lori Wallach of Public Citizen; Erich Pica and Bill Warren of Friends of the Earth; Julia Paley and Ron Carver of the Institute for Policy Studies; Wilson Muñoz of Committee for the Development of El Salvador (CODESES); Jean Stokan of Sisters of Mercy; Scott Wright of the Columban Center for Advocacy and Outreach; Joe Eldridge, Geoff Thale, and Maureen Meyer of the Washington Office on Latin America; Marie Dennis of Pax Christi; José Artiga of the SHARE Foundation; Lindolfo Carballo and the workers of CASA; Fray Jacek Órzechowski and his congregants at St. Camillus Church; Jim Boyce; Deborah Barry; Barry Gills; Bob Denemark; Ana Sol Gutierrez and her father, the late Jorge Sol. Also the late Robert Goodland, who encouraged us in our work for decades and, among other kindnesses related to this book, introduced us to the late Robert "Bob" Moran and also to ICSID legal expert Luis Parada. Also to Jonmin Goodland and her salon gatherings, and Eric Hershberg and American University's Center on Latin American and Latino Studies. And others who have requested anonymity.

In Australia: Sean Cleary of the Edmund Rice Centre in Sydney; Kevin Bracken of the Maritime Union of Australia; Luke Fletcher of Jubilee Australia.

In Bolivia: Jim Shultz of the Democracy Center; and Thomas McDonagh, Aldo Orellana, Leny Olivera, and Philippa de Boissiere of Terra Justa.

In the Philippines: former congressman Walden Bello of Focus on the Global South; Jaybee Garganera of Alyansa Tigil Mina; Enteng Bautista of Kalikasan-People's Network for the Environment; Governor Carlos Padilla and provincial planner Edgardo Sabado of Nueva Vizcaya; the late Isagani "Gani" Serrano and his colleagues at the Philippine Rural Reconstruction Movement; Joseph Purugganan and colleagues at Focus on the

Global South; Rico La Viña of the University of California at Davis; and Tony La Viña and Lisa Dacanay of Ateneo de Manila University. Members of DESAMA, ANNVIK, and SAPAKKMMI showed us local impacts of the OceanaGold mine.

For being pillars of support and knowledge, and for being there whenever we needed their expert opinion (as well as for accompaniment on a couple of trips to El Salvador): Manuel Pérez-Rocha and Jen Moore (formerly of MiningWatch Canada) of the Institute for Policy Studies. We are also indebted to the rest of John's IPS colleagues, notably Sarah Anderson, Phyllis Bennis, Chuck Collins, Netfa Freeman, and Kathleen Gaspard.

For deepening our understanding of water and watersheds at multiple levels even before we knew it would become central on our own radar screens: Maude Barlow and the organizations she built, the Council of Canadians and the Blue Planet Project; Chip Fay; and the late Maximo "Junie" Kalaw.

For extending our grasp of mining-related issues: International Allies member organization MiningWatch Canada and especially Jamie Kneen, Catherine Coumans, and Kirsten Francescone; Jen Krill, Payal Sampat, and Ellen Moore of Earthworks.

For strengthening our insights into the workings of ICSID: Luis Parada and University of Costa Rica International Law Professor Nicolas Boeglin.

For interpreting for us across El Salvador: Jan Morrill (now of Earthworks), Damian Vasquez, and Maggie Von Vogt.

Special thanks to Rachel Nadelman, who wrote her dissertation on the pre-2009 period of this struggle, for generously sharing some of her transcribed interviews and other primary sources. We were extremely fortunate that between the arbitration case and Rachel's documents, we had access to a trove of documents from Pac Rim and other global mining companies seeking permits to mine in El Salvador. These allowed us to follow the thinking and actions of the set of actors we call Big Gold far better than we could have ever imagined.

Whatever mistakes this book contains are ours and ours alone. But the following individuals read all or part of the manuscript (in English or translated into Spanish) and provided invaluable feedback on both fact and analysis: Luis Parada, Antonio Pacheco, Vidalina Morales, Miguel Rivera, Manuel Pérez-Rocha, Rachel Nadelman, Sarah Anderson, Jan Morrill, Jen Moore, Geoff Thale, John Feffer, José Hernandez, and Ellen Moore.

American University graduate student Adrienne Castellon read and copyedited a draft of each chapter and translated chapters into Spanish. Other research assistance was provided by American University graduate students Rachel Nadelman, Pauline Abetti, Nasiruddin Mahmud Chowdhury, Hilary Kung, Audrey Manahan, Wazim Mowla, and Adam Needelman.

We are grateful for financial support that helped us and International Allies do this work. For Robin: the John Simon Guggenheim Foundation and also American University. For International Allies and IPS: Tom Lee of the Sigrid Rausing Trust, Conniel Malek of True Costs Initiative, and Ellen Dorsey and Scott Fitzmorris of the Wallace Global Fund. (Fitzmorris was part of the International Allies May 2013 delegation to El Salvador.) Thanks also to Voices for a Sustainable Future.

For publishing three of our articles on this story in *The Nation*, Katrina vanden Heuvel and Roane Carey. In the Philippines, editors Chay Hofilena and Maria Ressa of *Rappler*.

Permission to use the lyrics of "Water for Gold" was given to the authors and Beacon Press by musician Joe Uehlein of the U-Liners. The song, written by Uehlein after he read our 2011 article in *The Nation*, is on the U-Liners' second album, *Sweet Lorain*. For more about the band, see https://www.uliners.com. We are extremely grateful to him for writing the song and for granting us this permission.

For encouraging us to write creatively and to experiment with new ways of telling stories: the late Dick Barnet, the late Marc Raskin, the late James Chace, Barbara Ehrenreich, E. Ethelbert Miller, Tope Folarin, Frederick Clairmonte, Harriet Barlow, Adam Hochschild, Frances Moore Lappé, Naomi Klein, Deborah Rhode, and Mark Kramer and his Boston University Narrative Nonfiction conference. Also thanks to Richard Falk, Bill Moomaw, Gus Speth, and Arun Agrawal for supporting Robin's application to the Guggenheim Foundation.

In addition, Robin's International Studies Association "support group": Pamela Martin, Manuela Picq, and Nora McKeon for reading umpteen of our academic papers and providing feedback and encouragement; and J. Ann Tickner and Henry Alker and those at the International Studies Association who selected Robin as 2016 recipient of the J. Ann Tickner Award for "pushing boundaries" in the field of international studies, which helped us decide to try to push boundaries a bit more with this book.

We found a home at Beacon Press and great care from our team there: editor Amy Caldwell (who understood and believed in this book from the start), editorial assistant Nicole-Anne Keyton, associate director Gayatri Patnaik, director Helene Atwan, contracts director Melissa Nasson, managing editor Susan Lumenello, production coordinator Beth Collins, marketing liaison Isabella Sanchez, copyeditor Chris Dodge, cover designer Louis Roe, and publicist Caitlin Meyer, as well as Sanj Kharbanda, Priyanka Ray, and Travis Cohen.

Robin had the luxury of studying narrative nonfiction writing and working on this book as a John Simon Guggenheim Fellow and under American University research and sabbatical leaves. But much of this book—and our collaborative work—consumed our weekends, evenings, and so-called holidays as John worked full-time as director of the Institute for Policy Studies in Washington, DC, and Robin taught courses on development, environment, and globalization at the International Development Program in the School of International Service at American University. Both sets of colleagues gave us the space to complete this book. Deep thanks to our dear friends Thea, Mark, Helen, Jonny, Walden, Nikki, Billy, Mae, Erica, Harold, Vidya, Nanette, Jennifer, Chip, Nonette, Cathy, Andy, Marcy, Ernesto, and our families—including especially our son Jesse—who put up with us during our absences and were there for us throughout.

SOURCES

This book is primarily based on our fieldwork and interviews from trips to El Salvador in 2011, 2012, 2013, 2014, 2016, 2017, 2018, and 2019. In addition, we relied on the below sources, which are presented in the order in which they appear.

CHAPTER 1: WHITE MEN IN SUITS

Tom Shrake's quotes are primarily from his written testimony at the International Centre for Settlement of Investment Disputes (ICSID): "Witness Statement of Thomas C. Shrake," ICSID Case No. ARB/09/12, December 31, 2010. The Shrake testimony also provides a history (on page 15 and elsewhere) of how the El Dorado mine changed hands from the old owner New York & Honduras Rosario Mining Company, to Kinross El Salvador, which in turn was owned by Mirage Resources, to Mirage's merger with Dayton Mining Corporation (with Robert Johansing as its El Salvador project director) and then with Pacific Rim Mining, as well as the overlapping individuals who bound these companies together.

Our sources on Butters include Thomas Rickard, *Interviews with Mining Engineers* (San Francisco: Mining and Scientific Press, 1922), including Butters's words quoted; "Central America in 1913," *Engineering and Mining Journal* 97, no. 2 (1914): 140; and Percy Falke Martin, *Salvador of the Twentieth Century* (New York: Longmans, Green, 1911).

The information on the World Gold Council is from its website: https://www.gold.org.

On mining and gold, see Eduardo Galeano, *Open Veins of Latin America: Five Centuries of the Pillage of a Continent* (New York: Monthly Review, 1973); Roger Moody, *Rocks and Hard Places: The Globalization of Mining* (New York: Zed, 2007); Stuart Kirsch, *Mining Capitalism: The Relationship Between Corporations and Their Critics* (Berkeley: University of California Press, 2014); and Peter Bernstein, *The Power of Gold: The History of an Obsession*, 2nd ed. (New York: John Wiley & Sons, 2012).

On the corporate control of water and the global backlash, see Maude Barlow's
    trilogy of water books, *Blue Gold*, *Blue Future*, and *Blue Covenant*, and the work
    of two organizations of which Maude Barlow has been a leader: the Blue Planet
    Project (https://www.blueplanetproject.net) and the Council of Canadians
    (https://councilofcdns.ca).
For more on the Lempa Massacre that Don Carlos describes, see Warren Hoge,
    "Slaughter in Salvador: 200 Lost in Border Massacre," *New York Times*, June 8,
    1981, which we quote.
For a broader sweep of the history of the civil war, see Roberto Lovato, *Unforgetting:
    A Memoir of Family, Migration, Gangs, and Revolution in the Americas* (New York:
    HarperCollins, 2020); and Robert Armstrong and Janet Shenk, *El Salvador: The
    Face of the Revolution* (Boston: South End Press, 1982). See also Raymond Bon-
    ner, *Weakness and Deceit: U.S. Policy and El Salvador* (New York: Times Books,
    1984); Mark Danner, *The Massacre at El Mozote* (New York: Vintage, 1994); and
    Cynthia Arnson, *Crossroads: Congress, the President and Central America, 1976–
    1993* (New York: Pantheon, 1989).

CHAPTER 2: A NEW PACT WITH THE DEVIL
As in chapter 1, Tom Shrake's quotes are primarily from his written testimony at the
    International Centre for Settlement of Investment Disputes (ICSID): "Witness
    Statement of Thomas C. Shrake," ICSID Case No. ARB/09/12, December 31, 2010.
Robert Moran's quotes come from his technical report and his testimony to ICSID,
    supplemented by our meeting with him in Washington, DC, in 2016. *Technical
    Review of the El Dorado Mine Project Environmental Impact Assessment (EIA), El Sal-
    vador* (October 2005); and "Witness Statement of Dr. Robert E. Moran," June
    23, 2014. Moran was killed in a car accident in 2017.
The information on Marinduque Mine in the Philippines comes from a number of
    sources in addition to our own interviews in the Philippines in 2013 and 2017:
    the presentations of Carlos Padilla in El Salvador in March 2017; publications of
    Alyansa Tigil Mina (ATM) and of MiningWatch Canada's Catherine Coumans;
    and William Holden and R. Daniel Jacobson, *Mining and Natural Hazard Vulner-
    ability in the Philippines: Digging to Development or Digging to Disaster?* (New York:
    Anthem Press, 2012).

CHAPTER 3: STATE OF SIEGE
On Shrake and Pac Rim: Thomas Shrake testimony before the Standing Committee
    on Foreign Affairs and International Development of the Canadian Legislature,
    June 8, 2010. Other of Shrake's quotes and information about Pac Rim are from
    the ICSID case *Pac Rim Cayman LLC v. The Republic of El Salvador*, especially
    El Salvador's Rejoinder on the Merits (July 11, 2014), summarized in Robin
    Broad, "Summary of El Salvador's Rejoinder on the Merits (11 July 2014) in *Pac
    Rim Cayman LLC v. The Republic of El Salvador*," Blue Planet Project, September
    4, 2014, http://www.blueplanetproject.net/index.php/summary-of-el-salvadors
    -rejoinder-on-the-merits-11-july-2014-in-pac-rim-cayman-llc-v-the-republic
    -of-el-salvador.
Beyond the documents from Pac Rim, among the sources for this chapter are nu-
    merous documents from Au Martinique/Minerals Martinique/Intrepid Mines.

These include "The Potonico Brief," by miner Robert Johansing, a three-page internal memo to Marco Montecinos of Tribune Minerals and Jorge Mario Rios of Intrepid Mines on October 29, 2007. These were shared with us by Rachel Nadelman, whose dissertation committee Robin chaired. See Rachel Nadelman, "Sitting on a Gold Mine: The Origins of El Salvador's De-Facto Moratorium on Metals Mining (2004–2008)," PhD diss., American University, 2018, http://hdl.handle.net/1961/auislandora:85258.

We also quote from Nadelman's interviews with Barrera, Robert Johansing, and Gavidia. The other quote about Barrera is from Lydia Chavez, "El Salvador," *New York Times*, December 11, 1983.

Beyond our interviews, the information on Archbishop Sáenz Lacalle is from other primary and secondary sources. The 1995 quote is from Religion News Service, "San Salvador Gets Archbishop; He Vows Less Political Stance," *Los Angeles Times*, May 13, 1995. The later quote was originally on the website of the Archdiocese of San Salvador (http://www.arzobispadosansalvador.org/index .php/sobre-nosotros); it now can be found in Gene Palumbo, "Spurred by Catholic Leaders, El Salvador Becomes First Nation to Ban Mining," *America: The Jesuit Review*, April 3, 2017, https://www.americamagazine.org/politics -society/2017/04/03/spurred-catholic-leaders-el-salvador-becomes-first-nation -ban-mining.

Complementing our interviews, the information on Manuel Hinds is from Hinds's report; a publicly available source for Hinds's calculations is Thomas M. Power, *Metals Mining and Sustainable Development in Central America: An Assessment of Benefits and Costs* (Boston: Oxfam America, 2008), 15–19, Hinds's quote can be found on p. 15.

CHAPTER 4: LOCAL TERROR, GLOBAL EXTORTION

Bautista's quotes are from Leonard Morin, "El Salvador's Misfortune in Gold: Mining, Murder, and Corporate Malfeasance," *Alterinfos America Latina*, April 21, 2010, http://www.alterinfos.org/spip.php?article4368.

Tom Shrake, "Pacific Rim Response to [Steiner] Report 'Gold, Impunity, Violence in El Salvador,'" August 20, 2009. The Business & Human Rights Resource Centre invited Shrake to submit this response. See also interview with Tom Shrake, February 10, 2012, quoted in Kari Lydersen, "Pacific Rim and Beyond: Global Mining, Global Resistance and International Law," *Colorado Journal of International Environmental Law and Policy* 23, no. 2 (2012): 367–87. Shrake's quote, after Marcelo's murder, is from p. 4 of his 2010 testimony in Canada, listed with the sources for chapter 3.

On Funes's election: Mary Anastasia O'Grady in the *Wall Street Journal*, Blake Schmidt and Elizabeth Malkin in the *New York Times*, and Catherine Bremer and Alberto Barrera (Reuters).

We were told of the text messages. But, to ensure that we have the phrasing correct, the ones we quote in this chapter (unless otherwise noted) were compiled by Radio Victoria, "Radio Victoria: Chronology of Threats and Actions," 2011, which can be found online at http://www.dghonline.org/ and also as appendix 3 in Richard Steiner, "El Salvador—Gold, Guns, and Choice: The El Dorado Gold Mine, Violence in Cabañas, CAFTA Claims, and the National Effort

Ban Mining," http://indypendent.org/wp-content/uploads/2012/01/Steiner
%20Salvador%20Mining%20Report.pdf.

On ICSID: the Pac Rim law firm's attempt to hire Luis Parada for this case as early
as 2007 is detailed in a four-page document submitted by El Salvador's lawyers
for this case, ICSID Case No. ARB/09/12, "Witness Statement of Luis Alberto
Parada," March 14, 2011. For the "Tokyo No" history, see Robin Broad, "Corporate Bias in the World Bank Group's International Centre for Settlement of
Investment Disputes: A Case Study of a Global Mining Corporation Suing El
Salvador," *Journal of International Law* 36, no. 4 (2015), 851–74, http://scholarship
.law.upenn.edu/jil/vol36/iss4/1. Nicolas Boeglin, a Costa Rican law professor,
also wrote about the Tokyo No in "ICSID and Latin America: Criticism, With-
drawal and the Search for Alternatives," December 3, 2013, https://www
.brettonwoodsproject.org/2013/12/icsid-latin-america. We interviewed Boeglin
in Costa Rica in 2014. For statistics on the number of ICSID cases: Sarah Anderson and Manuel Pérez-Rocha, "Mining for Profits in International Tribunals: Lessons for the Trans-Pacific Partnership," Institute for Policy Studies,
April 2013. See also Manuel Pérez-Rocha and Jen Moore, "Extraction Casino:
Mining Companies Gambling with Latin American Lives and Sovereignty
through International Arbitration," MiningWatch Canada, Institute for Policy
Studies, and Center for International Environmental Law, May 2019, https://
ips-dc.org/wp-content/uploads/2019/07/ISDS-Mining-Latin-America-Report
-Formatted-ENGLISH.pdf.

Details of Marcelo's funeral, in addition to our interviews, are from US–El Salvador
Sister Cities, "Anti-Mining Activist Marcelo Rivera Tortured and Murdered,"
July 15, 2009, https://www.elsalvadorsolidarity.org/anti-mining-activist-marcelo
-rivera-tortured-and-murdered-july-15-2009. See also Jamie Moffett. "The
Mysterious Death of Marcelo Rivera," YouTube, July 31, 2019, https://www
.youtube.com/watch?v=yvXm52BhSHQ.

Sources for Honduras include Robin Broad and Julia Fischer-Mackey, "From
Extractivism toward *Buen Vivir:* Mining Policy as an Indicator of a New Development Paradigm Prioritising the Environment," *Third World Quarterly* 38, no.
6 (2017): 1327–49, which largely uses information from MiningWatch Canada,
including Jen Moore, "Canada's Promotion of Mining Industry Belies Claims of
Corporate Social Responsibility," Projet Accompagnement Solidarité Colombie,
July 18, 2012, http://pasc.ca/en/article/canada%E2%80%99s-promotion-mining
-industry-belies-claims-corporate-social-responsibility. Also see "Honduras: The
Deadliest Country in the World for Environmental Activism," Global Witness,
January 31, 2017, https://www.globalwitness.org/en/campaigns/environmental
-activists/honduras-deadliest-country-world-environmental-activism.

CHAPTER 5: WITH A FAT CAT AND SUN TZU, THE RESISTANCE GOES GLOBAL

Karin Wells, "High Stakes Poker (2012 Documentary Encore)," CBC Radio, January 11, 2013, https://www.cbc.ca/radio/thesundayedition/high-stakes-poker
-2012-documentary-encore-1.1473331. The background information on
Catherine McLeod-Seltzer is from the section titled "Personal and Professional
Background" in "Witness Statement of Catherine McLeod-Seltzer," December
31, 2010, one of the witness documents for the ICSID arbitration stage.

For more specifics on this case through 2014 and 2015 by International Allies authors: Manuel Pérez-Rocha, "When Corporations Sue Governments," op-ed, *New York Times,* December 3, 2014, https://www.nytimes.com/2014/12/04/opinion/when-corporations-sue-governments.html; Robin Broad, "Corporate Bias in the World Bank Group's International Centre for Settlement of Investment Disputes: A Case Study of a Global Mining Corporation Suing El Salvador," *Journal of International Law* 36, no. 4 (2015): 851–74, http://scholarship.law.upenn.edu/jil/vol36/iss4/1; and Robin Broad and John Cavanagh, "The Global Fight Against Corporate Rule," *Nation,* January 15, 2014, https://www.thenation.com/article/archive/global-fight-against-corporate-rule. See also Maude Barlow and Meera Karunananthan, "Save Our Water, End Investor Rights," *Huffington Post,* May 13, 2015, https://www.huffingtonpost.ca/maude-barlow/water-crisis_b_7258782.html.

Perhaps the most outspoken of the investor-state "insiders" who have gone public with their criticisms of ICSID is prominent trade lawyer George Kahale III. We quote his "Inaugural Brooklyn Lecture on International Business Law: 'ISDS: The Wild, Wild West of International Practice,'" *Brooklyn Journal of International Law* 44, no. 1 (2018). His many other writings and speeches include his keynote speech at the Eighth Annual Juris Investment Treaty Arbitration Conference, Washington, DC, March 28, 2014, https://s3.amazonaws.com/cdn.curtis.com/news-attachments/8TH-Annual-Juris-Investment-Treaty-Arbitration-Conf.-March-28-2014.pdf.

Pacific Rim filed its Notice of Intent in December 2008 and its Notice of Arbitration in April 2009, before the Funes administration took office. June 15, 2009—just two weeks after the Funes presidency began and just days before Marcelo disappeared—is the date that ICSID registered the request. ICSID held three hearings on this case. In a preliminary hearing, the ICSID tribunal rejected the first application made under CAFTA Article 10.20.4 raising preliminary objections that the claims could not succeed in law. The decision: Pac Rim Cayman LLC v. The Republic of El Salvador (ICSID Case No ARB/09/12), Decision on the Respondent's Preliminary Objections under CAFTA Articles 10.20.4 and 10.20.5. The decision for the second hearing, the jurisdictional one: "In the Matter of an Arbitration Before the International Centre for Settlement of Investment Disputes ('ICSID') Brought Under the Dominican Republic–Central America–United States Free Trade Agreement ('CAFTA') and the Investment Law of El Salvador (ICSID Case No. ARB/09/12) Between: Pac Rim Cayman LLC, Claimant v. The Republic of El Salvador, Respondent," June 1, 2012, https://www.italaw.com/sites/default/files/case-documents/ita0935.pdf. The merit hearing, where the Fat Cat appeared, held on September 15, 2014, is discussed more in chapter 6. Other key ICSID documents include Pac Rim Cayman LLC v. The Republic of El Salvador, ICSID Case No. ARB/09/12, The Republic of El Salvador's Rejoinder on the Merits, July 11, 2014, http://www.italaw.com/sites/default/files/case-documents/italaw3321.pdf.

The International Allies report: Jen Moore et al., *Debunking Eight Falsehoods by Pacific Rim Mining/OceanaGold in El Salvador* (International Allies Against Mining in El Salvador, 2014), https://ips-dc.org/wp-content/uploads/2014/03/Eight-Falsehoods-Final-March-17-2014-WEB.pdf. Moore's coauthors include Robin

Broad, American University; John Cavanagh, IPS; René Guerra Salazar, SalvAide; Meera Karunananthan, Council on Canadians; Jan Morrill, International Allies/ Sister Cities; Manuel Pérez-Rocha, IPS; and Sofía Vergara, Oxfam. The report was published jointly by Council of Canadians/Blue Planet Project, the Institute for Policy Studies, Maritime Union Australia, and MiningWatch Canada.

From May 10 to May 13, 2013, an international delegation of nearly fifty delegates from twelve countries on four continents, representing twenty-two human rights, social justice, and environmental nonprofit organizations and advocates, along with academics, journalists, artists, and grassroots activists, carried out a three-day tour of El Salvador to examine experiences with gold mining operations and the defense of water. Robin was part of this delegation as was Raul Barbuno from Common Frontiers. See Robin Broad and John Cavanagh, "A Road Trip to Save El Salvador's Water," International Allies Against Mining in El Salvador, https://www.stopesmining.org/campaigns/oceanagold-el-salvador /fact-finding-mission.

CHAPTER 6: JUDGMENT DAY AT THE KANGAROO COURT

The ICSID Award document: Professor Dr. Guido Santiago Tawil, Professor Brigitte Stern, V. V. Veeder, Esq (President), and ICSID Tribunal Secretary Marco Tulio Montañés-Rumayor, "Award in the Matter of an Arbitration Before the International Centre for Settlement of Investment Disputes ("ICSID") Brought Under the Dominican Republic-Central America-United States Free Trade Agreement ("CAFTA") and the Investment Law of El Salvador (ICSID Case No. ARB/09/12) Between Pac Rim Cayman LLC Claimant, the Republic of El Salvador Respondent," October 14, 2016.

Kahale's writing is listed with chapter 5 sources. For analyses of ICSID cases by mining and other extractive corporations: Manuel Pérez-Rocha and Jen Moore, *Extraction Casino: Mining Companies Gambling with Latin American Lives and Sovereignty Through Supranational Arbitration* (MiningWatch Canada, Institute for Policy Studies, and Center for International Environmental Law, May 2019), https://ips-dc.org/wp-content/uploads/2019/07/ISDS-Mining-Latin-America -Report-Formatted-ENGLISH.pdf; Cecilia Olivet and Pia Eberhardt, *Profiting from Injustice: How Law Firms, Arbitrators and Financiers Are Fueling an Investment Arbitration Boom* (Brussels: Corporate Europe Observatory and the Transnational Institute, 2012), https://www.tni.org/files/download/profitingfrominjustice .pdf; and Lori Verheecke, Pia Eberhardt, Cecilia Olivet, and Sam Cossar-Gilbert, *Red Carpet Courts: 10 Stories of How the Rich and Powerful Hijacked Justice* (Brussels: Friends of the Earth Europe and International, Transnational Institute, and Corporate Europe Observatory, 2019), http://10isdsstories.org/wp -content/uploads/2019/06/red-carpet-courts-WEB.pdf. Also: UNCTAD's Investment Dispute Settlement Navigator, https://investmentpolicy.unctad.org /investment-dispute-settlement. See also the work of Lori Wallach and Public Citizen's Global Trade Watch: https://www.citizen.org/about/staff/global -trade-watch; and the Columbia Center on Sustainable Investment at Columbia University, http://ccsi.columbia.edu.

On "regulatory chill," see the work of Kyla Tienhaara, such as "Regulatory Chill in a Warming World: The Threat to Climate Policy Posed by Investor-State

Dispute Settlement," *Transnational Environmental Law* 7, no. 2 (2018): 229–50. See also Robin Broad and John Cavanagh, "El Salvador Ruling Offers a Reminder of Why the TPP Must Be Defeated," *Nation*, October 19, 2016, https://www.thenation.com/article/archive/el-salvador-ruling-offersa-reminder-of-why-the-tpp-must-be-defeated.

CHAPTER 7: DECISION TIME

OceanaGold, "ICSID Tribunal Finds in Favour of Government of El Salvador in Arbitration Process," press release, October 14, 2016; and "Open Letter to OceanaGold: OceanaGold Must Pay up and Pack up from El Salvador," International Allies Against Mining in El Salvador, February 21, 2017, https://www.stopesmining.org/campaigns/oceanagold-el-salvador/letter-to-ocenagold.

For the back and forth between members of International Allies and OceanaGold, see letter to Karen Hudlett, from Robin Broad et al., March 26, 2017, https://www.business-humanrights.org/sites/default/files/documents/Rejoinder_Allies_OceanaGold_for_BHRRC.pdf.

On the SER and the Blue Ribbon Committee (also called the Technical Committee): Anthony Bebbington, Robert Goodland, and Ann Maest, "Observaciones acerca de los desafíos de la gobernanza ambiental y el sector minero en El Salvador: aportes para la elaboración de una política pública," Report to the Ministry of Environment, 2012, shared with authors. On the idea of no-go zones, see Robert Goodland, "Responsible Mining: The Key to Profitable Resource Development," *Sustainability* 4, no. 9 (2012): 2099–2126, https://www.researchgate.net/publication/278106950_Responsible_Mining_The_Key_to_Profitable_Resource_Development. For more on the debate on the term "responsible mining," see Robin Broad, "Responsible Mining: Moving from a Buzzword to Real Responsibility," *Extractive Industries and Society Journal* 1, no.1 (2014): 4–6.

The March 23 OceanaGold communique that was also sent to Gallegos: R. Timothy McCrum and Ian Laird, Crowell Moring, Letter to Luis Parada and Derek Smith, Foley Hoag, "Re: Pac Rim Cayman LLC v. Republic of El Salvador (ICSID Case No ARB/09/12), March 23, 2017, in possession of authors.

Also: Broad and Cavanagh, "El Salvador Votes for Water over Gold: Against Overwhelming Odds, an International Grassroots Campaign Has Won the World's First Comprehensive Ban on Metals Mining," *Nation*, April 4, 2017, https://www.thenation.com/article/el-salvador-votes-for-water-over-gold; and Andrés McKinley, "In El Salvador, a Moment More Precious Than Gold," *National Catholic Reporter*, April 26, 2017, https://www.ncronline.org/blogs/justice/eco-catholic/el-salvador-moment-more-precious-gold, which also has a photo of the meeting with El Salvador's president.

EPILOGUE: THE VOTE HEARD AROUND THE WORLD

On OceanaGold in the Philippines, see websites of the two national coalitions, Alyansa Tigil Mina (ATM), https://www.alyansatigilmina.net, and Kalikasan People's Network for the Environment, http://kalikasan.net. Robin Broad, John Cavanagh, Catherine Coumans, and Rico La Vina, *OceanaGold in the Philippines: Ten Violations That Should Prompt Its Removal* (Business and Human

Rights Resource Centre, October 2018), https://www.researchgate.net
/publication/330912670_OceanaGold_in_the_Philippines_Ten_Violations
_That_Should_Prompt_Its_Removal.

On other countries moving to ban or limit mining: Robin Broad and Julia
Fischer-Mackey, "From Extractivism Towards *Buen Vivir*: Mining Policy as an
Indicator of a New Development Paradigm Prioritising the Environment," *Third
World Quarterly* 38, no. 6 (2017): 1327–49, http://dx.doi.org/10.1080/01436597
.2016.1262741.

On other ICSID cases: Manuel Pérez-Rocha and Jen Moore, "Extraction Casino:
Mining Companies Gambling with Latin American Lives and Sovereignty
through Supranational Arbitration," MiningWatch Canada, Institute for Policy
Studies, and Center for International Environmental Law, May 2019, https://
ips-dc.org/wp-content/uploads/2019/07/ISDS-Mining-Latin-America-Report
-Formatted-ENGLISH.pdf; Focus on the Global South, Alyansa Tigil Mina,
and the Philippine Rural Reconstruction Movement, "Cancelled Contracts
and the Corporate Backlash," "concept note" for a forum on mining and ISDS,
Philippine Rural Reconstruction Movement, July 28, 2017, in possession of
authors. See also the work of Kyla Tienhaara, including "World Bank Ruling
against Pakistan Shows Global Economic Governance Is Broken," *Conversation*,
July 22, 2019, https://theconversation.com/world-bank-ruling-against-pakistan
-shows-global-economic-governance-is-broken-120414.

On factors leading to the win, such as the key role of a private sector not connected
to mining, see Robin Broad and John Cavanagh, "Poorer Countries and the
Environment: Friends or Foes?" *World Development,* 72 (2015): 419–31, http://
www.sciencedirect.com/science/article/pii/S0305750X15000662.

On metals recycling: Rick LeBlanc, "An Introduction to Metal Recycling," *Balance
Small Business*, June 25, 2019, https://www.thebalancesmb.com/an-introduction
-to-metal-recycling-4057469. See also Jake Halpern, "Scrappers: The Big Business of Scavenging in Post-Industrial America," *New York Times Magazine,* August 25, 2019; Payal Sampat, "Keeping Clean Energy Clean, Just and Equitable:
Earthworks Position Statement," Earthworks, April 16, 2019, https://earthworks
.org/publications/making-clean-energy-clean-just-equitable-earthworks
-position-statement; and "These Six Metals Are Key to a Low-Carbon Future,"
Carbon Brief, April 2018, https://www.carbonbrief.org/explainer-these-six
-metals-are-key-to-a-low-carbon-future.

On gold demand: publications of the World Gold Council, including "Gold Demand Sectors," https://www.gold.org/about-gold/gold-demand/sectors-of
-demand, which notes that around 50 percent of the gold is used for jewelry and
that this "remains the single largest use for gold," "Gold Demand Trends Full
Year and Q4 2019," January 30, 2020, https://www.gold.org/goldhub/research
/gold-demand-trends, and "Retail Gold Insights: India Investment," 2020,
https://www.retailinsights.gold/regional-spotlights/india.html. On falling demand by younger generations in India, see Shruti Srivastava and Swansy Afonso,
"The Younger Generation Is More Focused on Buying Smartphones than
Gold—Indians Are Falling Out of Love with Gold—and Millennials Are Partly
to Blame," *Financial Post*, July 4, 2018. https://business.financialpost.com
/commodities/mining/indians-are-falling-out-of-love-with-gold.

On arrests and sentencing for Marcelo Rivera's murder: "Ambientalistas declaran que homicidio y otros crimenes estan impunes" [Environmentalists declare that homicide and other crimes are unpunished], Observatorio de Conflictos Mineros de America Latina, September 24, 2010, https://www.ocmal.org /ambientalistas-declaran-que-homicidio-y-otros-crimenes-estan-impunes; Gabriel Labrador Aragon, "Pandilleros mataron a los ambientalistas de Cabañas, dicen Fiscalia y PNC" [Gang members killed Cabañas environmentalists, prosecutors and PNC say], *El Faro,* June 7, 2011, https://elfaro.net/es/201107 /noticias/4692/Pandilleros-mataron-a-los-ambientalistas-de-Caba%C3%B1as -dicen-Fiscal%C3%ADa-y-PNC.htm; "Clamor de Justicia" [Clamor of Justice], *Diario Co Latino,* March 2, 2017, https://www.diariocolatino.com/clamor-de -justicia; and "Three Convicted for the Murder of Marcelo Rivera," Voices on the Border, September 22, 2010, https://voiceselsalvador.wordpress.com/2010 /09/22/three-convicted-for-the-murder-of-marcelo-rivera.